Así es la humanidad, compadre, que cuando uno quiere hacé una gracia le sale una morisqueta. Pero yo lo que digo es que si las cosas están malas, toavía se pueden poné más piores.

That's humanity for you, compadre, you try to do something nice for folks and you end up falling on your face. What I always say is, things might be bad now, but they can sure get a whole lot worse.

—General Parmenión Cunaguaro in *La Primera Versión de El forastero, novela inédita*, by Rómulo Gallegos, written in approximately 1922 and published after the author's death

Todo se puede poner peor.

Things can always get worse.

—Elías Jaua, former vice president to Hugo Chávez, speaking at a conference in Caracas in 2019

CONTENTS

Things Are
Never So Bad That
They Can't Get Worse

Prologue: Mene Grande

Venezuela's first oil well sits on top of a low hill in a town called Mene Grande, near Lake Maracaibo, in the far western state of Zulia. The well was drilled in 1914. It was still pumping oil when I was there in 2014, a few weeks after the government held a celebration marking a hundred years of Venezuela as an oil-producing nation. The well had been spiffed up for the ceremony. There was a small pumpjack, painted in the national colors, yellow, blue, and red, with eight white stars. It nodded up and down, patiently measuring out the national diastole and systole. A pipe that carried away the oil was painted a shiny silver. The well is called Zumaque 1. A century ago there were sumac trees here—*zumaques*—but I didn't see any on my visit. The pumpjack stood behind a metal railing in the center of a newly paved parking lot. Shadeless under a punishing sun, the black asphalt absorbed and radiated the intense heat.[1]

The history of Venezuela and oil flows through Mene Grande like the crude oil through the silver pipe. The first oil workers' strike occurred here (and was put down here) in 1925. In 1976, during the country's first petro-delirium, when oil prices quadrupled, President Carlos Andrés Pérez came to Mene Grande to declare the nationalization of the oil industry. Three decades later, in the midst of an even bigger boom, President Hugo Chávez came here to announce a second nationalization, changing the terms by which foreign oil companies operated in Venezuela and giving the government a controlling stake in everything that happened in the oil fields. There were information boards at the edge of the parking lot commemorating the dual nationalizations; in their telling, Chávez got all the glory.

Chávez had died a year earlier, in 2013, after fourteen years as president. A former soldier, he called himself a socialist and a revolutionary and he delighted in thumbing his nose at the United States, the imperial power to the north, to which he sold most of his country's oil. His successor was Nicolás Maduro, a less talented politician who styled himself as the ideological heir of the man he called the eternal comandante. In Maduro's short time as president, there had been waves of protest, the economy had begun to contract, inflation was soaring, and shortages of food and other goods were becoming acute.

The word *mene*, in the name of the town Mene Grande, comes from an indigenous word for oil seep, a place where oil bubbles up naturally from the earth. That is typical of Venezuela's oil. It is so close to the surface in many places that it seeps out of the ground on its own. Or you poke a hole and out it comes—like the opening credit scene in *The Beverly Hillbillies*, when Jed Clampett shoots at a varmint and misses, striking oil instead. Mene Grande has numerous oil seeps. The oil surges up, and over time it congeals and becomes a mound of something like tar or asphalt.

Behind the tricolor park with the first oil well was a barrio, tumbling down the back of the hill, where people lived in hovels. Wandering around the barrio, I came upon a woman who was probably in her thirties or forties, but she looked twice that age. Her bones showed under the skin of her arms. She wore a housedress so threadbare that it was almost sheer, and whatever color it once had was gone. She seemed faded too in the white-hot sun, bleached instead of burnt or tanned. She lived in one of the worst hovels I'd seen in Venezuela or anywhere else, a teetering collection of corrugated metal, cardboard, and wood. The most striking thing of all was that it had been assembled on top of a mene. Shiny slicks of oil stained the earth all around. To keep themselves out of the muck, the woman and her family had built up a kind of midden, maybe three feet high, from chunks of hardened oil residue and debris. It was like a big, broad pitcher's mound with a shack on top.

Using a rectangular metal can for a stool, she sat in front of her hovel, on top of this mound of oil in its various states of coagulation, spooning rice and beans from a tin plate into her mouth. She told me that her name was Ismara Barrios. She lived there with her husband, three daughters, and a cousin. Her husband sold soft drinks and fried plantains in town.

The sun was a hammer. I stood on the spongy ground, between puddles of oil, and squinted up at her. I tried to strike up a conversation. Venezuela was a country of extroverts, but Ismara cut against the grain. She seemed mistrustful of a stranger asking questions.

"Things are going really well for me here," she said, as though wary that someone might suggest otherwise.

I asked what she thought about the government. She told me that the government gave people what they needed. This was a Venezuelan truism, whether or not it was true in practice: Venezuela was a petrostate, and in the eyes of its citizens, it existed to parcel out the riches pumped from the ground.

What did she think about Chávez? She said that he was her comandante.

And Maduro? The son of the comandante.

That was all.

* * *

As Ismara and I spoke in September 2014, the country was poised on a fulcrum, like a pumpjack about to tip downward from the top of its cycle. For most of the year, oil prices had been close to $100 a barrel—continuing a historic run of high prices. But now the price had begun to fall. By January, oil would have lost half its value—spelling disaster for Venezuela, which depended almost entirely on oil exports for its economic survival.

I lived in Venezuela from 2012 to 2016, when I was the Andes region correspondent for *The New York Times*. After my stint as correspondent was over, I kept returning to Venezuela, sometimes to cover the news and sometimes to visit friends. I was back in 2018 to report on Maduro's reelection in a tainted vote—to ensure his victory the government had barred most opposition parties from running a candidate against him. I returned again the following year after a young opposition legislator named Juan Guaidó, recently chosen to lead the National Assembly, mounted a challenge to Maduro by declaring himself interim president, with the support of the United States and dozens of other countries. By then Venezuela had slipped into permanent crisis and economic free fall: hyperinflation, joblessness, hunger, and a massive outflow of refugees second only to Syria, which was undergoing a civil war. Venezuela sat on the world's largest reserve of oil. It had once been one of the richest countries in the hemisphere. Now it was being compared to Syria and Haiti, the poorest country in the region.

* * *

ON THAT DAY in Mene Grande, with the country's collapse still beyond the horizon, I said goodbye to Ismara and stepped around the patches of sticky oil that slicked the muddy track in front of her home. Two men came walking along the path, and I greeted them.

Without prompting, one of the men pointed at the puddled oil, in the Venezuelan manner, by pursing his lips and turning his head. "Look at the riches of Venezuela," he said.

PART ONE

1

Blackout

On a typical Thursday afternoon, before the crisis, before the collapse, before hyperinflation, before the bottom dropped out from under the price of oil, before the bolivar was worthless, before your whole monthly salary went to buy a chicken and then just half a chicken and then some chicken parts, before cash disappeared, before everyone left, before the refugees, before doctors and nurses and engineers and managers and workers with skills and time on the job started leaving the country, before the stampede to the exits, before all of that; simply put, *before*—on a typical Thursday afternoon there would have been three or four operators watching the computer screens in the central control room in Caracas that monitored the electrical grid for all of Venezuela. But that was *before*. Today, on this Thursday afternoon, March 7, 2019, there was just one man watching the computer screens at the National Center for Power Distribution: Darwin Briceño.

Darwin Briceño has a calm, understated demeanor, which is useful in his job, because when things go wrong, it can get stressful in a hurry. He has thick black hair and a closely trimmed Abe Lincoln beard, a long oval face with a strong, prominent nose and big deerlike eyes. He uses a styling product that makes his hair shine in the light.

Light is Darwin's business. Light and power, in the form of electricity.

And on that afternoon, he was the only person in Venezuela in charge of making sure that there was a smooth flow of electricity to every city and town and millions of homes and businesses, with their air conditioners, refrigerators, televisions, and appliances, and all the airports and seaports, government offices, oil wells, refineries, and everything else in the country that used electrical power.

Venezuela has one national control room because the country is composed of a single integrated power grid. About three-quarters of Venezuela's electrical generating capacity resides in three large hydroelectric plants in the far eastern part of the country, in what is known, for the purposes of the electrical grid, as the Guayana sector. Those generating plants provide virtually all the power used in Caracas and a large portion of the electricity used in Maracaibo, Venezuela's second-largest city, all the way across the country, close to the western border with Colombia. There are smaller regional control rooms that collect information and feed it into the national center in Caracas.

At forty-two, Darwin had been working nearly half his life in the central control room. He'd gone through the merger, after 2007, of the country's regional electrical companies into one government-run company called Corpoelec. He'd been through the "electrical emergency," declared by Chávez in 2009 and 2010, when a severe drought caused the water level in the reservoirs behind the big dams to drop. More recently he'd watched as his coworkers disappeared. Your salary wasn't enough even to buy food for your family. Some drifted off to find other work in Caracas. Others had taken jobs with electrical utilities in Chile or Colombia or Ecuador.

But Darwin and a few colleagues had stayed. No one *wanted* to leave Venezuela. Your people were here—your family, your parents, your friends. It was the life you knew. There was a kind of light in Venezuela that you didn't find anywhere else: the honeyed light of a Caracas evening, filtered through the dark green leaves of the mango trees, against the eternal backdrop of the forested Ávila mountain that stood like a guardian between the city and the sea; the intense white light of the Caribbean littoral, which makes you squint and washes the world clean of color. And the warmth of the people. You couldn't find that anywhere else. Leaving was a last resort. You had to be desperate to leave, and Darwin wasn't desperate, not yet. He also felt a sense of responsibility, to the electrical company and to the country that relied on his work. And to the Revolution. Darwin was a member of the United Socialist Party of Venezuela; he believed in the dream of a better, fairer Venezuela for everybody.

"There came a time when we had to choose between leaving or assuming responsibility and working hard," Darwin said. "We decided to stay and make our bet, to say, 'We're here and we're sticking around.'"

The control room used to be a busy place. There were three or four operators on a shift, with three shifts a day. Now there were only six operators left. It used to be that you'd come in and see your friends and you'd have someone to talk to, joke around with. Now you worked alone, on a twenty-four-hour shift.

On any given day, all sorts of things could happen—a brush fire under a transmission line could cause a spike in current, a transformer could blow—and then you had to think and act fast. And if it occurred at peak consumption, you had to scramble to keep power flowing. It was like being the pilot of a jet plane when an engine goes out in flight. You had alarms going off and split-second decisions to make. These days the whole system was under strain, held together with chewing gum. Equipment was going longer without being replaced; less maintenance was being done. You felt the weight of responsibility. The whole country depended on you. And now that it was just you, all alone, for twenty-four hours—well, it was even more stressful.

The central control room looked like a low-budget movie set. A line of desks, arranged in an arc, faced a wall on which a big screen showed a schematic of the electrical grid, with the generating plants and the transmission lines. Each desk held four computer screens that displayed a constant feed of data from all the components of the system.

On that Thursday, March 7, 2019, Darwin was less than halfway through his twenty-four-hour shift when a series of alarms flashed on the screens in front of him. It was 4:50 P.M. In that instant, the lights in the control room blinked and went out. That in itself was unusual. The control center was on a priority circuit—it wasn't ever supposed to lose power, even when other areas of Caracas went dark. Darwin didn't know it yet, but this wasn't a local problem. Power had gone out all across the country. From one moment to the next, as though someone had thrown a switch, all of Venezuela had no electricity. In some places it would stay out for five days. Millions of people would run short of food and water. Hospital operating rooms went dark. Banks and grocery stores couldn't function. In a few days the looting would start. Two weeks later the lights would go out again. And then again less than a week after that. And again in early April. The system was falling apart.

But that was all in the future. For now, at the central control room, the building's backup generator kicked in and the lights blinked back on. In that brief span between light and no light the computers had remained on because they had a separate backup battery system. But now Darwin noticed something that he'd never seen before. Although the computers were still on, the screens were frozen. The steady stream of data from power lines and generating plants was not being updated. It was the first of many *holy shit* moments for Darwin as afternoon shaded into evening and a deeper darkness than usual descended on Venezuela. No new information was coming in. Sitting there at the brain center of the country's electrical grid, Darwin was isolated. He was in every sense alone.

He picked up the white telephone on his desk and started calling around. Or he tried to.

First he called the Corpoelec headquarters in Caracas. The number was busy. He called the regional control room in Guayana, where the hydroelectric plants were. Busy again.

Darwin felt a kick of adrenaline. He called the other regional control centers. One after another, they were all busy. (Investigators later discovered that many of the backup battery systems designed to keep communications open and computers running at Corpoelec facilities around the country were disconnected or no longer working, because of a lack of maintenance or the failure to replace aging equipment.) At last he called the control center in Zulia state, in the far west of the country, and someone answered the phone. "I asked them, *coño*, holy shit, what's going on there? And they tell me, 'The whole system here is down.'"

Finally he got through to Guayana. They told him: "We're down here too."

By now his phone was ringing as well. Headquarters was calling. They wanted to know the same thing he did: What was going on?

Everywhere it was the same: no one had power, the whole system had crashed. And he knew what that meant. "Okay," he told himself, "now it's up to me to bring back the electrical system for the whole country." He felt the fear rising in him. He told himself to stay calm, to remember his training. "Your nerves are a little bit on edge because it's an emergency," Darwin, always prone to understatement, told me when we spoke a few months later. "It's a heavy situation."

Darwin's colleague, Carlos Sánchez, had worked the previous twenty-four-hour shift in the control room. Now Carlos was driving home, listening to the radio, when the signal went out. He changed stations, working his way along the dial. No signal anywhere. Then he noticed that the traffic lights weren't working and there were no lights on in the stores. When he arrived home, he found that his house too was without power. He took out his cell phone and called Darwin, but the cellular lines were overloaded. Eventually he got through and Darwin told him that there was a nationwide blackout. Carlos turned around and headed back to work.

When Carlos arrived at the control room, it had been about three hours since the blackout hit. Carlos and Darwin were close friends. Years ago, they'd done their training together, graduated together, and been hired on the same day. Now Darwin explained what he knew, which still wasn't much. The first alarms that had come in, the ones that had remained frozen on the computer screens, pointed to a problem with the high voltage lines that made up the spinal column of the nation's electrical grid, connecting the hydroelectric plants in the east with the center of the country. Transmission lines are divided into segments, each with a kind of circuit breaker that is automatically triggered in case of trouble, such as a sudden increase in current. The idea is to isolate the problem to the segment where it occurred and keep it from spreading to other segments. In this case, it appeared that something had happened to trigger a chain reaction, knocking out segments up and down the power grid.

Darwin hadn't paused since that first flickering out of the lights. Now, with Carlos there, he could take a minute to catch his breath. He went into a break room, with a large window, and looked out over the city.

Night had fallen, and the valley of Caracas lay before him, plunged in blackness. There was no twinkle of a thousand bare lightbulbs in the shantytowns climbing the hillsides, no lights from the giant housing blocks, no yellow glow from the wealthy enclaves to the south, no lights in the middle-class neighborhood that spread out below his window, no tangerine-tinged streetlamps. There was only darkness. The headlights of cars slashed white channels through the night, but that only seemed to accentuate the blackness all around.

"I go out there and I see everything in darkness. You couldn't see a thing. It made a tremendous impact—" Darwin's eyes grew wide and he made an asthmatic, suffocating sound, *eeeeee*—the sound a vacuum cleaner makes when something is stuck in the tube and the air is forced to go around it. That sound, the sound of Darwin's deepest fear, has stayed with me, and the look on his face: the doe eyes enlarged into big circles inside the elliptical halo of the Honest Abe beard and the thick, pomaded hair. He said, "I went back immediately, I mean, I didn't catch my breath. I went back inside right away because, just imagine, the capital without—the nation's capital without electricity. It really hit me."

He sat down at his console and said to Carlos, "*Vamos a darle.*" "Let's do this."

2

The Shouting Country

In 1989, I was living in Mexico City, and I watched on television as Caracas was swept by riots and looting. Police and soldiers opened fire on the looters and hundreds of people were killed. My Mexican friends were stunned. For them, Venezuela was a place apart, a country touched by the blessing of wealth. Mexico had oil too, but nothing like Venezuela. La Venezuela Saudita, people called it: a Latin American Saudi Arabia. The chaos on television belied all that. It was like the crushing of a dream. The riots exposed Venezuela as a hollow fantasy—a pretty bauble on the outside, with rolls of money and shopping trips abroad, while inside, there was pulverizing poverty and the usual curse of promises never kept. The rioting came to be called El Caracazo—which roughly means the Caracas blow, as in the blow of a fist. It had that kind of impact: a gut punch. During the oil boom of the 1970s, money had poured in and politicians spun fairy dreams of a country rocketing out of underdevelopment. The slogan then was La Gran Venezuela. A Great Venezuela in the making. Other countries had similar aspirations, but Venezuela seemed poised to achieve them. Instead it woke to a familiar tale of debt, mismanagement, pauperism, and corruption. The 1980s were a lost decade; the rioting in 1989 was the bitter coda.

Three years after the Caracazo, a young lieutenant colonel named Hugo Chávez led a coup against Venezuela's democratically elected government. The coup failed, but Chávez became a celebrity. In 1998, he ran for president as a change candidate and won.

By the time I moved to Venezuela, as a foreign correspondent, in January 2012, the country was deeply divided. You could say that division is what defined it. Pro-Chávez versus anti-Chávez. Poor versus well-off. Red T-shirt versus any other color T-shirt. You were for or against. On one side or the other. The division was obvious everywhere I went and in nearly every conversation I had. In interviews with poor people standing in line at a government store to buy subsidized food. In conversations with rich people over dinners served by maids in fancy houses. In interviews at pro-government rallies and anti-government demonstrations. People were talking across one another, over one another; they were full of anger and incomprehension; they'd given up trying to understand one another. They were frustrated and pissed off, and when they talked about it, the words often came out at top volume. The causes of the division were historical, but the rift deepened with Chávez. He had mined it and encouraged it until it became part of the landscape, something that people took as a given.

I thought of Venezuela as the shouting country. Venezuelans were like two groups of people facing each other on opposite sides of a street, shouting at the top of their lungs: insults, arguments, slogans. And each of them was shouting so loud, and with so much intensity, that they couldn't hear what the people on the other side of the street were shouting. Meanwhile, the street itself was a ruin, full of potholes and debris and trash. And no one cared. All they wanted to do was keep shouting at one another. Maybe once, long ago, someone had shouted about the bad condition of the street: that something should be done to fix it, maybe even that they should work together to get it done. But by now the street wasn't the point anymore; the shouting was the point.

* * *

I HADN'T BEEN in Venezuela long when I went to see a politician named Ismael García, who was the head of a small party called Podemos. He'd started out as an ally of Chávez and then broke away and joined the opposition. He was an old-style pol, a brawler in the trenches who'd paid his dues. The party headquarters was in a leafy middle-class Caracas neighborhood called El Bosque. Big trees hung over streets of one- and two-story houses tucked behind walls topped with broken glass. He had a crowded office with too much furniture and too many people. I had the feeling that he didn't spend much time alone, that he was always accompanied by an entourage. Acolytes. Aides. A driver. A bodyguard. Hangers-on.

García came across on this morning as a man bursting with barely constrained energy. He was in his late fifties, with a mustache that pushed his mouth into a frown, wire-rim glasses, and graying hair in full retreat behind the dome of his head. I recall a dress shirt, open at the collar, and a soft brown leather jacket. He seemed impatient, a man for whom time was a fast-food sandwich to be eaten as quickly as possible, in big bites. We sat in low-slung chairs at opposite ends of a small coffee table.

"Let's get down to it," García said. The recording goes on for forty-one minutes. Mostly we talked about the politics of the moment. Chávez had been treated for cancer and was about to run for reelection, although there was speculation that he was too sick and would make way for another candidate. García dismissed it as nonsense: Chávez was a messiah to his followers and irreplaceable. "That's a part of Venezuelan politics that we need to look at," he said, "not just on the Chavista side but on our side too. We've gotten used to creating messiahs." What stuck with me about the interview, however, wasn't what García said, the specific catalog of grievances and predictions, but how he said it. García didn't talk to me. He shouted at me. He gave me a forty-one-minute tongue-lashing. I started to wonder if he was angry at me. Had I said the wrong thing? Had I done something to offend him? I asked questions, but they hardly mattered before the verbal enfilade, the percussive sentences delivered without pause at full volume, as though he were standing on a stage and wanted to make sure that the very last guy in the very last row could hear him.

García began in the 1970s as a member of a small leftist party called Movimiento al Socialismo, or MAS. Long before Barack Obama popularized the phrase during his first candidacy for president in the United

States, the slogan of MAS was "*Sí podemos,*" "Yes we can!" The MAS supported Chávez when he first ran for president in 1998, but over the years the party repeatedly split, with factions coming out against Chávez and breaking off. Through it all, García stuck with the pro-Chávez wing until he decided to create his own pro-Chávez party, which he called Podemos (he took the MAS slogan, *Sí podemos,* with him). But nothing lasts forever. In 2007, García finally made his own break—he objected to a proposed constitutional amendment that would have allowed Chávez to be reelected indefinitely—and he took Podemos over to the opposition. At the time that I spoke to García, Chávez was in the process of wresting control of Podemos away from him in the courts and handing the party over to a loyalist; soon García would be a political orphan.

What meaning was there in all this splitting and changing sides? Ismael García had spent ten years shouting from one side of the street, but now he was shouting from the other. In his view, he was the one who'd stayed consistent. It was Chávez who'd lost García's trust. But what insight had García brought with him, what nuanced understanding of his former companions? He'd added his bugle voice to the choir. The change was geographical, Sidewalk A to Sidewalk B, and chromatic, the color of the T-shirt. The problem was always on the other side of the street. The solution? Maybe if we shout a little louder . . .

I sat and listened to him haranguing me from three feet away, across the little table. The volume squeezed the meaning out of the words; like water wrung from a washcloth, it trickled down the drain. What had I done to invite his anger? Then it occurred to me that maybe he wasn't angry with me after all. Maybe he was hard of hearing. Maybe he spoke loudly because he couldn't gauge the volume of his own voice. He didn't know that he was shouting. It was like texting with your mother, who doesn't realize that she's WRITING IN ALL CAPS. I took a deep breath. It seemed a likely explanation. Not angry. Just deaf.

I waved the white flag and thanked him for the interview.

We stood up. He grabbed my hand and, out of reflex, repeated the old shibboleth "*Sí podemos,*" "Yes we can," a phrase uttered a thousand times, devoid of meaning.

It was the first thing that he'd said in forty-one minutes that wasn't shouted.

I stumbled out into the sunshine, Caracas's great blessing. A blue sky. Green trees.

* * *

LATER THAT DAY I had another interview scheduled, with Luis Britto García, a prizewinning writer of short stories who was one of Chavismo's house intellectuals. I would see him often on television, presenting the government side of things in a soft, confident, educated voice that said: *reason resides with me.* He came across on television as both self-effacing and supercilious, the distracted, disheveled egghead.

Britto García (no relation to Ismael García) lived on a street with a wide, park-like divider in the middle, shaded by tall trees. His house had a high stucco wall separating it from the street, with a black metal door. I pushed the doorbell button and waited. No answer. I pushed again. Again nothing. I waited some more, not wanting to be rude or overinsistent. I called Britto García's number on my cell phone. There was no answer.

A newcomer to a country always wonders whether he's missing some social cues that everyone else is attuned to. There's a note of doubt, like a distant bell struck just within the range of hearing. As a foreigner traveling in Latin America, I try to observe and match my behavior to those around me. I don't want to be the clueless gringo barging in. As a newspaper reporter, you have to strike a balance between being pushy—get that interview, ask that question—and hanging back, observing, not assuming that things are as you expect them to be. These are countries where the brassy directness of a New Yorker won't get you very far, where people often prefer to talk around a subject, skirting it, avoiding it, before they're ready to discuss it. Sometimes you're more likely to get where you're going by taking the long way around.

Still, in this case, I couldn't understand what had gone wrong. I'd confirmed with Britto García the night before. Perhaps he'd been called away on an emergency. Or gotten stuck in traffic. I was determined to wait. I'd made a decision when I'd arrived in Venezuela not to accept received wisdom, not to adopt the opinions of others who had been there before me. I wanted to see and understand for myself. Above all, that meant speaking to people from all sides.

So I waited. The street was quiet. I sat under a tree in the green strip in the middle. Every once in a while I would call the phone number or go over and ring the bell—just in case he somehow hadn't heard it before. Finally, after more than an hour, I called the phone number again. This time Britto García picked up.

I told him who I was.

"Who?"

"The journalist. From New York. We had an appointment."

"Ah! Yes! How are you?"

"I'm fine. I'm outside your house."

"Excellent. I was asleep." He said it as though it were the most natural response in the world. As though what you did when you had an appointment was take a nap and wake up an hour later. "I'll let you in."

I went to the black door and waited a while longer. I heard a movement on the other side and the metal door scraped open.

Luis Britto García was short and thin, about seventy years old, with soft white hair that encircled his face. There was a tall domed forehead with a thin beach of white hair above it and then a beard of the same color completing the circle below. He had a white pencil mustache and untrimmed eyebrows. He had on a much-worn white T-shirt, loose white pants, and black sandals. His thin arms stuck out of the shirt sleeves like pink drinking straws. He glanced at my face without meeting my eyes, and then he looked down at the ground. He never looked at me again.

I entered. He shut the gate and turned around and I followed him along a concrete path through a wasteland. Weeds, knee-high, rioted in what was once a garden. Everything was yellowed and parched. To the left was an abandoned pool or cement-lined pond. I remember it being round, a shallow circle of black liquid at the bottom. The whole place had a feeling of abandonment.

We entered a house that seemed almost a continuation of the garden: a dusty couch with stained cushions and ancient throw pillows, some unhappy chairs, and a few houseplants, one of them tumbled over, spilling soil across the floor. Britto García indicated that I should sit on the couch and asked if I wanted some water. I said yes. He disappeared into the kitchen, looking down at the floor, barely picking up his feet as he walked. He returned, and without looking at my face, he put a glass in my hand. The glass was dirty. I set it down.

Britto García sat on the couch, not facing me but facing out, toward the room. Sometimes he gazed at the floor; other times he looked up, as though staring at a sort of middle distance, beyond this room, beyond our conversation.

We started out talking about books and movies, detective novels, science fiction. Eventually I steered the conversation to politics—but this was 180 degrees from my earlier interview. Britto García spoke so softly that sometimes I had to ask him to repeat himself. His voice was high-pitched and distant, as if he was speaking to me from a long way off. It had a sort of whistle to it, on another register, an accompaniment like the drone string in Indian music.

And here was a new phenomenon. After that first fleeting glance at the gate, Britto García never looked at me. I began to wonder—can he see me, is he partially blind, does he have impaired vision? There was the spilled plant, the dirty glass of water, the wreck of a garden, the downcast eyes. He sibilated on, touting the accomplishments of Chávez and his government, defending it against its enemies.

He said that there was a campaign against Venezuela in the international media. Outside the country you'd think it was a dictatorship. But it was the opposite. He pointed out that Chávez and Chavismo had won dozens of elections. He'd never seen a government so evenhanded with its enemies. The newspapers in Venezuela said terrible things about the government all the time, and there was no censorship. The same was true with TV and radio. I asked about RCTV, a stridently anti-Chávez TV station that was forced off the air when its broadcast license wasn't renewed. It was at the discretion of governments everywhere to grant or withhold licenses to the public airwaves, Britto García said. I asked about the president's cancer. Who would be the candidate if Chávez was too sick to run? Commenting on that would be speculation, he said, political gossip, which he found pointless and boring. But shouldn't people be concerned about the health of a president running for reelection? "I can't tell you the date of my death because I don't know it. By the same token I can't tell you the date of anyone else's death. You need to talk to an astrologer." I asked if there could be Chavismo without Chávez. It was a question that had been voiced frequently since the president fell ill. "If my grandmother had wheels, she would be a bicycle." I asked if what was happening in Chávez's Venezuela could be defined as a revolution. "It's a process of transition that one supposes is heading toward socialism," he said. "A revolution is when there is a radical change in the ownership and control of the means of production." In Venezuela the government had gone part of the way, taking over the oil industry, steel mills, aluminum. "It's complex. It doesn't get resolved from one day to the next."

This went on for more than an hour. Where Ismael García was a cudgel, Britto García was a scalpel, sharp and precise, so that you didn't know how deeply you'd been cut until it was over. I thanked him and said goodbye. I retreated through the blasted garden, past the black eye of the pool.

The day had left me stunned. In the morning, Ismael García, shouting, seemingly deaf to everything but his own words. In the afternoon, Luis Britto García, softly polishing the beautiful world of Chavismo, head down, unseeing, blind to the wreck of his garden, the wreck of the country.

I went out through the gate to the street, where the light was beginning to fade. I still wasn't used to the early sunsets near the equator.

3

Blackout

The blackout played tricks with your mind. It was like jujitsu. It put you off balance, it saw your weakness, and it flipped you. It brought things out of you that you didn't know were there. You were a different person, before and after the blackout. One of the ways it did that, one of the ways that it threw you off balance, was that it messed with your sense of time.

"The thing is, those days seemed like years," Marlyn Rangel told me. "You didn't know what day it was. To make things worse, without electricity you couldn't charge your phone. So you didn't know what time it was. Or the day of the week. You didn't even know the date."

You were isolated. There was no news. No TV. No radio. No cell phone signal. No data plan. No internet, no social media. No one from the government ever came to say what was going on. The government never sent water, never sent food or medicine. No police officers, no firemen, no rescue workers, no one to tell you what was happening and how long it would last. That was the most important question as the days dragged on, Thursday into Friday, Friday into Saturday, Saturday into Sunday, Sunday into Monday: How long would it last?

You were on your own. Alone, you and your family and your neighbors, every neighborhood an island surrounded by silence and darkness. The city an archipelago.

One day. Two days. Three days. Four. Five . . .

Power started to come back in Caracas and some other parts of the country within twenty-four hours. But in Maracaibo, the country's second-largest city, with nearly 2 million people, where Marlyn lived, the power stayed out for five days. And it didn't come back on all at once. Some parts of the city were without power for longer periods of time, and in some areas it returned, only to go out again.

Think about it. The power goes out. At first you think, *No big deal, it'll come back on in a few hours.* Then as black night settles down all around, you think, *It'll come back in the morning.* Then in the morning you think, *Later today we'll have power.* Later that day: *Certainly the lights will come back on by tomorrow.* And as the days go by and there is no power and no news, you start to wonder: *What if it doesn't come back on at all?* And then the food runs out. Or it spoils in the heat. And you have no cash (hardly anyone has cash anymore, because on top of the shortages of food and medicine, there's a cash shortage). And without power the bank machines don't work. And the stores can't sell you food because the card readers don't work. And it's over 90 degrees. And there's no air conditioning. And there's no running water. And you can't bathe. And you can't sleep. And still no one tells you what's going on. Or how long it will last . . .

And time starts to bend.

"We never thought," Marlyn said, "we'd be without power for so many days."

Marlyn was twenty-five. She studied computer science in a two-year public university. Her goal was to graduate and get out. Move away from all this, to somewhere more like her old definition of normal. Somewhere with electricity, running water, gasoline, cooking gas, cell phone service, internet. In other words, someday she wanted to live in the modern world again.

While the March 7 nationwide blackout made headlines around the world and dismayed and inconvenienced people in Caracas and other parts of the country, here in Maracaibo, the residents had been coping with blackouts and electrical rationing for more than a year. When the big blackout hit, they were already desperate *before* the power went out.

When people in Maracaibo start counting blackouts, they go back to Christmas Eve, 2017. The power started to fail as families gathered for their holiday dinner. By midnight the whole city was without power. Merry Christmas, Maracaibo.

That, for the purposes of counting, for Maracuchos, as the people of Maracaibo call themselves, was the first blackout. It lasted in some areas until about noon on Christmas Day.

The second blackout came a week later, on New Year's Day, 2018. After that the power rationing started. Power would be shut off for about four hours a day, in different areas at different times, to ease the overall load on the grid. By April, the rationing had increased to about six hours a day. Over the next few months, it would fluctuate, sometimes longer, sometimes shorter. The schedule was erratic: you never knew when your turn would come. It was like a giant behavioral experiment to see how hundreds of thousands of people would react in an environment of increasing uncertainty and stress.

Maracaibo and the rest of Zulia state are at the far end of the nation's power grid, almost as far as you can get from the big hydroelectric plants and still be in Venezuela. Yet they are reliant on those plants for most of the electricity they consume, which has created chronic problems. The state has several thermal generating stations, which operate on natural gas or diesel fuel. If they are operating at full capacity, they can provide nearly enough power to satisfy local demand. But most of those plants are either shut down or barely functioning.

The chronology of the blackouts and power rationing was related to me by Nataly Angulo, a journalist who lives in Maracaibo and has become a keeper of such facts. During 2018, Nataly counted a total of twenty-five blackouts, some lasting just two or three hours, some more than a day. The longest blackout in 2018, in August, lasted three days. After that, the rationing became more intense: many people would go without electricity for up to half a day at a time. Toward the end of the year, it improved, and on some days there might be no rationing at all. Then it became worse again, and by February some areas of the city would be without power for up to sixteen hours a day. Then March 7 came and the lights went out all across the country.

While Maracaibo is Venezuela's second-largest city by population, Maracuchos think of it as being first by every other measure. Maracuchos are, by their own account, happier, funnier, smarter, and better-looking than people in other parts of the country. They're superior singers and they have more melodious songs and they tell funnier jokes and more entertaining stories and they have tastier food. Maracaibo is the Texas of Venezuela. Everything is bigger in Maracaibo. The hamburgers are bigger. The women's fake breasts are larger, and their silicon-injected butts are firmer.[1] Their high heels are higher. The men's bellies are bigger too (Maracuchos are prodigious eaters—and a big belly on a man is a sign of success and sex appeal). They're louder and more outgoing. In a country of extroverts, they're more extroverted. Maracaibo is the Texas of Venezuela because it learned from the real thing. The oil industry started here in Zulia state (at Mene Grande, site of the first oil well), and for a long time the foreign oil companies kept their headquarters in Maracaibo. For Texans working in the oil fields, Maracaibo and Zulia were home. Zulia also had large cattle ranches, and in the 1940s, Nelson Rockefeller (whose family owned Standard Oil and its Venezuelan subsidiary, Creole Petroleum) imported Texas bloodstock to ranches in southern Zulia.[2] Maracaibo had Venezuela's first bank, its first electric streetlights, its first telephone service, its first movie theater. Or at least it lays claim to all that. But most of all, Maracuchos are big—they're fat and jolly and loud, and they love to go to extremes. That, at least, is how it was before the crisis.

* * *

I HAD MY first conversation with Marlyn two months after the big blackout and the looting that followed. It was May, the sky was overcast. It had rained and brown puddles filled the pockmarked streets. "So many holes," Marlyn said, "it looks like a sieve."

We were at the house of Marlyn's grandmother, Grandma Minerva, sitting in chairs made of bent iron rods covered with stretchy plastic bands, in front of a zinc-roofed carport on the side of the house. Behind us slumped a broken-down blue Fiat Uno that looked like it hadn't run in a long time. Many people stopped driving their cars once they broke down, either because no spare parts were available or because they couldn't afford them. The car's left rear taillight was missing, and one of the tires was flat and had come off the rim. The car was covered in a thick coat of dust. On the grimy back window, someone had drawn a smiley face and written, "Wash me."

The house, inside and out, was crammed with tchotchkes: kitschy painted plaster owls and gnomes and Santas. On a pillar in the front of the house was a painted metal bracket for mounting a flag. It was fashioned in the form of the national seal: a pair of cornucopias, a shield, a clutch of weapons, a shock of wheat, and a white horse running toward the right while looking back toward the left. You could tell with the precision of carbon dating that the thing had been made before 2006; that was when Chávez had ordered the seal changed. He wanted it to show the horse galloping to the left, just like the country. And there would be no more looking back.

Marlyn wore a gray Hard Rock Cafe T-shirt, flip-flops, and even though it was midafternoon, plaid pajama pants. Her long dark hair was pulled back in a ponytail. She seemed tired, with circles under her eyes and a listlessness to her smile, as though that small movement of the facial muscles was the limit of her energy. Each time I saw her, Marlyn seemed to be in a state of enervation that was out of place for someone so young. You might think that the frequent absence of electricity would be conducive to better sleep—no lights to disturb you, no TV to watch, no bars or clubs to go to. But Maracuchos in general wear the irritable, beleaguered demeanor of the sleep-deprived. And it's easy to see why. They spend nights in their cars, waiting in line to buy gasoline. They have to wake up in the middle of the night when the water suddenly comes on (often after weeks without running water), at which point they set to work filling tanks, washing clothes, bathing.

Most important for Maracuchos, without electricity there's no air conditioning. Maracaibo, where the average high temperature every month of the year is over 90, used to be known as Venezuela's coldest city: the air conditioning was always cranked to the max. The kind of air conditioning that gives you a headache when you walk in from outside. Not anymore. Now the nights are hot and full of mosquitoes. Maybe you have no power. Or maybe you do and your air conditioner sits like an outsize brick in the window because it burned out in one of the countless power surges. So you stay in your sweltering room with the windows closed against the bugs, tossing tangled up in the clammy sheets, or you lie outside in a hammock, sweating and slapping at mosquitoes.

Marlyn lived in a barrio called Raúl Leoni. It contained some of the poorest neighborhoods in Maracaibo, but this section was not so badly off, with solid cinder-block homes. Marlyn's father was a medical records clerk who worked for a hospital union. Her mother (who lived separately) was a housewife. Grandma Minerva used to work in a clothing store.

Raúl Leoni, the barrio's namesake, was the second president elected in Venezuela after the dictator Marcos Pérez Jiménez was overthrown in 1958 and democracy was established. When Leoni's term ended, he became the first president in the country's history to hand over power to an elected president from a different party. That was half a century ago.

Leoni belonged to Democratic Action, the dominant party in Venezuela after the dictatorship, similar to the social democrats in Europe. The man he passed the presidential sash to was Rafael Caldera, of the party known as COPEI, the equivalent of the Christian Democrats. After the dictatorship ended, the two parties, Democratic Action and COPEI, more or less alternated in the presidential palace, much like the Democrats and Republicans in the United States. Presidents could be elected more than once, but not to consecutive terms. Caldera served his term, and after him came another president from Democratic Action, Carlos Andrés Pérez. People called Pérez CAP, for his initials. CAP and Caldera both served two terms. The second term did not go well for either man. For CAP, it included the catastrophic Caracazo riot in 1989, two coup attempts, including the one led by Chávez, and a corruption scandal that ended in his impeachment and removal from office. By the end of Caldera's second presidency, the country had gone through a banking crisis, a recession, and a crash in oil prices, and the public's confidence in the mainstream political parties was destroyed. While Caldera was the first elected president to take over from a predecessor of a different party, he was also the last to hand off power in the same way. Caldera's successor was Chávez, who first took office in 1999. And the party of

Chávez, in the person of Chávez and, on his death, Maduro, had held power in Venezuela ever since: twenty-one years and counting.

* * *

ON THE FOURTH day of the blackout, a Sunday, at midday, Marlyn's family ate the last of the food they had in the house: spaghetti with nothing on it. They had no dinner Sunday night and no breakfast Monday morning. Marlyn was worried about her three-year-old half brother, Marlon (her father's son with his second wife), and her grandparents.

For a long time, people had been living day to day—money was short and food was so expensive that you couldn't buy more than you needed for that day or maybe the next. I was in many houses in Venezuela in 2019 where you opened the kitchen cupboard and there was nothing inside, not a can or a crumb. There is a special kind of emptiness to a bare cupboard and an empty refrigerator. You feel it in the pit of your stomach (which is probably empty too). I would often ask people to take me to their kitchen and open the cupboard. It was necessary to understand their lives. There's a strange intimacy involved in the act of sharing an absence, a void. It's like someone opening his shirt to show you a surgical scar. How does an amputee show you his absent limb? In general, the empty cupboards that were opened to me were so bare, so clean, I had the feeling that someone had run the palm of their hand across the shelf paper to pick up any crumbs that might have remained.

Venezuela used to be a land of plenty. People would say that to me all the time: *We're a rich country, we have oil.* During the Chávez years, the country filled up with oil money—oil was over $100 a barrel—and these people who were going hungry now used to eat three meals a day and had enough money to take their kids to the movies or to the beach or to a fast-food restaurant. Now many people were eating just once or twice a day, and what they were eating was lentils. Maybe some rice or pasta. Tomorrow existed only as a doubt: What will we eat tomorrow?

I've seen refrigerators with only a jug of water in them. Maracuchos have a fetish about cold water. They don't like to drink water that's not icy cold. They consider room-temperature water unhealthy and, more than that, uncivilized, un-Maracucho (the water in Maracaibo is colder than the water anywhere else). But now even that's a luxury—so many refrigerators have been burned out by power spikes following the blackouts and brownouts. There is a poor person's joke. Q: What's in the refrigerator? A: Water and light (because the light goes on when you open the door). Now there's not even that.

   When the blackout hit, people were caught unprovisioned. They had no food to last them till the power came back on. There was a day or two when the merchants were giving away perishables, like meat and dairy products, because they started to spoil. After that there was nothing at all. And people's desperation began to rise.

4

To Be Bolívar

Columbus reached South America on his third voyage across the Atlantic, in 1498. It was the first time since the Vikings, centuries before, that European eyes beheld one of the continents on the western shores of the Atlantic Ocean. But Columbus didn't realize what he was looking at as he coasted along the Paria Peninsula in what would later be called Venezuela. He noted its attractive climate and landscape and the immense quantity of fresh water pouring into the Gulf of Paria from the as-yet-unnamed Orinoco River. But he thought that he had merely discovered another island. Some of the indigenous inhabitants boarded Columbus's ship, and he was impressed by their beauty and temperate character (and their gold and pearl ornaments).

Then, as he sailed away, toward Hispaniola, he reflected on what he'd seen and he reached a remarkable conclusion. In his journal and letters, he referred to the land he'd left behind as "an Other World." He had reached, he said, the vicinity of the Terrestrial Paradise, the Garden of Eden. The signs were unmistakable, starting with the beauty and mildness of the climate and the people. The abundant pure water flowing into the gulf could only have come from the fabled fountain of Paradise, from which sprung all the earth's waters. Columbus sent a report to the king and queen of Spain, describing his discovery, and he gave the land a name, the first European christening of what would come to be known as Venezuela.

He called it Tierra de Gracia, Land of Grace.[1]

It wasn't long before subsequent explorers confirmed its status as a continent and it began to appear on maps with a more prosaic name: Tierra Firme, Terra Firma.

A year after Columbus's voyage, a Spaniard, Alonso de Ojeda, and an Italian, Amerigo Vespucci, sailed together along the Caribbean coast of the continent and reached the entrance to Lake Maracaibo. There, the story goes, the explorers saw people living in stilt houses on the water's edge. The scene reminded Vespucci of Venice, prompting him to call the place Venezuela, or Little Venice.

That's the story that Venezuelan children learn in school. It is probably apocryphal.

A couple of decades later, another Spaniard, Martín Fernández de Enciso, offered an alternate version. He said that Ojeda and Vespucci, on reaching Lake Maracaibo, had encountered a village called Veneciuela.[2]

Whatever the origin of the name, the gulf where Lake Maracaibo has its outlet into the Caribbean Sea came to be known as the Gulf of Venezuela. Over time, the name was extended to the entire province.[3]

For a brief time, this new land would be the scene of the first commodity boom-and-bust in the New World. The pearls that Columbus saw worn by the inhabitants of Paria came from a group of small islands off Venezuela's Caribbean coast. From 1510 to about 1540, one of those islands, a tiny scrap of dry rock called Cubagua, became the center of a pearl fishery that brought immense wealth to the Spanish crown. Millions of oysters were harvested, yielding tons of pearls. Thousands of indigenous slaves, many taken from the mainland, were forced to work under brutal conditions as divers. It didn't take long for Columbus's Land of Grace to become a hell on earth. After twenty years, the oyster beds started to give out, and after another decade it was all over. Cubagua, the island of riches, was abandoned. The boomtown became a ghost town. In Venezuela, the pattern was set from the beginning.[4]

Its pearls depleted, Venezuela became a disappointment and an afterthought. The Conquest soon focused on Mexico and then Peru and the vast riches encountered there. Venezuela became a stopping-off place on the way to more profitable destinations. In the great grasping for booty that was the Spanish Conquest, Venezuela was the back of the line. And mostly it stayed that way. For a while it became the focus of the search for El Dorado, the golden kingdom fantasized by conquistadors and adventurers. But it always receded into the periphery, a not-very-profitable outpost of empire, a producer of cowhides and cacao and coffee beans.

* * *

VENEZUELA DECLARED ITS independence from Spain on July 5, 1811.

Simón Bolívar, a son of one of the wealthiest families in the colony, was twenty-seven years old and part of a radical pro-independence faction. The Bolívars owned copper mines and plantations with cacao, sugar, and indigo, and the slaves to work on them.

The éminence grise of the independence movement was Francisco de Miranda. He was born in Caracas in 1750 but spent most of his adult life abroad. From his home in London, he became a celebrity of revolution, agitating and conspiring for the independence of the Spanish American colonies.

Now, at the urging of Bolívar and other radicals, Miranda returned to Venezuela. He was given the title of *generalissimo* and put in charge of the rebel army. Miranda had the personality to match the grandiose title. He was arrogant and insufferable, puffed up with his own legend. But Venezuela's first spasm of independence was short-lived. Miranda's colonial recruits were raw, and he retreated in the face of superior royalist forces. Before long he capitulated and agreed with the Spanish to terms of surrender.

Bolívar and his fellow radicals wanted to fight on; they believed that Miranda had betrayed the cause. They confronted Miranda at the port of La Guaira, near Caracas, where he was waiting overnight to board a ship that would take him to safety. (Despite his surrender, he didn't trust the Spanish, his lifelong enemies.) Miranda was asleep when Bolívar and a companion entered his room. They woke him up and told him that they were arresting him as a traitor. Miranda raised a lantern (or perhaps an aide-de-camp did so; accounts vary) to get a better look at the faces of his accusers. Then he uttered one of the most famous sentences in the history of Venezuela: "*Bochinche, bochinche, esta gente no sabe hacer sino bochinche.*" *Bochinche* is noise, tumult, rowdiness, chaos. When your neighbors are having a party and playing music at top volume late at night, that is bochinche. Bochinche is sound and fury. If Shakespeare had been Venezuelan, he might have written that life is a tale told by an idiot, full of bochinche, signifying nothing. When a fight breaks out on the floor of the National Assembly in Caracas (not an uncommon occurrence), that is bochinche. When Venezuelans take off the weekend from demonstrating against the government to go to the beach and drink and dance, that too is bochinche.

Miranda had spent most of his life outside Venezuela, frequenting the salons of London and Paris. He had fashioned himself into a cultured European. He was shocked to come home and find an unruly, backward country full of rubes: untrainable would-be soldiers and squabbling, conniving criollos. And now this final midnight betrayal.

Lamp held high, Miranda looked Bolívar in the face and said: "Bochinche, bochinche. Chaos. Confusion. *The only thing that these people know how to make is noise.*"

It wasn't a curse so much as a prediction. Or a life sentence.

Bolívar had Miranda thrown in a dungeon. The Spanish forces soon arrived and made Miranda their prisoner. The world-famous agitator for revolution was turned over by his own brothers-in-arms to the empire he'd spent a lifetime conspiring to overthrow, deprived of liberty by the future Liberator.

Out of gratitude, the Spanish commander gave Bolívar a pass to depart for Curacao. Miranda was sent to Spain and died in prison there in 1816.

* * *

AFTER FLEEING TO Curacao, Bolívar went to New Grenada (today's Colombia), raised an army, and returned to Venezuela. Sweeping through a series of decisive battles, he defeated the Spanish forces. When he entered Caracas in August 1813, he rode on a white horse and was dressed in a uniform of scarlet, blue, and gold. An adoring throng acclaimed him the Liberator of Venezuela, and he was declared dictator, with absolute power to govern.

The euphoria didn't last. The country soon tore itself apart in what amounted to an undeclared civil war along lines of race, caste, and class. The white elite had preached liberation from Spain. The darker-skinned lower classes and the black slaves heard this and decided that they would like freedom too—from the white elite. They saw the best chance of achieving that goal was by taking the side of the Spanish Crown against their local masters. The bloodletting on all sides was ferocious.

Bolívar fled again, returned again. In 1819, he made an audacious move. He led his troops on a grueling march into the Andes and defeated the Spanish forces near Bogotá. Bolívar dreamed of creating a single great nation spanning the South American continent, from ocean to ocean. Made up of what are today Ecuador, Colombia, Panama, and Venezuela, it would be called Gran Colombia. In 1821, Bolívar came home and retook Caracas. A congress was convened and Bolívar was voted the first president of Gran Colombia.

Next Bolívar crossed the Andes again and captured Quito and Guayaquil. He continued south and drove the Spanish from Peru. Spanish forces had already been forced out of Chile, Argentina, Uruguay, and Paraguay by revolutionaries in those colonies. Peru was the last to fall, and with Bolívar's victory there, all of Spanish South America was now free.

His admirers gave Bolívar the title of Liberator of the Americas, showering him with adulation everywhere he went.

Bolívar had won the war, but he was soon to lose the peace.

He returned to Caracas. There was intrigue, calumny, and ruin all around. The promise of independence had given way to despair. The new nation that he had willed into being, Gran Colombia, was a three-legged stool with all the legs a different height. Bogotá, Caracas, and Quito distrusted one another, and each viewed the others as rivals rather than allies. Not for the last time, Miranda would seem prophetic: bochinche, bochinche, nothing but noise and confusion. In Bogotá in 1828 the Liberator escaped an assassination attempt by jumping out of his bedroom window. He was in poor health, suffering from tuberculosis. There were military uprisings. In 1830, against his wishes, Venezuela seceded from Gran Colombia and declared itself an independent nation. Ecuador broke away soon after. Gran Colombia was no more. It had taken Bolívar fourteen years to free South America from the

Spanish. His shining dream of a great nation spanning the continent had lasted barely eight years.

Dejected, Bolívar decided to leave for Europe. "If any one man were indispensable to a state's survival, that state should not and will not exist," he wrote. But he was too ill to make the journey. He wrote to a friend that in his years of struggle and glory he had learned only a few certainties. "America is ungovernable" was one of them. Another: "He who serves a revolution plows the sea." Bolívar died on December 17, 1830, in the town of Santa Marta, in present-day Colombia.[5]

* * *

VENEZUELANS HAD FOLLOWED Bolívar and fought and died across much of South America. But the war that took place on Venezuelan soil was the bloodiest of all. Towns, roads, and plantations were destroyed. Historians estimate that more than 30 percent of the population of Venezuela died during the war.[6]

At that point Venezuela was more a loose collection of regional fiefdoms, each headed by a caudillo, or strongman, than a coherent, unified country. The rest of the nineteenth century was the age of the caudillo: a series of civil wars and uprisings by local chieftains. The bloodiest of these, from 1859 to 1863, was known as the Federal War, with perhaps a fifth of the population being killed.[7] Venezuela seemed on the point of disintegrating, just as Gran Colombia had. That's when the victors of the Federal War raised up Bolívar and made him a symbol around which the wounded nation could cohere.

Bolívar, the hero who brought glory to the nation. Bolívar, the military and political genius, the Liberator, the Father of His Country. Today, the main square of almost every city and town in Venezuela is named Plaza Bolívar. And each one has a statue of the Liberator. Some show him standing, some on horseback. In the city named for him, Bolívar City, which is the capital of Bolívar state, there is of course a Plaza Bolívar, with a Bolívar statue: on a high marble pedestal the Liberator appears in the guise of a Roman emperor or senator, his cape wrapped around him to look like a toga, a sword in his right hand, a law scroll in his left.

All this fed what became a state religion: Bolívar as civic god. Venezuelan historians refer to it as Bolívar worship.[8]

In his eventful forty-seven years Bolívar said enough, wrote enough, gave enough speeches, corresponded widely enough, and changed his thinking often enough, that today you can find material in the vast Bolivarian catalog to support virtually any ideology, position, or cause. Bolívar ruled as a dictator—so Venezuelan dictators held him up as an example of how the country needed to be ruled by a firm hand. Bolívar said that elections were essential—so democrats embraced him. Bolívar warned that elections would lead to anarchy—so conservatives revered him. Outside Venezuela, both Mussolini and Franco saw Bolívar as a fascist precursor. Marx called him "the dastardly, most miserable, and meanest of blackguards." Cuban communists honored him. Chávez hailed Bolívar as a socialist.

Chávez once ordered Bolívar's remains, entombed in the National Pantheon in Caracas, to be exhumed. He then commissioned a computer-generated portrait of the Liberator, based on digital projections from the great man's skull. It looked a lot like the portraits of Bolívar painted by his contemporaries, but Chávez said that for the first time, modern Venezuelans were seeing Bolívar's "true face." This was a quaint notion. The true face of Bolívar is what you want it to be. He was a democrat. He was an autocrat. He was an egalitarian. He was an elitist. He was an abolitionist. He was a slaveholder. He was a cruel tyrant. He was a tolerant humanist. In fact, he was all those things at one time or another.

In the late nineteenth century, an amateur historian named Eduardo Blanco wrote a book-length panegyric to the Liberator. Called *Venezuela heroica* (*Heroic Venezuela*), it became a staple of the new civic religion. "Alexander the Great, Julius Caesar, Charlemagne and Napoleon—they all shared common traits," Blanco wrote. "Bolívar is like no one else. His glory is greater. To be the Liberator, that is above all greatness to which man's ambition may aspire."[9]

But there was a flaw built into this act of veneration. Venezuelans looked around—whether in the nineteenth century, the twentieth, or the twenty-first—and, with a few fleeting exceptions, saw nothing that came close to the past glories that they'd learned about as schoolchildren. "The historical narratives," wrote the historian Tomás Straka, "tell us the story of a country that doesn't look anything like the one we see on the street." In the act of its creation, Venezuela became a nation with a built-in inferiority complex: We were once great, and just look at us now. When the past is so grandiose, the present can only disappoint. And this disappointment contained within it a feedback loop. "The more they become disenchanted with the Republic," Straka wrote of his fellow Venezuelans, "the more they seek refuge in the glorious past."[10]

In 2019, as the country slid deeper into dysfunction and collapse, the government erected billboards around Caracas, showing pictures of happy Venezuelan families. They seemed to be not so much persevering through the hard times as living in a different, idealized country. The billboards carried a slogan with an echo from the past: "Heroic Venezuela."

5

Blackout

The looting started in Maracaibo late on Sunday, the fourth day of the blackout. The looters broke into a pharmacy and then an upscale mall. On Monday morning, Marlyn's boyfriend, Andrés, told her that people were looting stores in their neighborhood, in an area called La Curva de Molina. People were going down the street carrying packages of corn flour, rice, and pasta. In Marlyn's house they hadn't eaten since the day before and now food was literally walking past their door. Andrés and Marlyn's stepbrother, Anthony, set off for La Curva, as everyone called it, to see what they could find. Marlyn decided to go along.

La Curva was always a busy place, but Marlyn had never seen so many people there. They'd broken through the metal pulldown gates in front of the shops. People would run in, desperate to get their hands on something, anything. There was a chemistry in the air, almost a smell, you could sense it: desperation, adrenaline, a fever. It scared her. Suddenly Marlyn heard gunshots and she ran. A group of men with guns stood outside a variety store called Todo Regalado (Everything Cheap), and they'd fired into the air to keep the looters back. But this was the only store that was protected. All around, the other stores had been ripped open and people were swarming in and out: wasps around a broken nest.

The crush was so bad at some of the stores that many people couldn't get in. When that happened, the people outside would start to shout,

"*Guardia!*"—pretending to warn the looters inside that the National Guard had arrived. Scared of being caught, the looters inside would rush out. And then the people waiting outside would run in to take their places.

"It was like a game," Marlyn said. "'*Guardia!*' Run out. Run in. Out. In. Out. In." But there were no police, no soldiers. "It was absolutely out of control."

The stores were like dark caves. There was broken glass, jagged metal. People were bleeding. Marlyn was too scared to go inside. "I felt like I was about three feet tall, like a hobbit. Everyone else seemed like giants, and if I went inside, I'd be crushed."

She found a safe spot from which she could watch the parade of looters. People were taking more than food: electric fans, tables, chairs, a bed, blenders, pressure cookers, shoes, clothing, and even the shelves from inside the stores. "To me, that was just vandalism," Marlyn said. "You're not going to eat a shoe. You're not going to eat a big industrial fan that you're carrying on your back."

* * *

Later in the day, Marlyn, Andrés, and Anthony followed the crowds to a warehouse. Inside there was a bonanza: pallets of food stacked to the rafters. This time Marlyn was determined to go in. But Andrés pulled her back. He was afraid she would get hurt. The boys went inside and soon came out loaded with treasure. Sacks of pasta, a case of canned deviled ham, laundry detergent, toilet paper, catsup, and a box of caramel candy (the kind that comes in tubes). The boys dropped their booty and went in for more. Marlyn sat on top of the pile like a robber princess. They came out again with more stuff and now decided to head home.

Their haul was a burden to carry, so they stopped to rest in front of a yellow and green house with a black gate set in a wall that separated it from the street. Two elderly women stood inside the gate. They saw all the food and asked if they could have a few bags of pasta. One of the boys offered a trade: if they could stash their things at the old women's house while they went to find someone with a car, they'd give the women pasta and more.

The women agreed and opened the gate. They carried the things inside. Andrés and Anthony went off in search of transportation. And Marlyn stayed behind with the two elderly women in the little yellow and green house, like in a fairy tale.

Here the story becomes stranger.

It turned out that the warehouse had a big stash of tires. Tires are valuable in Venezuela. They're hard to come by and expensive and necessary for certain tasks—like smuggling loads of cheap Venezuelan gasoline across the border into Colombia. After Marlyn and the boys had left the warehouse, a group of armed men showed up. The men told the looters at the warehouse: take whatever you want but don't touch the tires. Then some of the men went out into the neighborhood to find the tires that had already been looted.

Around this time, a man and a woman, about Marlyn's age, came down the street, toward the yellow and green house. The man carried two tires. The woman carried one. Word had spread quickly about the armed men and the tires and the old women told the newcomers to bring the tires inside until the coast was clear. Marlyn helped carry the tires to the back of the house, where they would be out of sight from the street.

But one of the armed men was right behind them and he pushed his way in at the gate. When Marlyn emerged from the house, he pointed an automatic pistol at her and demanded the tires. The gun looked enormous; it had an extra-long clip extending below the grip. "I was scared for my life," Marlyn said. She brought him inside to where they'd left the tires but the man became incensed. Tires come in pairs. Why were there only three of them? Where was the other one? He aimed the gun at Marlyn again. From the way he acted, she thought that he must be a cop or a soldier. Finally the man put the gun away. He carried the tires to the street, loaded them into the back of a car, and drove off.

At last Andrés and Anthony came back, with Marlyn's dad driving her grandfather's white Daewoo. They loaded everything into the car. They gave the old women ten bags of pasta and a bag of laundry detergent. Then they went home.

After they'd divvied the food up, Marlyn took some of her share to her mother, who lived nearby. But instead of thanking her, her mom chewed her out. What was Marlyn thinking? She could have been shot! She could have been killed! And for what? For a few bags of noodles and some toilet paper? Marlyn went back to her dad's house, and this time it was his turn to yell at her. What was she doing taking food to her mother when they didn't have enough for themselves? Marlyn shut herself in her room and lay down in the dark and cried. Her whole body shook. Her mom was right. She could have been shot. The guy who came for the tires could have shot her. Or the men protecting the store at La Curva.

Her father called her to dinner. After everything she'd been through, it looked like a feast. A big plate of noodles and deviled ham. They sat in the dark and ate. Marlyn didn't know it, but the lights were starting to come back on in parts of Maracaibo.

* * *

THE BLACKOUT GOT inside your head. It threw you off balance. You weren't the same after as you were before.

"Morality, your sense of right and wrong, everything you learned when you were little, everything they taught you when you were growing up, everything they teach you in school, all the way up to college, was completely lost," Marlyn said. "Why? Because people got to a point where they couldn't think past tomorrow. What are you going to eat tomorrow? That's the only thing that they have in their head anymore . . . We were like that American movie *The Purge*. No one cared about anybody else. If you die from hunger, what do I care, as long as I've got food. There's no more lending a helping hand. People here, we have a tradition of helping each other out. If you come to my house: 'Here, have some coffee. Do you want something to eat?' People don't do that anymore. You wait for the person to leave before you sit down to eat because you haven't even got enough for yourself." Many of the stores that had been looted had been around for years and, against long odds, had remained open despite the country's economic crisis. But after the looting, some of them had shut down, and the people who worked there were out of a job. "The situation carries people to extremes. I'm sorry about what I did. If you look at it, the ones who suffered were the shop owners, the ones who were still around, who'd stayed open—the ones who were making an effort to stay in business here. And it's sad, but we stole from them. But I didn't have food. What was I going to do? Of course, everyone has their own conscience, everyone has their own way of thinking, every head contains its own world, but at the end of the day that's what it was: I had food on my table that night. But what did that do to me? What about my conscience? Where was I? Where was Marlyn Rangel at that moment? I didn't know her anymore."

Marlyn took night classes in computer science at a school called the University Institute of Technology, and when there was no power, which was often, classes would be canceled. Oh, and by the way, the computer science department at the University Institute of Technology had no computers. They were all stolen.

I asked Marlyn: "How do you study computer science without computers?"

"Theory."

Marlyn was fortunate because she had an aunt who lived in Bogotá, who sent the family food and clothing and other essentials. Aunt Carmen used to live in Maracaibo, working as an administrator in PDVSA, the government oil company. In 2003 and 2004, the opposition conducted a petition drive in support of a recall referendum seeking to remove Chávez from office. More than 2 million people signed. Many of them had government jobs and thousands were fired in retaliation.[1] Aunt Carmen was one of them. After that she moved with her family to Bogotá. (The recall vote was held in August 2004; Chávez won.)

A few years ago, Aunt Carmen bought Marlyn a laptop computer. But that led to another problem. Marlyn needed the internet to do her schoolwork, and in her barrio and in most other neighborhoods in Maracaibo, thieves had stolen the telephone wires that provided landline and internet service. The wire was made of copper, and the thieves sold it to scrap dealers. As a result, there was no internet at Marlyn's father's house, where she lived. It was the same at her mother's house and her grandmother's house and at the homes of everyone else she knew. Instead Marlyn used the data plan on her cell phone to connect her computer to the internet. But service was erratic and often too slow to get much done.

A while back, when thieves stole the wires for the telephone lines on Grandma Minerva's block, Grandma Minerva went to the local office of the government-run telephone company to report the theft. The people in the office told her that they couldn't process her complaint because the internet wasn't working.

"A little bit of black humor," Marlyn said. "There's no power at the electric company and the phone company doesn't have internet."

Marlyn suddenly sat up in her chair and her face brightened. "*Llegó la luz!*" "The electricity's back on!"

She pointed across the street to where a lightbulb had blinked on in the patio of another house, pale in the daylight.

As an outsider, I wasn't attuned to the comings and goings of electricity. The whole time that we'd been talking, there had been no electricity at Grandma Minerva's house. It was the power rationing. Each day they would receive a few hours of electricity, but you didn't know when it would come or how long it would last.

The lightbulb across the street blinked out again and Marlyn slumped back in her chair. Easy come, easy go.

"Venezuela takes one step forward and four steps back," she said. "It's like a crab. The president goes on TV and says, 'We're going to solve the electricity problem in two weeks.' Two weeks go by and it's 'We're going to solve the electricity problem in a month, two at the most.' Three months go by, and then he doesn't talk about the electricity problem anymore."

Marlyn wanted to earn her degree and leave the country, maybe go to the United States. "I have aspirations. I aspire to graduate. I aspire to get out of here. I aspire to build a better life, better than the one I'm living."

Marlyn worried that people had become accustomed to just scraping by, putting up with what would have been unthinkable a few years or even a few months earlier. When power first started to go out, people were indignant. Now they hardly reacted. They used to have reliable running water. At first, when the water went away, people protested.

Now they woke up in the middle of the night every few weeks when the water sputtered on and started washing clothes. "We've decided to become conformists, to just be here and to take whatever they give us, and that's it."

* * *

ON MY FIRST night in Maracaibo I was at a restaurant and the power went out. Everything went black and people went on talking and eating as though nothing had happened. Someone started to sing "Happy Birthday," just the first two words, "*Cumpleaños feliz.*" This was a joke, but with a birthday cake you light the candles *before* you turn out the lights. I was with Nataly, the local reporter who kept a running tally of the blackouts. She told me that when the lights went out at home, her two-year-old daughter kept on playing, without interruption. When her daughter walked through the darkened rooms, she never bumped into the furniture, navigating by memory. She was a few months old when the blackouts started. It was the only world she knew.

But for adults, living in an aleatory world created an ever-present stress that took its toll. People slept poorly or not at all; they didn't bathe; they didn't eat much, and what they did eat was mostly cheap calories: pasta, rice, lentils, with few fruits and vegetables and little protein. They lived attenuated lives whose limits and constrictions were set by the irregular comings and goings of electricity, water, phone service, the internet, food, cooking gas, gasoline. It was all out of their control, a constant reminder of the power and the incompetence and the arbitrariness of the state. And of your own state of uncertainty.

People developed new forms of superstition. If they were waiting for the power to come on, for instance, they wouldn't talk about it, so as not to jinx it. Or the opposite occurred. People would get nervous if the power came on and stayed longer than the six or so hours that they assumed was the amount allocated to them under the rationing.

"Last Saturday," Marlyn said, "the electricity stayed on almost the whole day. The first thing you think is, okay, now they're going to punish us, they're going to take away electricity for a full day. And sure enough, the next day we had maybe four hours of electricity the whole day."

What Marlyn actually said was "*Nos dejaron la luz*," "They left us with electricity."

The way Venezuelans talk about it, electricity is given and taken away. The government gives electricity just like it gives boxes of food or houses. And like gasoline, electricity is so cheap it might as well be free. With the devaluation and hyperinflation, the government electric company had essentially stopped charging customers. Whatever it might receive in payments wasn't worth the cost of processing them.

In Spanish, people typically refer to electricity as *luz*, light. When Marlyn saw the bulb go on across the street and perked up, she said, "*Llegó la luz!*" "The light has come!" When the power goes out, people say, "*Se fue la luz*"—"The light went away."

American English is less fanciful.

Light is electricity's most visible product, but in the United States we call electricity what it is: *power*. Electricity is power, and here in Venezuela it is power in the rawest sense. When Marlyn said, "Last Saturday they left us with electricity [light] for almost the whole day," in no way did she mean, "They left us with power." The government gives away many things: apartments, washing machines, television sets, pensions, gasoline, water, electricity. But it never gives away power.

The light on the patio across the street came on again, and this time it stayed on. Someone flicked on a switch in Grandma Minerva's house. It worked. "*Hay luz!*" "There is light!" It was 3:40 P.M. and Marlyn guessed that if they were lucky, the lights would stay on for five or six hours. She needed to charge her phone and her laptop too, and she had homework to do.

But suddenly there was an emergency. The whole time that we'd been talking, Grandma Minerva had been sitting in a rocking chair in the open front doorway. She was seventy-two and had low blood pressure. She sat limp, head tilted back, pale, eyes closed, her bony arms resting on the arms of the rocker. Every once in a while she gave out a weak moan. Now the heat and humidity had become too much for her. (Even with the electricity on, there was no relief: the air conditioners and fans had all burned out during past outages.) Another relative helped Grandma reach the bathroom. She couldn't hold herself up, could barely drag her feet across the tiled floor. There was a flurry of concern. A phone call was made and a relative arrived in a pickup truck. They lifted Grandma into the truck and drove off. Marlyn rode in back.

I checked with Marlyn that night, and she told me that they'd gone to a government-run clinic, but there was no doctor and no medicine. When they returned home, the lights were still on.

Crude

The first well began pumping oil at Mene Grande in 1914. Eight years later and fifty miles north, near the town of Cabimas, a drilling crew hit the first gusher. In Cabimas, it rained oil for nine days.[1]

In 1926, the value of oil exports, for the first time, exceeded the value of agricultural exports, including coffee, which for a century had been Venezuela's main commodity. By 1928, Venezuela was the world's top oil exporter and the second-biggest oil producer, after the United States.[2] By 1935, nine out of every ten export dollars came from oil.[3] Government revenue, from taxes on oil exports and concessions, soared. At the same time, exports of coffee and cacao, another staple crop, were falling.[4] Oil hadn't just taken over the economy. It was the economy.

The president was Juan Vicente Gómez, a cruel cartoon dictator with a waxed mustache that curled up at the ends. Labor unions and political parties were outlawed. Gómez's torture chambers were notorious, and their specialty was a method for hanging men upside down by the testicles.[5] Except for the secret police, the government under Gómez was minimal. The country was mostly empty space. Epidemics of malaria and yellow fever helped keep the population in check. Gómez treated the country like his personal hacienda. He grew rich off the oil concessions, and he gave the foreign oil companies, mostly from the United States, value in return—he let them draft Venezuela's 1922 petroleum law. It was low on regulation and taxes.[6]

Gómez died in December 1935, after twenty-seven years as president. He left behind a country that was so backward that the historian Mariano Picón Salas would say that the twentieth century didn't begin in Venezuela until 1936, after the death of the dictator.[7]

Stumbling out of the roadless decades of insurrection and malaria and coffee bushes and testicle-hanging, Venezuela found itself blinking in the klieg lights of the twentieth century. It was only then that it began to coalesce as a modern state and society.

It's not so much that Venezuela produced oil; it's that oil produced Venezuela. The country that emerged from the depths of this underdevelopment was in almost every way shaped by the economics of oil and the social and political relations that oil imposed on it.

After Gómez, there was a succession of military governments and coups and then another strutting general as dictator. Marcos Pérez Jiménez fancied himself a builder and a modernizer. He took the oil money and built highways and cloverleafs and airports and housing blocks. Like Gómez, he threw his opponents in jail and tortured or killed them. He outlawed labor unions and censored the press. He decided that Venezuela's problem was the color of its skin (too dark), and he encouraged Europeans to immigrate, to make the country whiter (like him).[8]

Then there was another coup, this time by a group of officers committed to a transition to democracy. Pérez Jiménez was forced out on January 23, 1958 (the date was once celebrated in Venezuela with more fervor than Independence Day). Later that year, Rómulo Betancourt, the head of the center-left party, Democratic Action, which had led opposition to the dictator, was elected president.

The young democracy fended off military coup attempts and a leftist guerrilla insurgency. The two main political parties, Democratic Action and COPEI (the Christian Democrats), signed a pact pledging to share power and to work together to preserve democracy. Oil prices were stable, the economy grew steadily, elections were held peacefully, and presidents passed the sash from one to another.

And then the world tilted.

In 1973, the Arab members of OPEC, the Organization of the Petroleum Exporting Countries, declared an oil embargo. The price of oil soared. Venezuelan oil was selling for almost $14 a barrel by the end of 1974, up from less than $3 a barrel in 1972.[9] The result was a head-spinning windfall. In 1974 the Venezuelan government received $10 billion from taxes and other fees on the oil business, compared to $1.4 billion in 1970.[10] Developed countries like the United States called the price surge the oil shock, referring to the damage it did to their economies. But it was a shock also to the producing countries. What to do with this gusher of money? Most profound of all, the paradigm had changed: even when the OPEC embargo was lifted, prices remained high—expensive oil was the world's new normal.

In Venezuela, all of this coincided with the landslide election of a new president, Carlos Andrés Pérez, of Democratic Action, the man Venezuelans called CAP. Pérez took office in 1974. He was grandiose and grandiloquent, a man for the times. "You are actors in the great national transformation that will make Venezuela into one of the great countries of the world," he declared.[11] Together, he told Venezuelans, they would build La Gran Venezuela, a Great Venezuela.

It certainly seemed a time for greatness.

More money poured into the public treasury in the 1970s than in the previous seven decades combined.[12] Pérez launched an ambitious campaign to supercharge development. As fast as they could, officials approved plans to build or expand steel mills and aluminum foundries and hydroelectric plants, oil refineries, ports. The bigger and faster, the better.

The government shoveled money into its pet development projects. Huge amounts were spent by PDVSA, the government oil company, to modernize its facilities.[13] And because policy makers were convinced that oil prices would stay high, the government chose to borrow money, in order to front-load the spending and make progress faster. Foreign banks rushed to write loans. The country's foreign debt soared.

But there was little or no planning and no oversight. No one asked if there was a market for the steel and other products that the new mills and factories would produce (too often there wasn't). No one checked the plans to see if the construction schedules and budgets could be met (they couldn't). Contracts ballooned, millions of dollars disappeared, fortunes were made.[14]

Consumers went on a spending spree of their own. The country was flooded with cheap imports: American cars, Japanese television sets, new-fangled digital watches, VCRs, and other gadgets. Venezuela became one of the world's leading consumers of Scotch whisky. Those who could afford to flew to Miami to do their shopping. This was the era of "*'Tá barato dame dos*"—the unofficial motto of middle-class and upper-class Venezuelans traveling abroad—"It's cheap, I'll take two."

And then it all fell apart.

Inflation—always low before—had surged above 20 percent a year by 1979.[15] Even with wage increases, many Venezuelans were having a hard time getting by. Shortages set in as basic goods disappeared from store shelves. The non-oil sectors of the economy, like farming and man-ufacturing, stagnated or declined. Unemployment increased. Calls to restrain government spending were cast aside as everyone clamored for a piece of the pie, and despite having the highest revenue levels in history, the government started running enormous deficits. The ambi-tious plans began to spring leaks. News stories reported delays in big projects. Accusations of corruption were commonplace. Pérez, lionized as a national savior when he came into office, watched his popularity plummet.[16]

The nation received a brief reprieve when oil prices spiked again following the 1979 revolution in Iran and the subsequent Iran-Iraq war.

By now there was a new president, Luis Herrera, of COPEI. He prom-ised a course correction. But it was too late. In 1980 and 1981, with oil prices at record highs, the Venezuelan economy went into recession.[17] Eventually the price of oil started to fall. But even as the government's income declined, its spending continued to grow. Government spend-ing under Pérez had more than tripled. Under Herrera, it doubled again.[18]

The year 1983 was supposed to be a celebratory one, marking the two hundredth anniversary of Bolívar's birth. Instead, Herrera stunned Venezuelans by devaluing the bolivar. Venezuelans called the day of the devaluation Black Friday. It came as a shock, showing Venezuelans that their heightened expectations based on the oil bonanza were an illusion.

The full reckoning came at last in 1989. Carlos Andrés Pérez had been elected president a second time, promising a return to prosperity. In-stead, upon taking office, in February 1989, he announced a package of economic austerity measures. A hike in transit fares sparked the riots and looting known as the Caracazo. Security forces opened fire on unarmed citizens. The social fabric seemed to have unraveled. The oil genie showed a demon face.

One of the best indicators of a country's economic health, as it relates to ordinary people, is per capita gross domestic product, which is the total economic activity divided by the size of the population. That measure, GDP per capita, grew at a modest and steady rate from 1959, at the start of Venezuelan democracy, until 1978. Beginning in 1978—in the midst of the world-changing oil boom—GDP per capita fell every year through 1985. Real wages—that is, wages adjusted for inflation—peaked in 1978 and fell almost every year thereafter, continuing to decline for more than two decades.[19]

Economists have a name for what happened in Venezuela. They call it the Resource Curse. It's also called the Dutch Disease, after a boom-and-bust cycle that followed a surge in natural gas export income to the Netherlands in the 1970s.

The Dutch Disease works this way. A country has a sudden increase in export income from the sale of some natural resource commodity. It could be natural gas in the Netherlands or oil in Venezuela—or, centuries earlier, the gold and silver that rushed into Imperial Spain from its New World colonies. This could occur because new sources of the commodity are discovered (as was the case in the Netherlands and sixteenth-century Spain) or because the price of the commodity goes up (as with Venezuela in the 1970s). What seems at first like an unmitigated good—more money coming in—soon leads to problems, and oftentimes, disaster. Other parts of the economy, mainly manufacturing and farming, start to falter. Inflation spikes and there are shortages of basic goods.

The underlying reason for this cycle is surprisingly simple. The large increase in export income causes the value of the local currency to rise. That means the country's other exports, such as manufactured goods and farm products, become less competitive on the world market, so exports of those goods decrease, depressing those sectors of the economy. At the same time, a strong local currency means that imported goods are cheaper (each Dutch gulden or Venezuelan bolivar buys more than it used to), so the domestic market is flooded with inexpensive imports that consumers snap up. That again hurts local manufacturers and farmers, since now they're also facing tougher competition in the domestic market. Along with all this, wages in the commodity sector increase (such as oil workers' pay), which can force wages higher in the other parts of the economy (manufacturing and farming) that are suddenly struggling. Higher wages mean increased consumer demand (especially for all those cheap imported products), but the economy isn't set up to quickly meet the jump in demand. Bottlenecks form at ports, and distribution networks and shortages set in. That leads to inflation as more money chases fewer products and prices increase. If the country imposes price controls, it leads to a black market in goods and more inflation.[20]

That is the classic Dutch Disease scenario—where something good has disruptive consequences. And when the price of the commodity, such as gas or oil, falls, as it inevitably must, the distortions of the Dutch Disease can lead to more extreme outcomes (a deeper recession, higher unemployment). That helps explain why poor countries that are rich in natural resources often go through periods of boom-and-bust that can leave people poorer after a boom than they were before. Juan Pablo Pérez Alfonzo, the first oil minister of Venezuela's democracy, who helped create OPEC, called oil "the devil's excrement," and he warned that the country's wealth would be its ruin. He saw that the riches that attach to oil in the world economy were greater than with any other commodity, the price gyrations more extreme, and the consequences more severe. The peculiarities of Venezuela's history have made it even more vulnerable to these same processes.

Terry Lynn Karl, a political scientist who studied Venezuela's 1970s boom and 1980s bust, concluded that virtually everything in the country—its institutions and patterns of government, society and politics, and the economy—had been shaped by oil. Karl found that oil created a series of incentives and patterns of behavior that exacerbated the effects of the boom and propelled political leaders into a single course of action and set of policies.

What's distinctive about Venezuela is that its economy revolves entirely around oil. The government owns the oil in the ground and receives money from oil sales. The effect of that is to put the government at the center of economic life. And the government's main function becomes the distribution of the oil money to its citizens.

The way it works in practice is that the oil companies (including PDVSA, the government-run company) take the oil from the ground and sell it. They then hand over a large portion of the money they receive for the oil to the government in the form of taxes. Both things have value—oil and money. The only thing that has changed is the location of the valuable thing—in the ground or in the National Treasury.

And just as the oil companies pump the oil from the ground, Venezuelan citizens then pump the oil money from the government.

Karl saw that over time this led to a series of distorted and often perverse relationships between the government and its citizens.

It accentuated an existing tendency toward a highly centralized government with a powerful executive. Because an extreme amount of power (both political and economic) was concentrated in the government, an outsize amount of power was put into the hands of the president.

And because there was always money from oil flowing in, the government never developed a strong tax base outside the oil industry. Income taxes, value-added taxes, property taxes, sales taxes—all were either nonexistent or charged at lower rates and with lower rates of participation than in other countries in the region. All this resulted in a government that had an overdeveloped head (the executive power) and stunted or shriveled limbs. One of the things that modern tax systems do, on a practical level, is create mechanisms for governments to extend their reach throughout a nation's territory (to assess and collect taxes), where they touch many levels of social and economic activity.[21] Venezuela never had that.

"The state could only give; it could not take," Karl wrote in her book, *The Paradox of Plenty*.[22] "Rather than symbolize military conquest, national glory, cultural superiority, or territorial expansion, the Venezuelan state came to be viewed primarily as an enormous distributive apparatus, a huge milk cow that benefited those who were able to suckle at her teats."

And since distributing oil money was the main function of the state, it developed a patron-client relationship with the citizenry, whereby each constituency lined up to get its slice of the pie. Labor unions got a big bureaucracy with a large workforce and state-owned companies that hired more workers than they needed. The business community got state contracts and subsidies, including low-interest loans and reductions or exemptions to the already low taxes. Old people got pensions. Poor people got housing. The middle class got access to cheap dollars that subsidized trips abroad. Everyone got cheap gasoline, sold at some of the lowest prices in the world. And while governments in every country offer some or all of these benefits and pork directed at preferred constituencies, Venezuelans came to view them as essential attributes of citizenship—regardless of whether oil prices were high or low. It was like belonging to a special club—you expected all the good stuff and being born was the only dues you had to pay.

* * *

IN MENE GRANDE, not far from where I met the woman living in a hovel on top of an oil seep, I spoke with a woman named Mayerlis Flores, who lived with her husband and three children in a sturdy cinder-block house built and given to her by the government in 2012, when Chávez was running for reelection. I told her that she must have felt lucky to live in one of the few solid houses in a barrio of shacks.

"Take a look at it!" she said. Her anger brimmed over. "It's not painted! They never finished the job!"

I hadn't noticed until then: the outside of the house was unpainted gray stucco. It had been eating at her ever since she'd moved in, two years before. She'd complained to the housing ministry, but to no avail. "We're a country rich in oil," Mayerlis said. "So how come they haven't painted my house?"

I asked if she'd considered doing the work herself. She could even pick the color. And she wouldn't have to be angry anymore. Mayerlis crossed her arms and planted her feet. "If you give me a house, you should give it to me painted and finished."

Over the crest of the hill above Mayerlis's house, the pumpjack on the country's first oil well rocked up and down, just as it had for the last hundred years. Mayerlis was responding to a pull just as strong and just as old, something ingrained in the Venezuelan psyche. It goes much deeper than the superficial dismissal that you might hear in the United States, of poor people spoiled by government handouts. The Venezuelan state's function as the doler out of oil revenue has created an expectation and a relationship. Mayerlis was talking about paint, but what she was really referring to was oil.

"Classic political theory says that the society forms the state," Arturo Peraza told me. "Here the state formed the society." Peraza, a Jesuit priest, is a political scientist and the vice chancellor of Andrés Bello Catholic University in Guayana City. "The mechanism here is that the state has a commodity, oil, that enriches it directly and makes the society completely unnecessary." That, he said, leaves people only one option. "Just like an oil well connects you to the oil, what you do is connect yourself to those who control the country's most important resource, which is oil. You connect yourself to the state."

Venezuelans sometimes talk about the miraculous quality of oil. Oil is not like other forms of wealth. Oil seems like manna from heaven. It is the result of providence smiling down on you. You had the good fortune to be born in a land where the world's biggest pool of oil sits just under the surface. And fortune is what it was, in both senses of the word: good luck and treasure.

"Venezuela goes very quickly from being a country destroyed by civil wars, disease, malaria, yellow fever" to becoming a country that was suddenly rich with oil, said Chúo Torrealba, a former head of the coalition of opposition political parties. And in the 1970s, there was money beyond anyone's dreams. "People start to see that there is a thing called instant gratification, that improvements in quality of life aren't the result of hard work, occurring generation after generation, but that they're the product of a miracle, the miracle that is the injection of oil money into the daily life of Venezuelans." He went on: "Oil Culture didn't teach you that you have to work hard and build things so that things change for the better. You only have to wish for them."

The relationship is the same whether you're talking about poor people or the middle and upper class. In the Chávez years, the government subsidized foreign travel and even foreign college tuition, benefits used mostly by middle-class and upper-class families. The sons and daughters of well-off Venezuelan families attended elite American universities while paying a fraction of what their peers in the United States paid—because government exchange controls made it possible. Businessmen, already well-off, made even bigger fortunes from government contracts.

In the eyes of its citizens, the Venezuelan state is little more than an ATM—the magic box that stands between the oil in the ground and the outstretched palm, the device that performs the alchemy of turning oil into money in my pocket.

The Man Under the Palm Tree

My friend D. (he had a government job and didn't want me to use his name) immigrated to Venezuela from another South American country with his family in the 1970s, when he was a teenager. There was a dictatorship in D.'s country. His father wasn't involved in politics, but he had friends who were. One day a friend of D.'s father was arrested. His father received a warning: the police were working their way through the friend's address book; his name would come up soon. The next day, D.'s father boarded a plane and flew to Venezuela. D., his sister, and their mother followed a short time later.

It was a good time to come to Venezuela. The country was full of oil money and there were immigrants from all over South America. It was D.'s father's second go-around as an immigrant. He was born in Europe and left for South America after World War II. To the second-time immigrant, Venezuela seemed a place of endless possibility and beauty: the perpetual sunshine, the generous, friendly people. And the beaches. So many beaches. To D.'s father, it seemed a paradise. One day D.'s father announced to the family that they were going to visit every beach in Venezuela. They'd load up the car with a big canvas tent and coolers and other equipment, and on weekends they'd head out to explore. Sometimes the whole family went, but often it was just D. and his father.

One of their first excursions took father and son to Bahía de Cata, a gorgeous, isolated horseshoe cove, reached by a winding road up and down the coastal cordillera.

D. and his father parked their car and proceeded to haul their gear the length of the beach, to the spot where it seemed best to D.'s father to make camp. A man sat nearby, at the base of a palm tree, leaning against the trunk. Mostly he seemed to gaze out toward the blue horizon. But sometimes he would look their way as they schlepped back and forth. He was barefoot and wore an old pair of shorts and a T-shirt. He was thin and wiry and dark-skinned, because he was black and because he'd spent a lifetime outside in the sun. D.'s father waved to the man and said hello. The man said hello back.

Once camp was set up, they made lunch, and when the food was ready, the father walked across the sand to the man beneath the palm tree and invited him to share their meal.

No thank you, the man said.

D.'s father insisted. *We'd be honored to have you join us.*

Thank you, the man said, *but I've got everything I need right here.*

D.'s father was curious. *How is that?*

The man pointed above him at the palm tree. *Whenever I'm hungry, I climb up and cut a couple of coconuts, and then I've got food and drink.*

The man stood up. He shimmied up the palm tree. With a machete he cut down four large green coconuts. They fell on the sand—*plop plop plop plop*. Quick as a flash he was down on the ground, and with a few slashes of the machete he cut off the top of two of the coconuts and presented them to D. and his father. They tilted their heads back and drank the coconut milk. With a couple more whacks of the machete, the man sliced the coconuts in half and showed them how to scoop out the soft white meat.

D.'s father was impressed. *This is wonderful. You should sell coconuts to the tourists who come here.*

By now the man was sitting down again at the base of the palm tree, gazing out at the sea, through eyes half shut against the glare. *What would I want to do that for?* the man said to D.'s father.

To make money, of course.

The man replied, as he had before, *But I've got everything I need right here.*

D.'s father said, *With the money you made, you could invest and plant more palm trees and have more coconuts that you could sell to the tourists. You could buy things for your family. Food or a radio, or you could put a new roof on your house, whatever you need.*

The man repeated, like a Caribbean Bartleby, *No thank you. I have everything I need right here.*

Back home, they told D.'s mother and sister about the man under the palm tree. The story became a foundational one for D.'s family, one they told often and one whose meaning changed over time. It became a parable of life in Venezuela.

At first the encounter was a source of fascination for the newcomers. It was novel, exotic. It revealed a people free of materialistic excesses, content to live life day to day, with what Mother Nature handed them. Venezuela was a Garden of Eden.

Later on, D.'s father would invoke the story to very different effect. He worked in an office and he would complain about the poor work ethic of his colleagues. The man beneath the palm tree became a symbol of what was wrong with Venezuela: people were lazy; they didn't want to work; it was no wonder the country couldn't advance.

Some time after that, his father's attitude changed again. D.'s father discovered that while he'd been working his butt off to do the best job he could and get ahead, others who didn't work nearly as hard as he did would be paid the same, or would even be promoted to jobs where they were paid more. By then times were tough in Venezuela, and D.'s father's salary bought less and less. Then the man beneath the palm tree became a symbol of Venezuelan cleverness, what is known as *viveza criolla*, Venezuelan street smarts. How intelligent the man sitting beneath the palm tree seemed then: Why work hard when you can get what you need by hardly working at all?[1]

* * *

D. TELLS ANOTHER story.

A man owed D.'s father some money. Instead of paying him with cash, the man gave his father the title to a piece of land in the countryside near Caracas. D.'s mother told his father that he was crazy. "What are you going to do with a piece of land?" "I don't know," said the father. "Maybe I'll plant something on it." One day D. and his father drove out to take a look. They hired a local man to help and they spent a couple of days clearing the land. Once the land was cleared, they planted it with lechosa, a fruit related to the papaya but infinitely better: larger than a typical papaya, it has a texture like the richest, creamiest ice cream. Lechosa trees grow fast and produce fruit quickly.

They gave the land a good watering and then father and son went home to Caracas, with a plan to return periodically to tend their crop. But D.'s father caught a cold and then D. got sick with something or other and then his father grew busy with work and the return trip kept being put off. Finally, after many months, D. and his father drove out to the land. They figured that there would be nothing but brush, the land returned to jungle. Instead they were amazed to find a forest of lechosa trees, heavy with fruit. They'd borrowed a pickup truck and now they filled the back with the ripe lechosas. They drove into town and found the man who'd helped them all those months before, to thank him for taking care of the land in their absence. The man gave them an odd look. "I didn't do a thing," he said. "I haven't been back there since I was there with you."

D. and his father gave away some of the lechosa that they'd picked and then told the man and his neighbors to go out to the land and take all they wanted. Then they drove home to Caracas.

"We ate lechosa morning, noon, and night," D. told me. "We couldn't eat it all."

What, I asked, was the lesson of this story?

The lesson was that the lechosa grew on its own. They did nothing but plant it and water it once. They never watered it again or fertilized it or weeded or pruned it. And it grew, with almost no effort on their part.

"That's Venezuela," D. said. "Why should I work hard if nature gives me everything I need?"

It was the story of oil all over again. All you have to do is poke a hole in the ground and up it comes. Oil. Lechosa. Coconuts.

D. laughed when he told these stories, but afterward he said that this was Venezuela's punishment, to have all this wealth, all this abundance, and not to know how to manage it.

We were sitting in a café, drinking, in the Venezuelan style, small cups of espresso with foamy milk. The Caracas morning was suffused with a soft, limpid light and the Ávila mountain lay across the far end of the upward-tilted street like a benevolent spirit under the bluest of skies. A friend who shared the table with us listened to D.'s stories and said this: "It's a Catholic tale of sin, guilt, and punishment. It all comes back to the Land of Grace. Venezuelans were born into the Garden and they didn't know how to take care of it. But instead of being expelled, they stayed in the garden and became the custodians of its decline."

First, I Want to Say Good Morning

The first time that Venezuela saw Hugo Chávez was on television, at about 10:30 A.M. on February 4, 1992. Hours earlier, around midnight, soldiers in Caracas, Maracaibo, and two other cities had set in motion a coup d'etat against the democratically elected government of Venezuela. While the units in other cities took control of military installations and some government buildings, the troops in Caracas failed in their main objective, which was to capture the president, Carlos Andrés Pérez. Overnight, Venezuelans watched in disbelief as television cameras showed a tank mounting the front steps of the Miraflores presidential palace, *chunk chunk chunk* on its clumsy tracks, and trying to batter down the door with its big gun. Pérez escaped and went on television to assure the nation that the coup would be defeated.

The coup's leader was Chávez, an unknown, thirty-seven-year-old lieutenant colonel in charge of a paratroop battalion. He had been directing the action from a military history museum on a hill overlooking the center of Caracas. But then his troops at the palace surrendered. A commando unit that had been sent to seize a television station and put a videotaped declaration by Chávez on the airwaves had also failed, for one of those idiotic reasons that so often gum up the most carefully made plans: the video was in the wrong format and the station's technicians pretended (while the commandos held them at gunpoint) that they couldn't convert it to the right one. Chávez bowed to the inevitable and surrendered. But the rebel units in other cities continued to hold out and Pérez's high command decided to put Chávez on television to order his comrades to lay down their arms.

Chávez pulled his red beret firmly down over his ink-black hair and went to meet the cameras. He stood in a glaring light, in front of a group of TV reporters thrusting their microphones at him.

"First, I want to say good morning to the people of Venezuela," he began, this narrow-faced man with light brown skin, somewhere between young and middle-aged, clean-shaven, sharp-nosed, wearing combat fatigues. He spoke clearly, without pause or hesitation, and with an odd equanimity that did not square with the condition of a soldier giving up in defeat. Then he directed himself to his fellow conspirators. "Unfortunately, for now, the objectives that we laid out for ourselves were not achieved in the capital. That is to say, here in Caracas, we were not able to take power." He instructed all units to lay down their arms, thanked them for their bravery and signaled his philosophic allegiance to his hero, the Liberator, Simón Bolívar. "In front of the entire country and in front of all of you, I take responsibility for this Bolivarian military movement. Thanks very much."

Pérez had instructed his officers to handcuff Chávez and videotape his statement so that it could be edited before it was broadcast. But they were in a hurry. They ignored the president's directive and stood Chávez in front of the reporters and the cameras and let him talk.

His words, broadcast over and over again throughout the day, landed with greater force than all the shots fired overnight. Much has been said and written since then about two phrases that Chávez spoke that day. Venezuelans were not accustomed to hearing a public figure (and Chávez instantly became one) taking responsibility for a failure. That caught everyone's attention right off the bat. The other thing that impressed his viewers were the words *for now*. We haven't achieved our objectives *for now*. It was part veiled threat, part promise, part cockiness, part delusion.

But what strikes me now, watching, on video, the Chávez of nearly three decades ago, is that opening line: "First, I want to say good morning to the people of Venezuela," so casual, so offhand, so sure of himself and yet so oddly courteous and self-effacing. You just sent someone to ram a tank through the door of the presidential palace—but first you want to say good morning? In that moment, the first time in his life that the lights and the cameras were turned on him, Chávez was born fully formed before the eyes of his country and the world. He found, in the moment of his defeat, the formula that would bear him forward across the decades and into the embrace of history. He discovered then that he could speak directly to his true audience, "to the people of Venezuela." He was a reality TV star before there was reality TV, a viral tweet before there was social media.

Venezuela had emerged from a military dictatorship just over three decades earlier, and many people who watched the coup play out on their television sets and then saw this unknown and cocksure commander speak on television were appalled. For all its problems—and there were many—Venezuela was a democracy, and a group of soldiers trying to shoot their way to power was a return to a benighted past of might makes right, when any strongman who could raise his own army might seize power in Caracas. Others cheered the coup attempt. They were sick of inequality and corruption. Many people didn't have enough food to eat, while costs were soaring. They had lost faith in their leaders and their political parties and the empty promises of an oil boom gone bust and a democracy that seemed to serve only the elites. Someone had to take bold action and shake things up!

But people in both groups agreed on one thing—the coup was a warning, a definitive sign that the country was on the wrong path.

At the center of all that, the name on everyone's lips, was Hugo Chávez.

* * *

THE SON OF schoolteachers, Chávez grew up in a small rural town in the wide plains of western Venezuela. He had a happy, barefoot childhood, poor but not wanting. As a young man, he entered the military and was drawn to a current of leftist nationalism rooted in the conflicts and ideologies of the 1960s—inspired by the revolution in Cuba, antagonistic to the United States and its history of interventions in Latin America, suffused with vague notions of socialism and standing up for the downtrodden. He and his co-conspirators had been plotting for fifteen years.

Chávez went to jail, but he was an instant celebrity, a savior, a new Bolívar. Three years later, he was released from prison. In 1998 he ran for president as an outsider, an anti-politician who promised to set the country on a new course that would bring prosperity to all those who had been left out. The recent past was all bad—lies, corruption, broken promises. The distant past was the glory that Chávez promised to restore—the past of Bolívar. He named his crusade the Bolivarian cause and promised a Bolivarian revolution. Chávez tailored his message to his audience. In front of leftists, he was a firebrand. In front of the middle class, he was calm and reasonable. For all that, Chávez was deeply conservative in an essential way. His discourse was aimed at the past more than the future. It was about recapturing a golden age, returning to an imagined greatness that never really existed.

Chávez was given no chance to win. But he had read the national mood. Despite his disrupter's rhetoric, Chávez was backed by powerful people in the establishment, lending him airplanes for his campaign, giving him money, and ensuring he received media attention. They thought he was a rube, all bluster, someone they could control if he pulled off the upset.

And he did. Chávez won in a landslide and he was sworn in as president in February 1999.

The first order of business was to write a new constitution, fulfilling a campaign pledge. While it had many similarities to the old constitution,[1] it was symbolic of a fresh start and it was approved in a referendum by the people. Chávez carried around a miniature edition of the constitution. It fit in his breast pocket. He would take it out often, while giving speeches or talking on television, and hold it up like a talisman. It stood for a special kind of unity: Chávez, his government, the constitution, the will of the people, ratified at the ballot box. They were all one and the same thing.

* * *

LIKE NO OTHER politician, Chávez lived and governed on television, by television, for television, cutting out the middlemen of the press and speaking directly to his supporters, the ones he chose to call "the people." This was true from the very first moment that he burst into the cognition of his fellow countrymen to the very last time they saw him, live on television, twenty years later, when he announced that he was going to Cuba for a cancer operation that turned out to be the agonizing prelude to his drawn-out death. His political life began and ended live on television. Television become reality, reality become television.

In 2000, Chávez started broadcasting a regular Sunday-morning television show called *Aló Presidente* (Hello President). It started out as a call-in show, with Chávez sitting in a studio at a microphone, talking and taking calls from listeners. Anyone could call in and talk to the president. That was part of the draw. It was democracy in action. A direct channel to the most powerful man in the country, who took the time to listen and chat with ordinary citizens.

Over time the show became more dynamic. Chávez visited farms and factories; he rode horses, took walks, drove tractors. He sang. He danced. There were musical acts. There were special guests (Fidel Castro, President Daniel Ortega of Nicaragua). He issued orders to ministers, criticized them, embarrassed them, put them on the spot. He made surprise announcements, ordered troop movements, berated his enemies, carried out diplomacy. It started every Sunday at eleven A.M. but you never knew when it would end. It might last four hours or eight.

Aló Presidente was just a small part of Chávez's presence on television.

Chávez's identity with the medium was total. He was on television almost every day. He broadcast cabinet meetings and speeches and tours of public works projects and trips abroad. The government had its own TV station, Channel 8, and later it created a twenty-four-hour cable news station called TeleSUR. But Chávez would not only appear on government-operated television. He frequently commandeered the airwaves, breaking in and preempting the programming on all broadcast television and radio stations. They were required by law to carry his signal whenever he chose. From 1999 through 2012 he took over the airwaves in this way 2,377 times, for a total of 1,695 hours on the air, according to an organization called Espacio Público.[2] In 2004, the year he defeated a recall referendum that could have removed him from office, he averaged more than one commandeered broadcast a day. In 2012, when he was running for reelection, the average was one every three days. That gave Chávez's on-air presence an element of both surprise and inevitability. You never knew when you'd hear the strains of the national anthem that announced one of the preemptive broadcasts. And you never knew what they would mean. Was it a routine cabinet meeting that might drag on for hours or the announcement of some fantastic new proposal? There were people who left their TV set on all day, tuned to Channel 8, because they knew that at some point Chávez would come on.

"This idea of communicating directly with the people, not having any mediating institution or entity and setting a media agenda almost on a daily basis—he was the first to do that," said Tom Shannon, a former U.S. diplomat who worked extensively in Venezuela. "It was quite remarkable at the time and at the time it seemed a little folkloric, kind of like *The Jerry Springer Show* instead of government. But it was very effective."

"He was governing on television. It was something new," said Rhonny Zamora,[3] who worked as a producer on *Aló Presidente* in the early years. "The whole critical mass of Venezuelan society had to watch the program, whether you were for Chávez or against him. All the heads of institutions had to watch because you never knew if he was going to call you, you never knew what he was going to come up with, you didn't know if he was going to give you a direct order. It was about governing through the media, like what Twitter is now, where it became popular with presidents to give orders or make announcements on Twitter. Chávez was ahead of his time." (Chávez was an early adopter of Twitter also; he joined the platform in 2010, five years before Barack Obama.)

During an *Aló Presidente* in September 2000, a woman named Isabel Mavares called in to talk to Chávez. She said that she needed a job and a new house. "Mr. President," she said, "I always bless you on the television screen. I put my hand on the screen and I ask the guardian angel to guide you and to follow you in all that you're doing. God bless you, Mr. President."

That was the essence of Chávez's relationship with his audience. For Isabel, television wasn't a one-way medium. She could put her hand on the screen and bless the president.

Chávez used television to create a connection with his supporters. They were the people. He was one with them. But Chávez was always very aware of the other side too, the not-the-people, the ones who hated, opposed, and underestimated him, the ones he called worthless, the squalid ones. He used television to create and maintain the image of the enemy. He would taunt and mock and skewer his opponents, at home and abroad. He would make announcements that his supporters knew would enrage his enemies, and because of that, they loved him even more.

In April 2002, Chávez used an *Aló Presidente* episode to carry out a shake-up at PDVSA. He'd been in a long-running battle to increase his control over the government-run oil company, and a few weeks earlier he'd named several new members to its board. Ever since, the company's workers and executives had been in revolt, staging protests and reducing production at wells and refineries. It was a test of wills—a defense of PDVSA's independence from politics and a challenge to Chávez's authority as president. So the atmosphere was charged as Chávez took to the air on *Aló Presidente* and announced that he had a list of PD-VSA executives that he'd decided to fire. He read their names, one by one, from a sheet of paper. "Mr. Eddy Ramírez, thank you very much, sir. You're fired!" He continued down the list. "Juan Fernández, you're fired!" "Thank you for your services, Mr. Gonzalo Feijóo. You're fired, Mr. Feijóo, from PDVSA!" When he was done, Chávez picked up a whistle and blew a sharp blast. "Offsides!" he said. "Get out!"

Chávez's fans loved the whole thing. They ate it up. They cheered. They clapped, on screen and at home. Did you see what he did? He fired them on TV! He fired them with a whistle! He showed those elite sons of bitches who's boss.

This was in 2002, two years before Donald Trump would make entertainment out of firing people on TV. Chávez beat him to it.

* * *

"*ALÓ PRESIDENTE* WAS always a mise-en-scène," Andrés Izarra told me, "*un pote de humo.* It was all show." Izarra and I met in a café in Berlin. We mostly spoke in English, but sometimes he switched to Spanish.

Pote de humo means a smoke screen, in the sense of something meant to distract, to cover up reality. *Aló Presidente* was a television production, Izarra said, and so it was normal for it to offer a more polished version of reality, as when a school or a clinic got a new coat of paint before the president's visit. But there were times when it went much further. If Chávez was visiting a farm and there wasn't any livestock, the producers would truck in cows and release them in a pasture behind the comandante. Idle factories would receive the materials or equipment they needed to produce.

Izarra had worked for Spanish-language news ventures operated by NBC in Charlotte and CNN in Atlanta. But he eventually went home and Chávez made him information minister, a post that included responsibility for *Aló Presidente*. After Chávez died, Maduro appointed Izarra as minister of tourism. But Izarra eventually broke with Maduro and left the country. He belonged to a riven family. His father was a hard-line leftist who fiercely supported Chávez and then Maduro. Izarra's wife was the stepdaughter of a prominent opposition politician, Antonio Ledezma, who had been imprisoned by Maduro and later went into exile. Izarra had publicly criticized Maduro for his handling of the economy, but he hadn't gone over to the opposition—he still defined himself as a Chavista. Izarra had settled in Berlin with his wife and children. Some opposition activists had found him there and staged protests in front of his house until the police forced them to stop.

Izarra described *Aló Presidente* as a televised Potemkin village—a stage set created for Chávez and the viewers that showed a shinier, more prosperous Venezuela than the one that existed.

Izarra said that when something was faked on *Aló Presidente*—a factory rushed into production, a farm gussied up to look more prosperous than it was—Chávez generally wasn't in on the deception. He was being fooled too. I asked why government officials would lie to Chávez. "People wanted to be in good standing with him," Izarra said.

It seemed a painful admission. He had worked for years to produce a program that ended up being an elaborate effort to fool both the country and the president, the program's star, to make failures appear like successes.

When I met with him in Berlin in late 2019, Izarra told me that he'd been thinking over the events of the last twenty years, trying to make sense of it all. "If you had consistency, you wouldn't have the crisis you have now," he said.

Then he laughed: It's still going on. He said that when he was the minister of tourism, in 2014, he attended a televised event with Maduro for the opening of a refurbished airport on the small Caribbean island of Coche. Nearby Margarita Island was a major tourist destination. Coche had nice beaches but was hard to get to—and an improved airport would be a significant boost to tourism. A few days after the event with Maduro, Izarra wanted to return to the island. But when he tried to arrange for a plane, he was told that it was not possible to fly there—the airport wasn't working. He called Maduro. "They're doing the same thing to you that they did to Chávez," he told him. There was a tone of bitterness to his laughter. "It was all a smoke screen, a pote de humo."

9

Irrevocable, Absolute, Total

In 2011, Chávez announced that he had cancer. The details of his illness, and his treatment by doctors in Cuba, remained a mystery. He wouldn't say what type of cancer it was or exactly where it was found in his body. But there was a presidential election scheduled for the following year, so in January 2012, Chávez announced that he was cured and he prepared to start campaigning. Presidential elections normally took place in December, but this year the vote was moved to October—there was only so much time to bring Chávez over the finish line. Oil prices were high and the government ramped up spending. It built thousands of apartments and houses and broadcast weekly televised giveaways, like game shows, where Chávez presented grateful families with the keys to their new homes. It spent millions to import washers and dryers and televisions and cars, which it gave away or sold at subsidized prices. And it announced new public works projects and rushed to show progress on those already under way.

One of those projects was an elevated train line in a big Caracas slum called Petare. Construction had been puttering along for years. Now crews started working twenty-four hours a day. Petare, with its tens of thousands of poor families, had long been an important base of support for Chávez. But in 2008, an opposition mayoral candidate had won a majority of votes there. The loss set off alarms within Chavismo: something had to be done to shore up the base.

The project, called the Bolivarian Cable Train, was more about politics than transportation. It would have three stations and three-fifths of a mile of track. In theory the cable train was to be part of a grand interconnected transit plan, linking to new subway and commuter rail lines. But the other projects were never built, and the Bolivarian Cable Train became a train to nowhere, connecting nothing.[1]

It was being built by Odebrecht, the giant Brazilian engineering company, and Doppelmayr, an Austrian company that specialized in cable-operated trains. As election day approached, government officials informed the contractors that Chávez wanted to hold an event to showcase the Bolivarian Cable Train. Could he ride the train on its inaugural run? Or take a test run over the tracks?

The contractors replied that this was a nice idea but they weren't that far along yet. The elevated structures and the tracks were in place—you could see the pristine concrete columns rising above the barrio. But the drive system needed to power the train—the cable, the motors and bull wheels and other machinery—had not been installed. Neither had the computerized system to control the automated trains. They didn't even have the electricity hooked up yet.

In other words, there were tracks, but there was no way to make a train run on them.

The government officials listened to this explanation and repeated: The president wants to ride the train.

In a meeting in August, Haiman El Troudi, the minister of ground transportation, laid down the law. Jorge González, a Spanish engineer working for Doppelmayr, had been explaining why the train couldn't be made to run and El Troudi cut him off. "No European engineer," the minister said, "is going to tell the people of Venezuela what can or cannot be done!"[2]

Doppelmayr had been doing lucrative work in Venezuela, and implied in all of this was that if the company wanted to continue to receive government contracts, it would be wise to make the president happy. Doppelmayr executives in Austria finally agreed and a price was negotiated. According to two Doppelmayr employees, company officials said at the time that the government paid an extra $1 million to make the train run for Chávez. One million dollars for what amounted to a stunt, a campaign event, to create the illusion that the train was working. (The number may have been higher—the government likely made an additional payment to Odebrecht as well.)

But now time was short. The election was coming up fast. Real work on the Bolivarian Cable Train project stopped. There was only one priority: make the train run.

The first task was to assemble a train. With a crane, they lifted the train parts onto the track: the wheels, the undercarriage, the car bodies, the seats and fixtures. Much of the work had to be done at night because the crane blocked traffic on a major road beside the train line.

That was the easy part. Making the train move was the challenge.

The line had three stations. The Doppelmayr crew placed the train at one end of the line, at a station called Petare II. At the other end of the line, three-fifths of a mile away, they installed an electric winch. Then they ran a slender cable along the tracks between the two stations. They attached one end of this cable to the train they had assembled. They fed the other end into the winch. Their plan was to winch the train along, very slowly, and hope that nothing went wrong.

The slender cable was a substitute for the much thicker metal cable, called a hauling rope, that would someday be installed to power the train. Less than half the diameter of the hauling rope, it was so thin that the Venezuelan workers on the project called it "the wire."

The big question was whether the substitute cable was strong enough to pull the train without breaking. The Petare II station was downhill from the other two stations. This was important. The train had no brakes (under normal conditions it would be attached to the hauling rope, which both pulls the train and acts as the brake). By going uphill, they could pull the train and control its speed with the winch. But if the cable snapped, the train would coast downhill, back to the Petare II station, gaining speed as it went. There would be no way to stop it. That is why the topography mattered. The rise from Petare II to the line's middle station, where Chávez would watch the simulacrum, was modest. But the rise was steeper from the middle station to the other end of the line, where the winch was located. And the steeper rise meant a greater strain on the cable.

Doppelmayr's engineers looked at all this and decided that, yes, the provisional cable could withstand the load if it pulled the train along the more gradual incline from Petare II to the middle station. And that was as far as they intended to go. Once they'd figured all this out and all the gear was in place, the technicians did some test runs. There were no disasters.

But there were concerns. One of them was that the cable might jump out of the system of sheaves that guided it between the tracks, since that system was designed for the much thicker hauling rope. If that happened, the cable could become jammed or break. Complicating things further, the track went around a curve between the first two stations. Jorge González, the Doppelmayr engineer who had traded words with the transportation minister, was assigned to ride in the front of the train and keep an eye on the cable—if it became displaced, he would have to radio the winch operator to stop the train.

It took them almost the entire month of September. They had to install generators to power the equipment. They had to dress up the station that Chávez would visit and hang banners to hide the unfinished areas. The platforms had automated glass doors that opened to allow passengers to get on and off the train. On this occasion they would be operated by hand. The train had to stop at exactly the right spot, to be in line with the doors. They had to practice several times to get it right.

The election was scheduled for October 7.

The day set for Chávez to visit the train project was September 29.

* * *

IT WAS A sunny day, Caracas as it was meant to be, filled with a generous light, a few clouds in a powder blue sky. Chávez arrived at the station at about 3:30 P.M. He wore a bright yellow windbreaker, the color of the sun.

The event was broadcast from start to finish on Channel 8, the government television station, and much of it was also carried by government order on all the other broadcast television stations, preempting their regular programming. On Channel 8 the event was narrated by a TV reporter named Boris Castellano. Boris was one of the station's most indefatigable personalities. Young, energetic, upbeat, with a toothy chipmunk smile, glasses, and a brush of dark hair, he seemed to be everywhere—on the street in Caracas, in some remote locale with the comandante, at a rally, in the studio. Boris was more repeater than reporter; more cheerleader than journalist. His job was to serve up, in happy, confident tones, the government line of the day.

The Channel 8 cameras showed Chávez approaching a group of a few hundred supporters gathered near the station entrance. Many of them wore red T-shirts or caps. Some held yellow, blue, and red heart-shaped Mylar balloons representing Chávez's campaign slogan: "Chávez, heart of the people." They chanted, "*Ooh-ahh, Chávez no se va!*" *Chávez isn't going anywhere!* As Boris narrated to the home audience, Chávez stepped up to the security barrier that held the crowd back. He reached out and grasped hands, kissed a young girl on the cheek, held a baby aloft. Boris said that he wanted to make an important point. Even though it wasn't part of the plan, Chávez had decided on the spur of the moment to speak to the happy people who had come out to see him. "It's no secret for anyone," Boris told his viewers, "that any time that the president has the opportunity to share directly with the people he does so, since it is perhaps the most direct and most expeditious way for him to know the true opinion of the people about the situations that they encounter in their lives."

After a few minutes, Chávez pointed to his wrist to signal that he was out of time. He waved goodbye to the crowd and climbed a set of stairs to the elevated station.

Maduro, who at the time was foreign minister, and El Troudi, the transportation minister, were waiting for him in the station. The camera showed Chávez and his ministers and then it pulled back to a wide shot. There, in the distance, was the train emerging from the Petare II station and heading, ever so slowly, along the tracks toward the president.

"What you are seeing is historic," Boris said. He sounded excited. "It's the first time that the Bolivarian Cable Train, in the testing phase, makes its run." He said that since 2008 about $440 million had been spent to build the Bolivarian Cable Train. (Boris didn't do the math for us, but that's a big number for less than a mile of track. A similar system built by Doppelmayr in 2014 at the Oakland airport cost $484 million. It had two stations and 3.2 miles of track, which works out to about $75 million per half-mile; the cost of the Petare train works out to $366 million per half-mile.)

The camera returned to Chávez. He held a microphone. He ordered the start of the preemptive broadcast. A few chords of the national anthem blared, and then the national colors swept across the screen. Chávez said that he was breaking into regular programming to take the event live to the nation. All of a sudden, anyone watching TV (except on some cable stations) or listening to their radio was seeing or hearing Chávez. He said that he was there to begin the testing of the Bolivarian Cable Train. "This is the work," Chávez said, "of socialist government so that the people will live better every day. That's the idea, to give, as Christ said, to God what belongs to God and to Caesar what belongs to Caesar and to the people what belongs to the people."

Chávez was in a fine mood. These events were candy for him. He loved the adulation. He loved the gizmos and the new stuff. The day before he'd gone on TV to preside over the launch of a new telecommunications satellite. The launch was in China, but Chávez gave the order from the presidential palace in Caracas, on live television, with the whole nation watching, as was happening again today. Yesterday the rocket soared into the sky and released the satellite to orbit the earth. "It's looking down on us now," Chávez said from the train platform.

Chávez held the microphone in his right hand. In his left hand he held a walkie-talkie. He noted that it was a Motorola. There was a false start when the volume of the radio needed to be adjusted. Then Chávez gave the order. "Train operator Jorge," he said, "start the test."

Chávez was like a child with a new train set on Christmas Day. "Here comes the train!" he cried. "Hee-hee. *Wooooo!*"

But the train crawled along so slowly that it was hard to tell if it was moving at all.

"Is it moving?" Chávez asked.

El Troudi told Chávez that the train was moving slowly because it was a test run.

Chávez turned in the direction of the crowd down on the street. There were speakers set up so they could hear him. He relayed the information: "It's moving slowly because it's a test." It was like a game of telephone with loudspeakers.

Chávez asked El Troudi when the train would open to the public. El Troudi told him that the tests would continue for two months and that the train would begin carrying passengers on December 10. (This, of course, was not true. El Troudi had been present at meetings where the project was discussed and where it was made clear that the train was not close to completion.)

Chávez turned to the crowd of spectators: "December tenth it goes into full operation!" he said. "That is only possible in . . ." He paused for the crowd to finish the sentence. This was a call-and-response that they were used to. On the television feed you couldn't hear the crowd's answer, but Chávez provided it for them: "Socialism!" But that wasn't all. "The kingdom of God on earth!" Chávez said. "The kingdom of Christ on earth!"

His voice rose in excitement: "Here it comes!" He meant the train, not the kingdom of God. Not yet.

The train crept toward them. "Today it's dancing a bolero," Chávez said. A bolero is a ballad, a slow song. "Tomorrow it will dance merengue!"

It was a beautiful day. The sky was blue. The clouds were white. Chávez was in a yellow windbreaker, the color of the sun. The train was silver with red doors. The Ávila mountain, so close you could almost touch it, was green. The crowd was full of smiling people who loved him: red shirts, red caps, heart-shaped balloons.

As the train approached, Chávez noticed that no one was driving it and he asked how it worked. El Troudi told him that the train was automated, that there was no operator inside the train. Chávez turned again toward the crowd on the street. "There's no driver!" he shouted. The president laughed. He really was having a good time. He seemed to single out a woman in the crowd below. "There's no driver!" he said to her. "Do you see that?" Then, laughing some more, he asked the crowd: "Have you heard the joke about Dracula's car?"

Chávez didn't tell the joke, but certainly some of the people in the crowd or watching on television would have known it. The joke goes like this: It's late at night. A young hoodlum, what Venezuelans call a *malandro* (literally, a bad man), has been out having a good time. He decides to go home and heads to a nearby highway, where he hopes to catch a bus or hitch a ride. On the way, he encounters an old man who points to the highway and tells him: Be careful, sonny, because every night, exactly at midnight, Dracula's car drives by that very spot. The malandro tells the old man to get lost, he doesn't believe in that sort of thing: "You can't scare me, old man." He goes to the highway and waits by the side of the road. Not a single car passes. As he waits, he thinks about what the old man told him and starts to get scared. The longer he waits, the jumpier he gets. Finally he hears a church bell strike midnight, and at that moment a pair of headlights appears in the distance. Slowly the headlights creep closer and closer. The car is moving veeeeery slowly (just like the Bolivarian Cable Train) and finally the malandro sees that it's an old black hearse. He keeps telling himself that he doesn't believe in vampires, but now he's really scared and he's desperate to get out of that place any way he can, so as soon as the car reaches him, he grabs the passenger side door, yanks it open and jumps inside. With his eyes squeezed shut, he sits there, expecting the worst. When nothing happens, he opens his eyes and sees that the car is moving but THERE IS NO DRIVER! There's no one at the steering wheel and no one else inside the car at all. He screams! Omigod, it's true! The old man was right! It's Dracula's car! He shouts: "Help! Help! I'm caught in Dracula's car! Help!" And a voice answers from outside, at the back of the car. "What kind of nonsense is this about Dracula? We had a breakdown. Now get back here and help us push."

Chávez was tickled pink by the driverless train. By the memory of the joke. By the sunshine. By the crowd. He laughed and said, "This isn't Dracula's car. This is the Petare train. Without a driver! Hee-hee!" He asked the minister again: "How does it run if it doesn't have a driver?" The minister answered: It's automatic. "Automatic!" Chávez shouted to the crowd. "*Pura modernidad!*"

What a country! What a time to be alive! Yesterday a satellite! Today an automatic train!

The train came to a stop in the station. The doors opened and Chávez stepped on board. So did his entourage. Maduro was with him, and El Troudi and other government officials and Chávez's security detail, as well as a television crew, a photographer, and people who worked on the cable train project. Chávez looked around the train. Everything was shiny and new. The plastic seats on the sides of the cars were red, the color of revolution. The seats at the end were blue, the color of hope. The windows were spotless.

Chávez said, "Close the doors. We're going for a ride."

At that point the television viewer may have been aware of some confusion. On TV you could see El Troudi seeming to shoo people off the train. Maduro said something that wasn't discernible but was apparently an attempt to persuade Chávez to skip the train ride. Chávez replied, "No, Nicolás. I'm not going to miss this ride." (It was the same argument that El Troudi had made a few weeks earlier to Doppelmayr's technicians: It's Chávez's train and he's going to ride it if he wants to.)

No one appears to have told the president, and certainly no one was telling the viewers at home, but there was a problem. With so many people on board, the train weighed much more than it had when it made its trip between stations.

The doors closed. Chávez was still on the air, still talking. Across the country people were watching in front of their TV sets or listening on their radios. They were unaware of the soul-wrenching uncertainty gripping the small group of people who were in the know, on the station platform, on the train, and in the machine room underneath the station at the far end of the line.

The wire had remained intact pulling an empty train. But would it hold with a full one? And would it hold pulling a heavier train up a steeper grade? What if the cable broke and the train, with Chávez on board, without brakes, went careering downtrack, downhill, down . . .

"I was worried about their safety," a person who was on the platform and knew what was happening told me much later. A person who was in the machine room with the technicians operating the winch, told me: "It was crazy. We were all worried the wire would break."

Chávez, however, seemed unaware of the panic rising around him. He was riffing now, talking to fill time on the air, waiting for the train ride that he'd been promised. He said that the new train would mean an increase in electrical use, so the country must advance in its plans to build more generating capacity. He mused about how the train would make people's lives better. "This," Chávez said, "is the revolution at work, and work is love. A revolution that delivers for the people." Chávez stood at the front of the train, looking out along the tracks, toward the far station. Those holding the TV cameras apparently had been kicked off the train, so we saw him now from the outside, through the train window. Finally the train started to move. To creep. In the direction of the next station. "Marvelous!" Chávez said. He liked being above the shanties of Petare. "It's like being in an airplane." Then the train stopped. It had traveled only a few feet from the station. The entire trip lasted 67 seconds.

You could hear a crisscross of unintelligible voices around Chávez and a command crackling on the radio. Then Chávez said, "We're going to go back. We took a short trip."

But the train wasn't moving yet. It wasn't going forward and it wasn't going backward. *Ooh-ah, Chávez isn't going anywhere.* A winch can only pull. The invisible owner of Dracula's car could push—but the winch could not. For the purpose of returning the train to its starting point a second winch had been set up, at the other end of the line, at Petare II. It too had a slender cable connecting it to the train. Now there was a pause while the second winch was activated to pull the train backward.

As the train hovered between going and coming and unseen hands grappled with machinery, a philosophical conversation ensued aboard the Bolivarian Cable Train and was broadcast to the nation. El Troudi, the transportation minister, told Chávez that the cable train would save people time by making their commute shorter. "That's very important," Chávez said. TV viewers saw the outside of the train, the station, and the crowd in the street while they listened to the disembodied voices on the train. The train was now sliding backward ever so slowly. It didn't make a sound: a silent, expensive metal tube with the comandante inside. "As Karl Marx said, man cannot end up becoming a waste product of time. In capitalism, human beings end up as slaves to time. Slaves to work." This seemed to Chávez to be a good moment to bring Maduro into the conversation. "What do you think, Nicolás?" he asked.

Maduro seemed taken by surprise, a pupil staring out the window, called on by the teacher. "It's time for life, Mr. President," he said. "And life . . ."—he fumbled for some new words, found only old ones—"with time."

"What," Chávez said, "does that mean?"

"Well," Maduro said, "a life with a new time." He paused. "A new era." He reached to find something that would please the teacher. "Of happiness."

Chávez burst out laughing. You could hear someone else laughing too, perhaps Maduro. It was absurd, filling time, killing time, talking about the train that was supposed to save people time as it slid slowly backward, powerless at the end of the slender wire, going nowhere, a slow-motion yo-yo on a string. "A new cycle," Chávez said. "A new life. It's a new Venezuela that's coming into being. The fruits of our sowing."

The train stopped at last and Chávez got out. His face was puffy and tired and he walked stiffly.

The election was eight days away. Chávez would win easily. After election day, the work on the cable train would continue in fits and starts. First they had to dismantle everything they'd put in place for the simulacrum. Even the train had to be disassembled and lowered from the tracks. The twenty-four-hour construction shifts ended. Despite the promise that train service would start in December, it would be almost a year later, the following August, that Maduro, who had become president after Chávez's death, presided over the opening of the Bolivarian Cable Train. Three stations. Three-fifths of a mile. Four minutes from end to end.

During the ceremony to open the line in 2013, Maduro said that the money to build the train had come from "the riches of the nation," by which he meant money from oil. Those riches, he said, used to go into the bank accounts of the parasitic bourgeoisie that had plundered the country. Now, Maduro said, the riches of the nation go to the people.

Odebrecht, the Brazilian company that was the lead contractor on the project, would soon be caught up in a massive corruption scandal reaching across Latin America. In 2016, the company pled guilty in federal court in New York City to charges of paying $788 million in bribes and kickbacks to obtain contracts in twelve countries.[3] That included $98 million in bribes in Venezuela. In addition, the head of Odebrecht in Venezuela, Euzenando Prazeres de Azevedo, told Brazilian investigators that the company had funneled millions in secret campaign contributions to government and opposition politicians in Venezuela, including $35 million to Maduro's presidential campaign in 2013.[4]

Where did all that money for bribes and kickbacks and contributions come from? Reuters reported that Odebrecht was awarded at least thirty-two projects by the Venezuelan government, worth $40 billion.[5] The contracts provided the money for the bribes. To use Maduro's words, it came from the riches of the nation.

* * *

WHAT WAS GOING on that day in September 2012, when an ailing Chávez took a 67-second ride on his Bolivarian Cable Train? Did Chávez know it was all a sham or was he also being fooled? Andrés Izarra, the information minister, was there, but he told me that he was unaware of the subterfuge. His only job that day was to make sure the television broadcast went smoothly. It wasn't like *Aló Presidente*, where he was in charge and he knew what was phony and what was real. When you spin fictions within fictions, if you do it long enough, even the fiction-weavers may wind up losing their way, caught in the hall of mirrors they created.

And yet Chávez teased Maduro: *I'm not going to miss this ride.* He brought up the joke about Dracula's car: a broken car with no driver that was being pushed from behind. Was he toying with his handlers? Or was he just a sick man trying to make it through another long day? The campaign had worn him out. His cancer, if it had ever left him, had returned. What was show and what was real? Why tell the comandante now that the whole thing was phony when so many times before you were happy to lead him on? When El Troudi told Chávez that the train would begin operation in December and Chávez repeated it, was he being fooled or was he taking part in the fooling?

The Doppelmayr workers, who labored day and night to jerry-rig Chávez's train with wire and winches, had a name for the simulacrum. They called it the Show.

It was the show of Venezuela unfolding on national television, pre-empting all other programming.

* * *

CHÁVEZ WAS A populist. The point of government for Chávez was staying in government. The point of power was staying in power. It wasn't using that power to improve lives or make the country better in a lasting way. To the extent that any of those things were attempted, the attempt was made with a different end in mind: Would it help him stay in power?

The core claim of populism, according to the political scientist Jan-Werner Müller, is this: only *some* of the people are really the people. There is no more succinct description of Chávez's fourteen years in power. Populism, according to Müller, a professor at Princeton University, incorporates a moral vision that pits the pure people against the corrupt elites.[6]

Chávez was neither a Marxist nor in any real sense, despite the rhetoric, a socialist. Chávez made no serious effort to dismantle the market economy. Because of its unique history and the state control of the oil industry, long before Chávez, Venezuela had a deeper state penetration of the economy than any country in the hemisphere other than Cuba.[7] Chávez simply continued what was already there and painted it a different color.

One of Chávez's greatest sleights of hand was convincing people that he was doing something new when the opposite was true. The Bolivarian Revolution, "twenty-first-century socialism," the social programs that he called missions—these were all just fancy titles for more of the same. Chávez's vision was deeply conservative. He wanted the nation to go backward—back to a golden age when Bolívar and other titans strode the land and Venezuelans were pure of heart and brave and conquered a continent in the name of liberty. No matter that such an age never was. Chavismo came to exist in a kind of eternal present, a circular time alive with links to the heroic past, both near and far: the Liberator's birthday, Bolívar's victory in a decisive battle, Chávez's coup, his first election. It all became part of the same sacred calendar.

Chávez's ideology was Chavismo, which is another way of saying that he was the boss and he would make the decisions. It was the same *caudillismo* that ran like a hauling rope through the nation's history. Chavismo wasn't a movement in any massive sense, but a following. The Venezuelan system of government has always been heavily centralized and weighted toward the presidency. And that suited Chávez and his cult of personality.

What Chávez understood intuitively was that the way to stay in power was to exploit the "us versus them" dynamic of populism.

"Chávez's tendency was always to polarize," said Izarra, Chávez's former information minister. "That was the only way a revolution like his could function. He would say, 'Polarize! We are good! They are bad!' . . . Class struggle. Social class warfare. There's no way to do that without polarizing. It has to be a no-compromise thing. There was no other way to move forward."

Izarra, who was also involved in Chávez's electoral campaigns, said that he and others would sometimes argue in favor of building bridges or toning down the rhetoric to try to gain the support of undecided and independent voters, people who might have liked Chávez without considering themselves Chavistas. Izarra said: "When we would discuss what direction the campaign would take, should we build bridges? Chávez would always—" Here Izarra scrunched up his face and pumped his fist. He meant that Chávez insisted on taking a hard line, on more us versus them.

* * *

IT IS OCTOBER 4, 2012. Caracas. Today Chávez holds the final rally of his reelection campaign. He is sick. You can see it. No one in the government will admit it, it is not discussed, but the man is dying. His face is puffy and he appears bloated, perhaps the effect of medication for the cancer that he pretends to have beaten. An immense crowd, dressed in red, turns out for what they seem to sense may be Chávez's last act. People come from all over Caracas or they are bused in from other states. They stream into the city center by the tens of thousands, filling the Avenida Bolívar and nearby streets. There is a huge stage with a wide runway that juts into the crowd.

Today, October 4, also happens to be the feast day of Saint Francis of Assisi. And on this day, tradition dictates that it will rain in Caracas. But not just any rain. This is the day of what is known as the *cordonazo de San Francisco*. On this day each year, it is said, the skies open up and unleash a torrent upon the earth. *Cordonazo* refers to the *cordón*, a rope or cord that a monk wore as a belt around his habit. The story goes that on his feast day Saint Francis removes his cordón and lashes the earth with it, punishing the wicked with lightning and thunder and pelting rain. In a more beneficent version, he flails the clouds to release the rain.

It's already raining by the time Chávez takes the stage in the early afternoon, a warm, welcome rain on a hot day. He leads the crowd in singing the national anthem. He is dressed in dark clothing, a surprising variation from the usual red.

The stagecraft is brilliant. He is all alone on the stage, a lone figure in dark clothing surrounded by and elevated above the adoring masses in red. He holds a wireless microphone. Sometimes he grips it in both hands like he's praying. His voice booms across the center of Caracas through giant speakers.

An enormous campaign banner declares "Together forever."

"Who is the candidate of life?" Chávez asks the crowd.

"Chávez!" they answer.

Chávez works the crowd like a master. They cheer, they wave flags. He sings to them and they sing along. Nothing less than the life of Venezuela is at stake, he tells them. They reach a kind of ecstasy together.

The rain falls harder. He seems to revel in the rain; it runs down his face, soaks his clothing. The crowd—the people, his people—is drenched too.

"We have been bathed in the holy water of the cordonazo of Saint Francis," he says. "With this rain of Saint Francis, we consider ourselves to be blessed by the hand of God, by Christ the Redeemer." It was all a prelude to his election victory three days hence. "*Gana Chávez!*" he says. "Chávez wins!"

When he finishes, he tosses the microphone to a retainer and continues, under the rain, to drink in the adulation of the masses. He dances and sprints about the stage, proving his vigor, his immortality.

It is an amazing performance. The rain falls hard but warm and purifying, a balm, a blessing.

You could really believe on this day, if you are so inclined, that God wants Chávez to win and to remain president of Venezuela. That God has arranged it so that Chávez will live forever, or at least not die soon from cancer. That God is a Chavista. Chávez on this day seems inevitable. A force of nature.

When he leaves the stage, he climbs into his campaign vehicle. No one outside his inner circle knows it, but he is so exhausted and so sick that he's on the verge of collapse. They cancel his activities for the rest of the day.[8]

* * *

ON DECEMBER 8, 2012, Venezuelans heard the familiar chords of the national anthem on TV, and a moment later, there was Chávez in the presidential palace. But this was no ordinary broadcast. Chávez told the nation that his cancer had returned and that he was about to fly to Cuba for emergency surgery. It was two months since he'd won reelection to a new six-year term, one that was to start after the New Year.

Chávez wore a dark blue shirt, vaguely military in style, with an open collar. Underneath was a red T-shirt. He sat at a table. The wood was dark and polished. A Venezuelan flag stood behind him to his right. A bust of Simón Bolívar was behind him to his left. Maduro, who had recently been named vice president, sat next to him, on the Bolívar side. Chávez spoke and made the fateful endorsement. If anything should happen to him, he said—for instance, anything that might, just maybe, prevent him from beginning his new term as president—"my opinion, resolute, fully formed like the full moon [he shaped his hands around an imaginary circle], irrevocable, absolute, total, is that in that scenario, which, as the constitution requires [he picked up a pocket-size copy of the constitution and held it up in both hands], would call for a new presidential election, you should elect Nicolás Maduro as president of the Bolivarian Republic of Venezuela. I ask you from my heart."

That was the last time that Venezuelans saw Hugo Chávez alive, and it was also the last time they saw him live, on television.

Chávez flew to Havana, where he had surgery. The rest was mystery. There would be periodic contradictory and cryptic announcements. Chávez was doing well. There were complications. He was growing stronger. His condition was delicate. After two months the government released two photographs of Chávez lying in bed, with a copy of the Cuban newspaper *Granma*, so that skeptics could verify the date. He looked jaundiced and his smile was a grimace. They were like the proof-of-life photos of a hostage. A few days later the government made a surprise announcement: Chávez had come back home and was resting in a military hospital in Caracas. It seemed clear that he had come home to die.

On March 5, 2013, it all came to an end. In the afternoon, Maduro went on television surrounded by cabinet ministers. He was dressed in white and leaned on a podium for support. "Dear countrymen," Maduro said, "listen to me and hear me." He said that he had "the hardest and most tragic information" to convey. His voice cracked. "At 4:25 P.M. today, March fifth, the president and commander, Hugo Chávez Frías, has died."

PART TWO

PART TWO

The Barrio

Gregorio had always been small. He was Hilda Solórzano's eighth child and her last one. He was a premie, and Hilda would say that when Gregorio was born, he was the size of a button. She would make a circle with her thumb and index finger. See, a tiny button. "You would look at him and say, 'Ooh, what an ugly little thing,'" Hilda told me, and she laughed. "And look at him now. He's one who really fought to be alive." As we talked, Gregorio played with a couple of his sisters on the cement walkway in front of Hilda's house. He had a buzz cut and wore a dark blue T-shirt and shorts that went below his knees. He was barefoot. When I first talked to Hilda, in May 2019, the family was eating just twice a day on most days, and mostly starch—rice or pasta and lentils. They hardly ever had milk or meat or fresh fruit and vegetables. Once or twice a month they'd buy a subsidized food box from the government, but it lasted for only a few days. One time, the box had powdered milk that gave the kids stomachaches. The milk, which came from Mexico, tasted salty. The next time she got that brand of powdered milk in the government food box, she sold it. She didn't want someone else's kids to get sick, but what could she do? Life was just a long list of things that you needed that you didn't have the money to buy. Food, clothes for the kids, shoes, school supplies. Hilda was thirty-five years old, and at the start of every day, she asked herself three questions: Is there food for breakfast? What will we have for lunch? What are we going to eat for dinner? On most days the answer to at least one of those questions was nothing. This went on for a long time, and then Gregorio's teeth started to turn black and fall out. Hilda took him to a doctor. Gregorio was four years old and he weighed just twenty pounds. The doctor told her that at his age he should have weighed at least thirty. (An average four-year-old in the United States weighs forty pounds.) The doctor said that Gregorio's teeth were falling out because he wasn't getting enough calcium. But what could Hilda do? The family couldn't afford to buy milk.

Gregorio, who has quick, thoughtful eyes, was eager to show me what his mom was talking about. He made a big ear-to-ear smile. His lips pulled back to show off his gappy gums, a few tiny, blackened teeth poking out.

* * *

HILDA LIVED IN Petare, the part of Caracas where Chávez built his Bolivarian Cable Train. Petare is often called the biggest slum in Latin America. Some 400,000 people live there on a concatenation of hillsides, ridges, and arroyos rising like a wall at the eastern end of the valley of Caracas. Petare started as a village, founded by the Spanish in the 1600s. It was swallowed up as the city grew. After the dictatorship ended in 1958, the new democratic government lifted the restrictions on squatting. People from the countryside poured into the capital and built their shacks on any piece of empty earth they could find. They started at the bottom and worked their way up the hillsides. The higher they went, the steeper it got, and where the roads didn't reach, they built narrow, zigzag concrete stairways. The growth of the slums was an unintended byproduct of democracy.

When Hilda's parents came to Petare in the early 1960s, there were only three houses on the piece of hillside where they settled. There was a stream with clear water. Now there are thousands of cinder-block houses, pressed against one another. Hilda was born here. She liked to bake, and as a kid she dreamed of opening a pastry shop in a nice part of Caracas. After high school she became pregnant and had her first child, a daughter she named Hilmaris. She thought about going to college but didn't want to wait too long for her second child. So she settled down to being a mother.

After Hilda had her fourth child, she started taking the pill. She got pregnant anyway. After that, they gave her an IUD. She got pregnant again. They tried a different type of IUD. Pregnant again. Finally she had her tubes tied. A few months later she went to the doctor with a stomachache. A sonogram showed that she was pregnant—again. That last one was Gregorio. "I came into this world," Hilda said, "to give birth." After Gregorio was born, Hilda told the doctor: "Do whatever you have to do, cut it, burn it, staple it, put cement over it, but I'm done." They tied her tubes again, and this time it worked.[1]

They were crowded but happy. Her husband, Alexander, was an electrician with steady work. Hilda worked in the kitchen of a Mexican restaurant in a high-end shopping mall. On the side she baked cakes and bread to sell in the neighborhood. The smell of the bread in the oven was all the advertising she needed: her customers came to her.

"I didn't think of myself as being poor," Hilda said. She had big eyes in an oval face framed by long straight black hair. "I had enough to provide for my children. There was plenty of food. I could take them out to do things. I could give them little luxuries and buy them things and have parties for them, and we would celebrate at Christmastime. I thought of myself as a person who had enough to make my children happy." She laughed. "And myself too. I'd take them to the movies. I'd take them to McDonald's, to Wendy's." Hilda's daughter Susana, who was listening, made a quizzical face. "She's looking at me like, 'Wendy's? I've never been to Wendy's.'" Hilda laughed again. "She's six. It's been six years since I could take these kids out. 'What's Wendy's? What's McDonald's?' Things used to be very different."

* * *

PETARE IS ONE of the most violent places in Caracas, a violent city on a violent continent. Gangs control the barrio and fight over territory, and if you stray across one of the invisible borders separating them, you might not return. When Hilda was twelve, one of her uncles was shot dead, in front of his family (Hilda happened to be there too), on Christmas Eve. When she was twenty-two, her seventeen-year-old brother was returning from a party when he was shot and killed in the street. Hilda was home with her parents, and they heard the gunshots. A neighbor came running to tell Hilda's mother that her son was dead. A couple of years later another uncle was hit by a stray bullet and bled to death.

And then there was Yara.

Yara was ten, Hilda's fourth child. It was December 31, 2016. There was always a special kind of sweetness about Yara. Something made Hilda give her a big hug that morning. She squeezed her extra tight. Yara went to the store, skipping down the crooked concrete steps. She never came home. The family spent days looking for her. They went to the police, but the police did nothing. They didn't care about a lost little girl from a poor family in Petare. The family printed posters with Yara's picture. They searched everywhere. Hilda sold an electric mixer to pay for the posters and the bus and cab fare. Days went by. They put up more posters. Some of the kids fell ill and had to go to the doctor. A man called asking for a ransom. They sold the refrigerator and their bed to raise the money. But the ransom was a hoax. The man didn't know where Yara was.

On January 6, Yara's body was found in a garbage dump. She'd been tortured. Her fingers and ribs were broken. Her hair was pulled out. Hilda was so stunned and exhausted she couldn't shed tears. She'd cried so much already. There was just an emptiness. But now that there was a body, the cops got interested. They put Hilda in a room and asked her why she'd killed her daughter. Hilda was furious. She told them to leave her alone and go find the killer. People in the neighborhood took up a collection to help with the funeral.

No one was ever arrested.

The part of Petare where Hilda lives is run by a gang boss named Wilexys. He is feared and revered. He is the law in a lawless place. He helps the needy.

Some months after Yara disappeared, Hilda received a phone call. It was Wilexys. He told her that he had found two men who had kidnapped Yara and sold her to another man, who owned a bodega. When the bodega owner tried to molest Yara, she'd resisted, and the man had beaten her to death. In the meantime, the bodega owner had been arrested for a different crime and was murdered in jail. One of Yara's kidnappers had left the country, so he was out of Wilexys's reach. But Wilexys had found the other one and he told Hilda that the man had confessed. I asked Hilda what had happened to the man. She said she assumed that Wilexys had him killed.

"That's how justice is done in the barrio."

* * *

AT SOME POINT after Yara was buried, when Hilda "returned to reality," she looked around and said, "Wow. There's nothing left." The stove, the refrigerator, even their bed. They'd sold it all to pay for posters and transportation and medicine and food and the funeral. Hilda never went back to work at the restaurant. She wanted to be close to her remaining children, to keep them safe. The country was in full crisis by then: 2017 was a bad year, inflation was out of control, food prices went higher and higher. They couldn't pay their rent and were kicked out of their house.

That's when they moved into the one-room shack where they were living when I met Hilda. Four tin walls and a tin roof on a concrete pad, barely big enough inside to spread your arms out. Alexander built a bunk bed out of pieces of scrap wood. The two oldest girls slept on the top bunk. The two oldest boys slept on a mattress that they pulled out from under the bed at night. Hilda and Alexander and the three youngest kids slept on the bottom bunk. Yara's picture was on the wall beside the bed, where Hilda could see it when she went to sleep and woke up. A small TV set with a fuzzy picture hung from the ceiling. There was one metal chair with a torn cloth seat in the space between the bed and the door. One chair for eight people. A toaster oven sat on top of a chest of drawers. A two-ring gas burner was on a small table next to a washbasin.

The first time I visited Hilda, the only food in the house was two small rolls in a thin green plastic bag hanging from a nail. The next time I visited there was no food at all. On that day the kids didn't eat breakfast and Hilda kept them home from school. What was the point of sending them if they were too hungry and weak to pay attention? Above the washbasin, there was an opening cut into the corrugated metal sheet of the wall, a window without glass. Through it you could see the brick-colored building-block homes of Petare, rising and falling along the contours of the hillsides, filling every bit of space. And in the distance, the glorious green expanse of the elongated Ávila mountain.

* * *

HILDA HAD ALWAYS voted for Chávez. She was born in 1983, the year of the post-oil-boom devaluation that Venezuelans refer to as Black Friday. ("Ever since then, all we've known is crisis," a friend once told me.) Hilda turned sixteen the year that Chávez became president and had her first child two years later. The price of oil was rising and the economy started to improve. It's easy to see why Hilda and so many others of her generation loved Chávez. Suddenly the country filled up with money. This was not because of anything that Chávez had done. Instead it was driven by events halfway around the world—because economic growth in China and other countries pushed the price of oil sky-high. But that's not how people in Petare viewed it. They voted to reelect Chávez for the same reason that people vote to reelect presidents in the United States when the economy is strong. Chávez was president and their lives were better. And he delivered for Petare. The government built medical clinics, installed water lines, and rebuilt the decaying staircases on the hillsides. It's not that previous governments hadn't done some of the same things. But oil prices had never been so high, and Chávez had more money to spend.

In 2009, Hilda went to a national meeting of pro-Chávez organizations and put her name down on a registration form. A couple of weeks later she learned that she'd been selected for a special program to train people for the dairy products industry. They told her that the government was going to take over a dairy plant and put people to work. She was sent to Argentina with thirty-nine others to study dairy farming and production. At the time, Chávez was in a fight with the international dairy companies, Parmalat and Nestlé. He accused them of hoarding milk and price gouging, and he threatened to expropriate their factories.

For Hilda, it was as if Chávez himself had reached out a hand to help her get ahead. That was the magic of Chávez. When he spoke to a thousand people, each person felt as though Chávez was speaking directly to them. When the government gave someone a job, it was Chávez who gave it to them.

The flights to Argentina and back were the only times that Hilda had been on a plane. They put her in first class. There was turbulence and she was terrified. Most of the people in Hilda's group had grown up in the countryside. Hilda never knew how she was picked. "I was from here, from Petare, from the barrio. I'd never seen a cow in my life." In Argentina they studied everything from bovine diseases to the manufacture of powdered milk on an industrial scale. "It was as if the president had said, 'If you're going to learn, you might as well learn everything.'"

When Hilda returned to Venezuela, she and the other students went to a couple of meetings and were told to wait. She was never contacted again. The plant that the government had promised never went into operation—if it had even existed. There were no jobs.

"It all came to nothing," Hilda said. "The president died [she meant Chávez], and from then till now, it's been total madness. When the president was alive, at least we ate well, we had clothes to wear, everyone had enough."

The only souvenir that Hilda retained from her trip to Argentina was a paper certificate from the National Agricultural Technology Institute in Argentina. It said that she had participated in a course titled Recent Advances in the Dairy Industry.

* * *

HILDA AND I walked up the concrete steps to where her cousin Elena lived. Hilda's shack looked like a mansion in comparison. If Hilda's life could be called marginal, Elena's was precarious. Elena, her husband, and their four children lived under a tin roof held up by wooden posts. There were walls on only two sides. They slept on a single mattress on the floor. Elena cooked on a wood fire on the ground, with cinder blocks to hold a pot above the flame. Elena coughed continuously, a ragged wet cough from deep in her lungs. She carried her four-month-old daughter,

Nahilet, in her arms. Elena had picked some mangoes from a tree in the neighborhood and boiled them to make a drink for the children. They'd had rice and lentils for breakfast. She was waiting to see whether her husband brought some food home for her to prepare that night. If not, they would go hungry. Two years earlier, Elena had an infant son who'd died from malnutrition.

I was struck by how matter-of-fact Hilda and Elena were about their suffering. They used to live better and now they lived worse. "We were rich and we didn't know it," Hilda said. It was a phrase that I would hear over and over as I traveled around Venezuela in 2019.

Hilda had a theory about how countries achieve progress. "There shouldn't be either too much capitalism or too much socialism," she said. "If there's no business, how are you going to work? And if you don't work, how are you going to buy things? But you also don't want a country to have too much poverty. That's no good, a country that doesn't progress, a country where people can't get ahead. I think there has to be a balance, socialism and capitalism, because they go hand in hand."

Hilda had voted for Chávez up to the end. But she never voted for Maduro. The two times Maduro ran, Hilda cast a blank ballot. She was distressed by the deterioration all around her, but she'd never been to a protest. She was afraid that if someone saw her and word got back to the local Chavista-controlled community council that distributed the monthly food boxes, she might be taken off the list and her family would get nothing.

Little Bird

On January 23, 1958, a popular uprising, with military support, forced out the Venezuelan dictator Marcos Pérez Jiménez. In December of that year, Venezuela held the first presidential election of the country's new democratic era. Three weeks after Venezuelans voted, another event shook Latin America. On January 1, 1959, the dictator Fulgencio Batista fled Cuba, ahead of the advancing forces of the guerrilla leader Fidel Castro. The winner of the Venezuelan election, Rómulo Betancourt, was sworn in as president on February 13.[1] Castro was named prime minister of Cuba three days later.[2]

Nicolás Maduro was born in 1962, in the shadow of these events. He grew up in Caracas in a working-class family. His father was a left-wing activist. He was a teenager during the unprecedented oil boom and turned twenty in time for the bust. It was an era of heavy-handed U.S. intervention in Latin America. In Chile, the CIA waged a covert campaign to destabilize the government of socialist president Salvador Allende, who was overthrown in a coup in 1973 that ushered in years of brutal dictatorship. In Nicaragua in 1979, the Sandinista guerrillas forced out the dictator Anastasio Somoza, only to come under attack by the U.S.-backed Contras. The U.S. supported brutal right-wing governments in El Salvador, Guatemala, Argentina, Uruguay, and other countries. In 1983, the United States invaded Grenada—barely a hundred miles off the Venezuelan coast. In 1989 the United States invaded

Panama and arrested its dictator, Manuel Noriega, on drug trafficking charges. Through all of this, the Venezuelan government remained a loyal ally to Washington.

In high school, Maduro played bass guitar in a rock band called Enigma. He became an activist in a militant group called the Socialist League. After high school, Maduro skipped college and went to Cuba for a year of political training at the Julio Antonio Mella National School for Cadre. In 1991, the Socialist League sent Maduro to take a job as a city bus driver. The league wanted a foothold in the transit workers union. Maduro drove a bus for a while, but he spent most of his time on union organizing and political activities. However brief, the experience gave him working-class bona fides. Many years later he would call himself the worker president, based on the few months that he'd spent behind the wheel of a Caracas bus.

In 1992 Chávez staged his unsuccessful coup. Maduro visited Chávez in prison and became part of his inner circle. After Chávez became president, Maduro was elected to the National Assembly. In 2006, Chávez named him foreign minister and then, in 2012, vice president.

Maduro was politically astute, affable, and loyal. And he'd learned better than anyone else how to be a survivor in Chávez's world. Others would earn Chávez's displeasure and be slapped down or cast out. Maduro took to heart the first rule of life around Chávez: Don't outshine the boss.[3]

* * *

TEMIR PORRAS MET Maduro in 2002. Porras had gone to college in France and returned to Venezuela to take a job as a foreign policy advisor in the presidential palace. Eventually Porras moved on to the ministry of higher education and then to the labor ministry. In late 2006, Chávez made Maduro foreign minister. But Maduro was rough around the edges and Chávez grew impatient. Maduro would send him reports from the foreign ministry and Chávez would send them back with the spelling and grammatical errors marked in red pen. Chávez wanted Maduro to become more disciplined. That's when Chávez remembered Porras, who had earned a reputation for being detail oriented. Chávez pulled Porras from the labor ministry and sent him to work as Maduro's chief of staff.

It was a fortuitous combination. Maduro was gregarious and good at anticipating the boss's wishes. Porras instilled a necessary level of efficiency. Maduro took the younger man under his wing. When Chávez named Maduro vice president after he won reelection in 2012, Porras went along as Maduro's right-hand man. After Maduro was elected to replace Chávez, Porras held the title of advisor to the president. Maduro also appointed him to head up the government's main economic development fund and a government bank. The bank and the fund kept Porras busy and Maduro complained that his protégé wasn't as attentive as he used to be.

Finally, they had a falling-out. Porras had been pushing for economic reforms, like the elimination of the fixed exchange rate and a renegotiation of the nation's debt. In September 2013, Porras got into a heated argument with the finance minister, Nelson Merentes. He'd also fought with the head of PDVSA, Rafael Ramírez. Maduro's top priority was to preserve the equilibrium within Chavismo. He couldn't afford to alienate powerful Chávez loyalists like Merentes and Ramírez. Maduro blew up at Porras. Afterward, another official called Porras on the phone and told him to submit his resignation. When I spoke with Porras in 2019, he said that he hadn't talked to Maduro since that day.

Porras felt as though he'd been sent into exile. He went into a funk and started asking questions about what he believed in and where the country was headed. He wrote a critical essay and circulated it among friends. Eventually someone posted it on the internet. Because of Porras's closeness to Maduro, it made a splash. The essay took aim at some sacred cows, including Maduro's habit (copied from Chávez) of blaming his enemies for everything that went wrong. "No one in his right mind, either in Venezuela or anywhere else, thinks that the blame for the country's problems lies primarily with the opposition," Porras wrote. Loyalists called him a traitor. Oppositionists pointed with glee to the breach within Chavista ranks. Since then, Porras has tried to position himself as a thoughtful critic on the left. At the same time, he kept his distance from the opposition. He told me that he was "careful not to nourish those I consider my political opposites."

But he wasn't doctrinaire. I met Porras in Washington, where he was taking part in a program to bring together Venezuelans of different political tendencies to speak to one another, out of the spotlight. We met in a white-tablecloth restaurant near Union Station. Porras wore a dark suit, with a white shirt and a black tie. He was in his mid-forties, but he looked younger, with a soft baby face and short hair with tight curls.

* * *

ONE OF THE things that everyone noticed about Maduro, after he became president, was that he seemed to hate to make decisions. The warning lights were flashing, the economy was deteriorating, but Maduro refused to change the policies that he'd inherited from Chávez. Was it out of loyalty to the eternal leader's legacy? Or was it some psychological inability to choose an option, discard other possibilities, take action? When Maduro came into office, the fixed exchange rate of the bolivar was causing unsustainable distortions in the economy, and the bolivar was rapidly losing value against the dollar on the black market. Nearly everyone was screaming for a change in policy, yet Maduro didn't act. There were other problems too. The country was losing billions of dollars a year by virtually giving away gasoline to Venezuelan drivers; maybe that was fine when times were good, but now the country was running out of money. Maduro said publicly that it was time to raise the price at the pump—and yet he kept putting off the decision.

I asked Porras what was behind Maduro's indecisiveness.

Porras paused to consider his answer. "Nicolás is a very mystical guy," he said. He paused again. "Very mystical in general."

It was well known that Maduro and his wife, Cilia Flores, were acolytes of Sathya Sai Baba, an Indian guru who died in 2011. They had traveled to India to visit the guru and kept an altar to him in their home. I asked Porras if he was talking about Maduro's attachment to Sai Baba.

It was more than that, he said.

"There are two things. He believes in predestination, in fate. Everything that's going to happen has already been written. There's not much you can do about it, and it's already going to happen anyway. And he believes in signs. When Maduro was foreign minister, he was always in a good mood and there was no way to stress him out. He told me more than once that if something was going to turn out badly, he would know because he would have received a sign."

In 2009, Porras and Maduro were on a small jet flying to Colombia. They were approaching the airport in Bogotá when the pilot suddenly pulled up and aborted the landing. The plane banked violently and the pilot appeared to lose control of the aircraft. The other passengers screamed and cried, certain the plane was going down. "The only imperturbable one was Nicolás," Porras said. "I asked him why, and he said that if he was going to die today, he would know it." He would have received a sign.

Sometimes Maduro's fatalism was on public display. In January 2015 Maduro gave his annual address to the National Assembly, similar to the U.S. president's State of the Union Address. Oil prices had fallen by more than half and the country faced difficult times ahead. Maduro acknowledged all that and then said: "God will provide." The opposition howled that Maduro wasn't taking the country's problems seriously.

But Porras heard and understood.

And then there was the little birdie, *el pajarito*.

Chávez had been dead for almost a month and Maduro was traveling around the country, campaigning for president. On this trip he was in Barinas, Chávez's native state. Maduro stopped for the night at a house that Chávez had occasionally used, on a cattle ranch taken over by the government. Chávez had a room there where he kept some books and clothes and other personal items. On his travels around the country since Chávez's death, Maduro had stopped at other places like this, where Chávez used to stay. "Chávez's things would be there," Porras said. "His clothes, the book left where he'd been reading it. It was very emotional and difficult." He said that it felt like they were on a pilgrimage, moving from one sacred shrine to another. At times Maduro would break down in tears. "Maduro cried at Chávez's death as if Chávez were his father," Porras said.

They arrived at the cattle ranch at night. In the morning, Maduro woke and went out into the garden. Porras followed at a distance, in case Maduro should need him.

There was a small chapel on the property, and inside it was a photograph of Chávez, draped with a black band of mourning.

Maduro entered the chapel and sat down. Porras stood in the doorway. Just then a small bird flew over Porras's head and into the chapel. It flew around the small space a couple of times and then flew out again. Porras thought nothing of it. But when Maduro came out, he said: *Did you feel it? There was a presence. Chávez was there.*

They went to breakfast and Maduro said the same thing to his wife, Cilia: *I felt the presence of Chávez. He was trying to tell me something.*

According to Porras, Cilia told her husband jokingly: *Don't tell anyone, they'll think you're crazy.* They all laughed. But later that day Maduro told the story at a televised campaign event. He said that the bird had flown around the chapel and perched on a rafter and looked at him. Maduro whistled like a bird into his microphone. "I felt his spirit!" he said. "I felt like he was giving us a blessing, telling us, 'Today the battle begins! Go on to victory with our blessing!'"

* * *

IF CHÁVEZ GAVE Maduro a sign before the election, it would have been the first and second fingers of his hand squeezed together to indicate: *thisclose.* Maduro declared himself "the son of Chávez," copied his style of speech and dress, and presented himself as a loyal follower of the man he called the eternal comandante. Maduro won by 270,000 votes, less than 2 percent, a far narrower margin than in any of Chávez's victories. All of Chavismo was stunned by its near miss.

Especially at the beginning, Maduro seemed to be gripped by a deep insecurity. Andrés Izarra, Chávez's former information minister, was named minister of tourism by Maduro. Izarra said that a resentful Maduro told him once in a phone conversation: "You don't recognize me as president." Rafael Ramírez said that Maduro told him the same thing. The accusation revealed Maduro's insecurity in those early months, but it was also based in truth—the old guard that had spent years around Chávez looked at Maduro as the class clown who suddenly became the quarterback of the football team. "The first thing he needs to do, he needs to impose himself as the leader: 'I'm stepping into Chávez's shoes,'" Izarra said. "But he couldn't fill those shoes. For me he was always Nicolás." He said that in the old days, when Chávez traveled abroad, there was always pressure and work to do, and Maduro would break the tension by cracking jokes. "He was always kidding about things." That's how Izarra continued to see him, as the joker, someone you didn't take seriously. There were those, like Porras, who immediately showed Maduro a new deference and addressed him as "Mr. President." And then there were those who kept calling him Nicolás.

For Maduro, governing was about survival. He focused on proving to the doubters that he was up to the task. The opposition accused him of winning the election through fraud (although it never presented any convincing evidence) and called him an illegitimate president. It vowed to remove him from office. Within Chavismo, Maduro was surrounded by skeptics, enemies, and factions; many within his own party wondered if he would last to the end of his term. Maduro proved them all wrong.

Maduro's keen political instincts helped him contain and manage the factions within Chávez's movement. And he took advantage of the mistakes of his opponents. For Maduro, Porras said, everything was tactics. There was no strategy. There was no long-term planning. Every day was taken up dealing with the obstacle immediately in front of him.

Inflation getting out of hand? Send in soldiers to mark down the prices in stores! Price controls causing shortages? Dispatch inspectors to enforce the controls! People can't buy food? Create a system of subsidized food deliveries! It was never about root causes; it was always about reacting and treating symptoms.

"Maduro governs week by week," Porras said. "One week after another he goes about building an administration that might wind up lasting twelve years." Porras laughed, but it was a hollow laugh of incredulity, without humor. "It's like a guy who battles day after day to stay in power and finally he's there for years, but in the end, those are lost years, because they were all spent in this state of immediacy, of short-term thinking."

* * *

FOR MANY PEOPLE, the question remains, *Why Maduro?* Why did Chávez choose a man who was guided by a belief in predestination, who believed in signs, who had distinguished himself more than anything as a yes-man, who was averse to making tough decisions?

Among the opposition, the speculation has always been that Chávez's Cuban advisors influenced him to pick Maduro. According to that the-ory, Cuba needed Venezuelan oil and Raúl Castro believed that he could control Maduro.

Izarra believes that Maduro and his wife, who was also a politician, had carefully planned and maneuvered to make him Chávez's choice. The sicker Chávez grew, the closer and more indispensable Maduro became.

Rafael Ramírez said that when he went off to Cuba to have surgery, Chávez thought that he might be incapacitated for a while and unable to start his new term. But he believed that he would survive and would be able to guide Maduro if Maduro took Chávez's place as president. "He didn't think he was going to die," Ramírez said.

But Porras said that it was specifically acknowledged that the oper-ation was risky. "In Cuba, they told him, 'We're going to operate, but there's a chance you will die.'"

Among the people that I spoke with, only Porras had no doubts: Chávez had picked Maduro because he had no other real choice. For years Chávez had governed as the lone caudillo, who slapped down any-one who might rival his popularity. That made Maduro the best of a limited set of options.

In addition, Chávez insisted on choosing someone who hadn't come out of the military. Chávez conceived of his revolution as a "civilian-military union." He idolized and privileged the military, but he also was wary of its power. Picking a military man as his successor would upset the balance. That eliminated Diosdado Cabello, a former soldier who, as the main Chavista party enforcer, was the second most powerful man in the country.[4]

Maduro came from a civilian background. And at over six feet tall, he looked the part of a potential president. "Maduro was big in stature," Porras said. "He had a big voice. He had run for election in the National Assembly. He was a politician. He had campaigned. He had international experience and recognition. He checked all the boxes."

When Chávez went on television to name his successor, Maduro, sitting next to him, looked physically ill. Afterward, the camera remained on Chávez alone, and he said, "Today our country is more alive than ever, burning with a sacred flame, a sacred fire."

Blackout

Three hours after the lights went out all across Venezuela on March 7, 2019, Maduro tweeted: "The electrical war announced and directed by U.S. imperialism against our people will be defeated!" A few minutes later, the communications minister, Jorge Rodríguez, went on television and announced that a foreign enemy had carried out a "cybernetic attack" against the large hydroelectric complex at Guri, in southeastern Venezuela. He said that electricity had been restored in the entire eastern half of the country (this was not true). And he promised that within hours the lights would come back on nationwide.

The minister was a familiar face to Venezuelans. Wearing a gray suit, a white shirt, and a royal blue tie, he stood in a courtyard of the Miraflores presidential palace that was brightly lit with power from a backup generator. But it's doubtful that anyone in Venezuela saw him, since virtually no one had power to turn on their television set.

Jorge had done a bit of everything within Chavismo. He was the head of the National Electoral Council, and he created the country's electronic voting system. He served for a year as Chávez's vice president. He was mayor of the largest municipality in Caracas, with about 2 million residents (and one of the world's highest murder rates). He was Chávez's campaign manager. Under Maduro he wore several hats, with cabinet-level responsibility for tourism, culture, communication, and information.

Before Jorge went into government, he was a well-respected psychiatrist and led a comfortable middle-class life. In the public sphere he often played on his professional bona fides, going on television to offer opinions about the psychological condition of opposition leaders. His conclusion was invariably that they were mentally depraved.

Jorge was often referred to by his first name, to distinguish him from his sister, Delcy Rodríguez, who had a similar Jill of all trades passage through government. Delcy's star didn't begin to shine until Maduro became president. She had been information minister and foreign minister and then Maduro's vice president. After the blackouts, Maduro gave her the additional job of heading a task force to address the electrical crisis. Together, Jorge and Delcy were among the most visible and ardent defenders of Maduro and his government.

On the night of the blackout, Jorge started out dead serious. The nation, he said, was under attack. Then he gave a cat-that-ate-the-canary grin that was typical of his TV appearances. "What a coincidence," he said. "Less than three minutes after the criminal sabotage occurred against the power generation system at Guri, Marco Rubio, the boss of the lackeys here, posted a tweet saying that Venezuela had no electrical power." He was referring to the Republican senator from Florida, who had been a cheerleader for aggressive action by Washington against the Venezuelan government; Rubio was also a vocal supporter of Juan Guaidó, the young leader of the National Assembly, who in January had declared himself president of Venezuela in defiance of Maduro. Now Jorge said that Rubio could only have known about the blackout so quickly if he had given the order to carry out the sabotage. (Jorge was wrong about the timing. Rubio's tweet was posted about an hour and a half after the blackout began.[1] By then the power outage had been widely reported.) Here's what the tweet said:

ALERT: Reports of a complete power outage all across #Venezuela at this moment. 18 of 23 states & the capital district are currently facing complete blackouts. Main airport also without power & backup generators have failed. #MaduroRegime is a complete disaster.

This plot against the people of Venezuela, Jorge said, was destined to fail. He promised that with a heroic effort power would soon be restored. "A little patience," he said.

The following evening, Jorge was back on TV, speaking again to a nation that for the most part couldn't see him or hear him. This time there was no talk about when the lights might come back on.

"We are here to denounce what, without a doubt, can be described as the most brutal aggression to which the people of Venezuela have been subjected in the two hundred years since the war of independence freed us from the yoke of Spanish imperialism," he said.

He said that Venezuelan scientists had determined that a cyberattack had targeted the computerized "automated control system" of the Guri hydroelectric plant, which he called the plant's brain. He said that as a result of the attack the generators at Guri had shut down, causing the blackout.

He held up a printout of Rubio's tweet of the night before. Now the crucial element wasn't the timing of the tweet but Rubio's mention of backup generators at the airport, which Jorge said was actually a reference to the computers at Guri. Rubio knew, he said, that the Guri computers were supposed to activate the generators at the airport. "For Mr. Rubio to be able to say that the backup generators didn't work, it's because he knew that what had been damaged was the automated control system." It was delivered with an air of absolute authority. But it made no sense because it wasn't supposed to make any sense. Jorge had to go on TV and say something, and the one thing that he couldn't possibly say was the truth—that the government had allowed the electrical grid to deteriorate to such a state that it had collapsed and they couldn't get it working again. The backup generators at the airport would be operated by a local fuel supply—diesel or natural gas. They would not be connected to a computer system that controlled the turbines at a power plant hundreds of miles away.

Next Jorge held up the printout of a tweet by Guaidó that said: "Venezuela knows the light will come with the end of the usurpation." It contained a play on words: *electricity* and *light* are synonyms. (The opposition called Maduro a usurper because he had used a tainted election to win a new term in office.) Jorge said that the tweet was both a

confession and a threat. He said that Guaidó was involved in the sabotage of the electrical system (he didn't say how) and that Guaidó was
telling Venezuelans that he intended to keep the power shut off until
Maduro was defeated. Jorge slashed at the air with his right hand. "We
are going to make an international denunciation," he said. "If on this
planet there is such a thing as international law, if on this planet there
are standards of coexistence among the countries of the world, then
women and men of goodwill must cry out against this barbarity."

The next day, day three of the blackout, Maduro spoke at a rally in
Caracas. Government technicians had been close to restoring power to
the entire nation, Maduro said, when another cyberattack had occurred,
which set the process back to the beginning. He also revealed a new type
of aggression. He said that the country had been the victim of an electromagnetic attack aimed at its power transmission lines. Maduro was
very angry. He said that the Venezuelan opposition and the U.S. government were behind the attack.

* * *

A SECOND NATIONWIDE blackout occurred on March 25.

This time Jorge said that snipers had fired on a transformer at the
Guri complex, causing the transformer to explode. He played a video of
Guaidó, with the speed slowed down to make Guaidó sound like Darth
Vader. In the clip, Guaidó said, "The darkness will end when the usur-
pation ends." Jorge said that Guaidó was a sociopath. "Believe me," he
said, "there is nothing in that frontal lobe."

The third big blackout occurred on March 29. This time Jorge said
that there had been two "synchronized and programmed" attacks against
transmission lines. He didn't specify what sort of attacks he was talking
about.

* * *

DESPITE THE EXTREME language and the shifting explanations, the
government's accusations should not be dismissed out of hand. The
first blackout came just a few weeks after Guaidó declared himself

president with the support of the White House. It wasn't out of the question that the Trump administration might try something to destabilize the country and help push Maduro out the door. But just because something was possible didn't mean that it had happened.

The U.S. government certainly has the ability to target computer systems. The most famous case was the attack, widely attributed to the U.S. (and Israel), on the Iranian computers that controlled the centrifuges used to refine uranium for that country's nuclear weapons program. Other governments have similar capabilities, and there has been much talk in the United States about the potential for an enemy to hack the computers that control the American power grid and generating plants, including nuclear reactors.

The United States and other countries have also developed weapons that use electromagnetic pulses. In 2012, Boeing announced the successful test of a weapon it had developed with the U.S. Air Force, called the Counter-Electronics High Power Microwave Advanced Missile Project, or CHAMP.[2] It was designed to emit "bursts of high-powered energy" to disable data or electronic systems. A 2018 report by the American Foreign Policy Council, a think tank (Newt Gingrich sits on its advisory board), surveyed the possible threats and concluded: "An ambitious terrorist with sufficient knowledge of the inner workings of the electrical grid could conceivably black out a major city."[3] And the U.S. government was concerned enough that, less than three weeks after the first big blackout in Venezuela, Trump signed an executive order directing government agencies to improve American defenses against potential electromagnetic pulse attacks.[4]

Sniper attacks on electrical infrastructure are another plausible concern. In 2013, snipers opened fire on an electrical substation in Metcalf, California, disabling seventeen transformers. While the shots did not ignite an explosion or fire or cause a blackout, the mysterious attack raised alarms among utility executives and security experts over vulnerabilities in the U.S. power grid.[5]

The Venezuelan government, however, never offered any proof that the country had been the target of computer or electromagnetic attacks. A sniper was never found and no serious evidence was presented.

There's something exhausting about going back to the videos from that time and watching the government's exercises in public shifting of blame. So much effort goes into covering over mistakes and pointing fingers at others—playing the victim—rather than fixing the problem. Casting blame on outside forces or internal double-dealers is one of the essential traits of populism. A shared sense of persecution helps build the us versus them identity. Chávez's utterance "I take responsibility," so impressive on the morning of his 1992 coup, had remained a unique event. One of the central attributes of Chavismo was playing the victim. Chávez indulged in it and Maduro excelled at it: the claims of coup plots, assassination attempts, and sabotage multiplied.

While Maduro and Jorge were claiming sabotage and outside aggression, other people were pointing to what everyone knew to be true: for years Venezuela's electrical system had been decaying, suffering from massive disinvestment and a failure to maintain its installations. Like virtually everything else in the country, it was falling apart.

One of the most likely causes of the initial blackout was a fire under the high-tension lines. All electric utilities make it a priority to cut the underbrush from beneath high voltage lines, in part because a fire can produce a spike in current that can disrupt the transmission system. For years all types of basic maintenance, including cutting brush, had been neglected by Corpoelec, the electrical utility. Years earlier, a Corpoelec manager had told me that the company was allowing brush to grow beneath power lines, with potentially disastrous consequences. In the days after the blackout, researchers pointed to satellite images that showed a fire in the vicinity of high voltage lines in eastern Venezuela at the time that power went out.

* * *

THE BLACKOUT OCCURRED during the dry season. Several people who were in the area where the blackout began told me that it was so dry that it was common to see fires blazing in the undergrowth by the roadside. But for the government, the obvious answer was the wrong answer because it would have had to accept responsibility for failing to keep the brush clear.

You couldn't blame the gringos for not cutting the grass.

Things Are Never So Bad

How extreme was Venezuela's collapse?

From 2013 through 2019, according to an estimate by the International Monetary Fund, nearly two-thirds of all economic activity disappeared.[1] That's a 65 percent drop in gross domestic product. What does that mean in people's lives? In broad terms, it would be as if, for every three people who used to have a full-time job, two are now unemployed. For every three shops on a block, two are closed. A family that used to eat three meals a day now eats just one (and often only lentils or pasta). Of course, the effects aren't even across the economy and across society: some families eat more, some less, some go hungry.[2] The United Nations estimated that in 2019, a third of the population had difficulty getting enough food to eat.[3]

This level of economic devastation is unknown in countries not at war.

During the Great Depression in the United States, the economy shrank by 27 percent during the four years from 1929 to 1933.[4] And then it started to grow again. After the disintegration of the Soviet Union, the Cuban economy, which relied on Soviet support, shrank by more than a third from 1989 to 1993.[5] And then it started to grow again.

By 2021, Venezuela had gone through eight consecutive years of economic contraction and it still hadn't hit bottom.

Episodes of hyperinflation are rare in modern economies. The IMF at one point projected that inflation in Venezuela would reach 1 million percent a year. That was merely a guess, a placeholder that signified: *A big number goes here.* For several years Maduro's government stopped publishing most economic data, as though by hiding the data it could hide the enormity of the problem. Finally in 2019 the Central Bank began releasing data again. It revealed that inflation in 2018 was more than 130,000 percent. For a variety of reasons, it was lower the following year: at almost 10,000 percent. Were those numbers accurate?[6] Did it matter to the people trying to buy food? Whatever the number, prices were out of reach. Sometimes stores would change their prices twice a day. If you had bolivars, you had to spend them today because they would be worth less tomorrow.

By contrast, next door, in Colombia, the annual inflation rate in 2018 and 2019 was about 3 percent.[7]

At the same time, the value of the bolivar evaporated against the dollar. When I came to Venezuela in 2012, one bolivar was worth 23 U.S. cents. As I write this in 2021, that same bolivar would be worth about one four-billionth of a cent, or $0.0000000000025.[8]

Millions of people, despairing of ever having enough work, money, or food and with no hope for the future, fled. The United Nations in 2020 estimated that more than 5 million Venezuelans had left the country since the crisis began.[9] That is one-sixth of the pre-crisis population of 30 million. In a world awash in refugees, the exodus from Venezuela was second only to the flight from Syria, which was in the midst of civil war.

* * *

WHAT WENT WRONG?

How did the nation with the biggest estimated oil reserves in the world turn into a disintegrating country where millions of people were going hungry and one in six residents had fled?

The short answer is that Venezuela ran out of money.

From 1999, the year that Chávez took office, through 2013, the year he died, Venezuela's total oil export income was $768 billion, a bonanza that far surpassed the oil boom of the 1970s and 1980s.[10] The windfall was the result of oil prices that rose from less than $8 a barrel the year that Chávez first took office to more than $100 a barrel—pushed upward by demand from China and other fast-growing economies.[11] In 2012 the value of Venezuela's oil exports reached its highest one-year level ever, surpassing $93 billion.

Then the price of oil started to drop. In 2015, the nation's oil export income fell to $35 billion. In 2016, it was just $26 billion.[12]

In 2017, Donald Trump became president and the United States cranked up sanctions. They landed with force on an economy that was already under stress, first cutting off Venezuela from international financial markets and then barring oil sales to the United States and greatly restricting the country's ability to sell oil elsewhere.

Oil production had started to decline sharply in 2016,[13] and even when prices started to recover that year, the nation's oil income did not—because it was pumping less and selling less. By 2019, with production dropping fast and U.S. sanctions biting deeply, oil exports were less than $23 billion,[14] a quarter of what they were at their peak.

When oil prices fell, Venezuela was like a two-income household in which one of the earners had lost their job. Suddenly there was a lot less money coming in. Then oil production dropped, and it was like the other breadwinner was fired too. A family in those circumstances would pinch pennies and live off savings, if it had them.

But during all those boom years, Venezuela saved nothing.[15] All the oil money had been spent or stolen. There was a law that said the government had to put money in a rainy day fund. Chávez repealed it and spent the money that had been set aside. When he died, the fund contained just $3 million.[16]

* * *

THE LONGER ANSWER is that several things happened before and after oil prices fell that contributed to the outsize scale of the disaster.

One of the main complicating factors was a foreign exchange system that grew increasingly dysfunctional as time went by.

In Venezuela there have been two primary areas of commerce or industry into which people could channel their energy.

One, of course, was oil.

The other was importing. Since oil exports boosted the value of the bolivar and created strong incentives against producing things locally (this was the Dutch Disease effect), it was natural that the import business should thrive in Venezuela.

Importing was also one of the ways that people could share in the oil revenues. The dollars produced by selling oil were used to bring in all sorts of things that consumers wanted. Food. Alcohol. Cars. Television sets. Clothing. Medicine.

In 2003 Chávez created a fixed exchange rate and a government agency, known by the acronym CADIVI, to decide who got dollars and for what purpose.

This had two important effects. First, it put the government in charge of handing out dollars—accentuating its permanent role as the distributor of oil money and creating new avenues for corruption. Second, it led to the creation of a black market for dollars.

Chávez promised that his government's regulation of the exchange system would guarantee that the poorest Venezuelans would have access to products at affordable prices. The nation's oil dollars, Chávez said, were for the people. They were not meant to buy fancy cars and whisky for the rich.

But there was a hitch. The gap that opened between the official exchange rate and the black-market rate created an opportunity to make money. For a long time the black-market rate was about double the official rate, which changed with periodic devaluations. In January 2012, the official exchange rate was 4.3 bolivars to the dollar. The black-market rate was twice that—8.6 bolivars to the dollar. That meant that if you could gain access to dollars at the official rate and sell them at the black-market rate, you could double your money.

In an ideal world a typical currency transaction might go like this: Let's say you wanted to import $1 million of tennis rackets from China. You would go to CADIVI, the government agency that sold dollars to importers, and request $1 million. If your application was approved, you would arrange for the purchase and have the tennis rackets shipped to Venezuela (for simplicity's sake, we'll assume that the price includes the shipping cost.) Once the rackets arrived and passed through customs, the government would sell you the hard currency you had requested. You would pay the government 4.3 million bolivars, and the government would give you $1 million. You would then take the dollars and pay your Chinese supplier. Now you could sell your tennis rackets at a reasonable markup to Venezuelans eager to improve their backhand, and you could take home a modest profit on the sales.

But Venezuela was far from that ideal world.

First off, not all applications for dollars were approved. So you might want to have a friend or a cousin in the government, who could grease the wheels for you, and you might want to pay bribes to this friend or cousin and their friends. Next, tennis rackets are nice, but money is nicer. So instead of spending the entire $1 million on tennis rackets in China, you arrange with your Chinese supplier to ship just $450,000 worth of tennis rackets to Venezuela, with a phony invoice that says the tennis rackets are really worth the full amount. Even so, once the merchandise arrived in Venezuela, customs officials might raise objections, and you might need to bribe them as well. In any case, once the tennis rackets had arrived and customs certified the shipment, just as in our idealized example, you would give the government 4.3 million bolivars and they would give you $1 million. But this time you would send just $450,000 to your Chinese tennis racket supplier. You would also need to pay the bribes you'd promised. Let's say that those add up to an additional $50,000. That leaves you with $500,000. You could then take that money and deposit it in a bank account in Miami or Switzerland. Or you could turn around and sell it to other Venezuelan businessmen who needed dollars. And you would sell it to them at the black-market rate, which was double the rate you'd paid for the dollars. At a black-market rate of 8.6 bolivars to the dollar, your $500,000 would fetch 4.3 million bolivars. Without selling a single tennis racket, you'd already broken even on your original investment. You could now take that money and spend it, or you could apply to buy more dollars. Venezuelans called that "the bicycle": using the profits of one currency transaction to finance the next one, and the next one, and the next one. The wheels kept turning. You were playing with the house's money.

This process of buying cheap dollars from the government and then over-invoicing the imported merchandise became a way of doing business in Venezuela. After oil, importing—and gaming the exchange system in the process—was the country's main economic pursuit. (None of this was new or peculiar to Chávez—a comparable system in the 1980s led to similar excesses.)

There was a joke that, in Venezuela, the honest businessman over-invoices by 50 percent and the corrupt businessman over-invoices by 100 percent.

The more you exaggerated the value of your shipment, the more you stood to profit. The incentives and opportunities for corruption were enormous for both importers and government officials.

Starting in 2012, the bolivar began to lose value on the black market. It started the year at 8.6 bolivars to the dollar, and by the end of the year it was at about 17 bolivars to the dollar. And the bigger the gap between the official fixed rate and the black-market rate, the bigger the profits to be had by gaming the system. And the greater the incentive to do so.

In February 2013, the government announced a devaluation to 6.3 bolivars to the dollar. But it also took other measures that restricted the amount of dollars it made available to importers. That had the effect of creating a dollar shortage, which drove the black-market price of the dollar higher. By the end of 2013, the black-market dollar was worth ten times the official rate of 6.3 bolivars to the dollar. That means that if our tennis racket importer operated in the same way at the end of 2013, instead of breaking even through his currency manipulation, he was showing a significant profit. An initial investment of 6.3 million bolivars would buy $1 million. If he spent half that on tennis rackets and bribes, the $500,000 that remained could be turned into 31.5 million bolivars. That's a 400 percent profit, without selling any tennis rackets. He could take that and buy $5 million from the government, and so on.

The orgy of dollars and bogus shipments became extreme. You could throw the tennis rackets you'd imported into the ocean and what would it matter? There were cases where importers didn't bother to bring in anything at all, or they shipped containers full of scrap metal. Importers abandoned containers of merchandise on the docks because they had already realized such an enormous profit that they couldn't be bothered to collect the merchandise and sell it.[17]

What had been a steady incentive for corruption under Chávez now became a huge and growing incentive under Maduro, with serious repercussions in the broader economy.

Oil dollars ceased to be primarily a means of importing needed goods at an affordable price and became instead an object of speculation and corruption.

By the second half of 2014, the price of oil had begun what would turn out to be a lengthy slide that would gut the country's revenues. (In June, the price was over $100 a barrel. In January 2015 it would drop below $50, and a year later it would bottom out at less than $25.)[18] But even before the oil price started to drop, recession had set in, and the economy in 2014 would shrink by nearly 4 percent. At the same time, inflation was increasing and so were shortages of basic goods and lines outside depleted supermarkets.

Maduro's response to inflation was price controls. Intended to keep basic goods affordable, they had the opposite effect. Cheap goods, including corn flour and other food staples whose prices were set below market value, were siphoned away from stores and resold on the streets at higher prices. The result was even more acute shortages and more inflation.

Many goods also disappeared into Colombia and Brazil. Anything subject to price controls or produced with government subsidies—corn flour, shampoo, cooking oil, and more—chased higher prices across the border.

But the biggest cross-border profits were to be had by selling gasoline. Venezuela had the cheapest gasoline in the world—you could fill up your tank for pennies. There had always been contraband traffic of gasoline into Colombia. But as the economic crisis set in, the incentive increased.

With oil revenues decreasing, the government had less money to spend. But Maduro, intent on shoring up his political position, wasn't willing to reduce spending. To cover the shortfall, he printed more bolivars, which produced more fuel for inflation. His response was more price controls and stricter enforcement.

Economists will tell you that in most cases price controls intended to keep products cheap end up making them more expensive and lead to shortages. There are several reasons. Low prices discourage companies from producing the controlled products, so there are fewer of them in the market. People rush to buy up the cheap products and stores run out. Then because the price-controlled products tend to be staples, those people who weren't quick enough to buy them in stores still need them—and so the people who bought them resell them on the black market at much higher prices.

According to the Venezuelan economist Francisco Rodríguez, the most fundamental item subject to price controls in Maduro's economy wasn't corn flour or gasoline, but the dollar. And it was from there that the distortions in the economy emanated.

The rationale for a strong bolivar (and cheap dollars) was so that products would be affordable to ordinary people, in keeping with Chávez's declaration that oil dollars were for "the people" and not to import luxury goods for the rich. The theory was that if the government provided cheap dollars to importers, they would bring essential goods into the country and sell them at low prices.

But by now the straightforward relationship between a strong bolivar and cheap imported goods had been broken. Because dollars were so cheap, everyone wanted them. Back in 2014, Rodríguez told me that the Central Bank might as well have put a sign on its door saying: "We sell $10 bills for $1." To keep its hard currency reserves from disappearing, the government restricted the sale of dollars. As with any other good, Rodríguez said, high demand and low supply meant the price of black-market dollars soared. As that happened, a growing portion of the dollars that the government sold to importers never resulted in goods coming into the country. The profits to be had by playing the spread between the official and black-market exchange rates were so great that would-be importers simply covered their costs and pocketed the money.

All that meant fewer imports and fewer products on store shelves, which meant higher prices. At the same time, the government's costs were going up too—salaries, pensions, military uniforms—and the government was printing money to finance its operations. As oil revenues fell, the government printing machine worked harder.

Maduro doubled down on price controls. He sent soldiers into electronics stores to mark down the prices of TV sets and computers. He added to the list of products subject to controls. He deployed an army of inspectors to audit stores and fine violators.

The effect was to push more and more products onto the black market (or across the border), and store shelves became emptier. Lines at stores became so long the government assigned shopping days to people based on the last digit of their national identification number, and it sent soldiers to patrol the lines to make sure people weren't shopping on the wrong day.

It was a Yogi Berra economy: stuff was so cheap that nobody could afford to buy it anymore.[19] Subsidized food and goods subject to price controls would be siphoned out of stores, and those same goods would show up on the street at elevated prices. Stores were left with the paradox of empty shelves and long lines of people waiting to get in to buy whatever remained. And cheap dollars from the government meant ever more expensive dollars on the black market.

All sorts of strange behavior resulted. Aside from selling cheap dollars to importers, the government had for years maintained a system for selling cheap dollars to ordinary Venezuelans who wanted to travel abroad. In those days, any Venezuelan with travel plans and a passport could buy up to $5,000 a year at the official exchange rate. This allowed many middle-class Venezuelans to take vacations abroad that they could not otherwise have afforded.

Of course Venezuelans found ways to milk the system, and the incentives increased with the price of the black-market dollar. A businessman I knew had a secretary who suddenly quit her job. The woman was a trusted employee and my friend offered to increase her salary, but she refused. The reason, she told him, was simple. She had received her government travel allowance, crossed the border into Brazil, and collected her dollars there (or Brazilian reals, which she could convert to dollars). She then returned to Venezuela, where she could exchange those dollars, little by little, on the black market. Why work when she could cover her living expenses for the next two years with the proceeds from her Brazilian "vacation"?

In early 2014, the minimum monthly wage, calculated at the official exchange rate, was about $500. At the black-market rate—which was more indicative of prices in Venezuela—it was about $50. By mid-2015, the minimum wage (having been raised in an attempt to keep up with galloping inflation) was about $1,200 a month when calculated at the official exchange rate and about $11 when calculated with the black-market rate. A survey of prices showed that a month's worth of food for a family of five cost more than six times the monthly minimum wage.

But if you had dollars, you were rich. You could buy a bottle of twelve-year-old Scotch for the equivalent of ten bucks, using bolivars bought on the black market. Dinner for two at a fancy Caracas restaurant, with drinks and wine, could be had for about $40 using black-market bolivars—though if you were filling out an expense account using the official exchange rate as the conversion, it would appear to have cost nearly $5,000.

Airfares became incredibly cheap because the airlines had to price them in bolivars calculated at the official exchange rate. A round-trip ticket that might cost $1,000 in the United States could be bought using black-market bolivars for the equivalent of $100 or less.

In the past, the airlines would sell tickets in bolivars and then exchange those bolivars for dollars with the government. But now, to protect its hard currency reserves, the government cut off the airlines' access to dollars. In response, the airlines started cutting flights. Delta once flew every day from Atlanta. By the middle of 2014, it was flying just once a week. American Airlines had forty-eight flights to Venezuela each week. In 2014 it cut the number to ten. It eliminated direct flights from New York and other cities and began flying only from Miami. For me, the direct flight from New York had been both a luxury and a revelation. On a good day, the direct flight from New York to Caracas would be in the air for just four and a half hours. Caracas, in what I had always thought of as faraway South America, was closer to New York than Los Angeles and about the same distance as Mexico City. Over time, the airlines cut back more flights, and the country, which had always been so open to the world, became isolated. Even then there were still many Venezuelans traveling and the flights were full. But as the economy continued to shrink, there was less demand and the flights simply disappeared. When I flew into Caracas in May 2019, there were just sixteen international arrivals a day. In July, the number was down to eleven.[20] By then the flights were full of elderly people who'd gone to visit children and grandchildren who had moved abroad because of the crisis, and now they were returning home to live out their days alone. Walking through the airport in Panama City or Miami you knew which flight was going to Caracas by the long line of older passengers in wheelchairs, waiting to board.

* * *

WHEN MADURO WAS elected president in April 2013, he was consumed by political challenges: tensions were high, the opposition questioned the legitimacy of his victory, and there were frequent protests. There were important decisions to be made about the economy and government finances, but Maduro kept putting them off. "He has a politician's frame of mind and he threw himself into the political confrontation," Rafael Ramírez, Chávez's longtime oil minister, said. "With that kind of thing Maduro is a fish in water: political confrontation, propaganda. But to sit down and govern? No."

In October, Maduro appointed Ramírez as vice president for the economy. By then the bolivar was sinking fast on the black market, inflation was accelerating, and shortages were increasing.

Ramírez said that he arranged a meeting with Maduro, the head of the central bank, Nelson Merentes, and a few others. Together they laid out for him the country's dire economic situation: the foreign exchange system, the devaluation of the bolivar, heavy debt obligations, a budget weighed down by costly social programs, financial pressures on PDVSA.

"I made a proposal to liberate the exchange rate," Ramírez said. "And everyone in the economy was waiting for that to happen. But Maduro wouldn't decide. And that's when the black market took off because people understood, the economists understood, that Maduro didn't have the capacity to make decisions. He would say one thing to me and Merentes: 'Yeah, you're right, we've got a problem here.' But he was talking to other people. He had other advisors."

For Ramírez, after twelve years beside Chávez, working with Maduro was a shock. "I found myself with a person who was like Jell-O. He moves this way and he moves that way and he doesn't make a decision. And the country, I felt like it was a boat that was sinking, down, down, down."

Over time, however, Ramírez concluded that Maduro was listening to a group of businessmen who had made a fortune through easy access to Venezuela's cheap dollars. And they didn't want the system to change. "Maduro decided in favor of an economic interest group that had been at his side and had supported him for years," Ramírez said. "Every time he either made a decision or didn't make a decision, it was to favor that group."

I asked Temir Porras, the former Maduro aide, about this. He said that when he came into the presidency, Maduro was intent on placating the vested interests within Chavismo and the government. That included officials who operated the exchange system and had been profiting from it, through transactions and the bribes associated with them. And many others in the private sector had become rich alongside them. Eliminating the government regulation of the exchange rate would have angered an important constituency. And Maduro's biggest priority at the time was to not rock the boat within Chavismo.

"The economic crisis is a creation of the Maduro government, of an absolute lack of comprehension of the laws of macroeconomics," Porras said. "Printing money, price controls. All that has an immense responsibility for the economic deterioration. Until 2016 or 2017, they didn't have a consciousness or awareness of the magnitude of the economic problem." Maduro, he said, combined ignorance of economic policy with overconfidence and a kind of insouciance born of fatalism. "To say the government was ill equipped to respond is an understatement. They had no think tank or brain trust or technical capacity to respond to it." Without advisors with economic expertise to guide him, Maduro acted true to form; he stalled, hoping that things would work themselves out. "He had no idea what to do," Porras said. "The crisis occurs and the government does the worst thing possible. It does nothing."

*　*　*

RUTH DE KRIVOY knows about economic crises. She was named the president of Venezuela's Central Bank in 1992, two months after Chávez's coup attempt. During her tenure, the Venezuelan banking sector went bust and it fell to her to stanch the bleeding and patch things back together.[21]

I met with de Krivoy a couple of times in 2018 and 2019 to talk about Venezuela's deteriorating economy. We met over coffee in New York City, in an atrium mall at the World Financial Center in Lower Manhattan. De Krivoy, an economist, is a fine-boned, pale woman in her seventies with a swirling aura of white hair that seemed to be illuminated from within.

During our first meeting, she ticked off a long list of the government's economic missteps. "You get this sense it's getting worse and worse and worse," she said. It was a phrase that she used more than once: "worse and worse and worse."

As we talked, the sky opened and a torrential rain beat against the glass ceiling of the atrium. Water started to pour in through the glass and men in dark suits with walkie-talkies appeared and then a diminutive woman with a mop. They put up a yellow plastic sign that said "Caution" and "Cuidado." The sign had a picture of a stick-figure person falling.

"At some point people and countries pay the price for their mistakes," de Krivoy said.

I asked when the breaking point in Venezuela would finally come. She gave me the kind of look that a teacher might give a pupil who hasn't mastered a lesson. "Things are never so bad that they can't get worse," she said. "They can."

I met de Krivoy a second time several months later, and true to her prediction, as grim as things had appeared before, they were orders of magnitude worse now. I recalled a recent conversation that I'd had with a man in Maracaibo who was spending the night in his car outside a gas station so that he could fill up in the morning. He told me all the problems that he faced: no water, no electricity, no gasoline. Venezuela, he said, had hit bottom. I challenged him: six months earlier he might have said the same thing. Six months later and surely the situation would be worse again. "You're asking me if we've reached our limit," he said. He ran through the litany of plagues again. "We don't know what to do anymore."

There's the old joke about how a guy went broke: gradually at first and then all at once. For many Venezuelans, the country seemed to have gone broke all at once—there was plenty of money and then there was none. Oil was at $120 a barrel; then it was at $20.

But de Krivoy saw Venezuela's crisis through a longer lens. In an *all at once* world, she saw the *gradually*.

Maduro might have been the one on hand to pay for the broken plates, but it was Chávez who threw the party where they were broken.

I asked de Krivoy how the country had come to this.

"You get into it through phases," she said. This time we were sitting on the other side of the mall, in front of a wall of glass looking out on the harbor and the Statue of Liberty. It was a sunny day with a strong breeze, and there were whitecaps and sailboats on the Hudson. "You start by weakening institutions," de Krivoy said. "Chávez reformed the law of the Central Bank and allowed the Central Bank to fund the government. That opened the door to printing money and hyperinflation . . . Chávez sacked twenty thousand professionals in PDVSA, changed the law [governing] PDVSA, turned PDVSA into a petty cash [source] for the government—and production started coming down." The process at PDVSA was complete, she said, when Maduro named a general with no oil sector experience to run the company. This was part of a broader pattern involving the military. First Chávez politicized the armed forces by making them loyal to his party, and then Maduro handed out key government posts to generals.

"Then you have the judiciary. Chávez increased the number of judges in order to control the Supreme Court, and the rule of law disappeared. Then you destroy property rights and overregulate the economy. Then you change the constitution and you start having yearly elections in Venezuela. So what used to be a five-year horizon for policy making ended up being a one-year horizon, because every election in Venezuela was a referendum on Chávez, so the quality of policy making also deteriorated."

De Krivoy held up her thin, pale hands in front of her and fluttered her fingers as she brought her hands downward. "It's like you think of a house of cards and one falls and the other one falls. It crumbles." But she didn't mean that the house crumbles and then it's over. Because there are still all the people who were making money off the status quo, all the factions and cohorts and mafias and centers of power, small and large. They're all still there, still fighting to hold on to their pieces of the pie. "It crumbles," she said, her hands coming to rest in her lap, "and leaves interest groups in place."

Outside the sun played off the water and lit up the Statue of Liberty.

Blackout

Four days after the lights went out all across Venezuela, Juan Carlos Pérez was at his house in Guayana City when a friend, an old work colleague, came to visit. It was Sunday.

"We need help," the friend said. "We can't get the system back up and running."

Juan Carlos had retired from Corpoelec, the national electrical utility, two years earlier. Over a thirty-year career he had worked at the country's three hydroelectric plants on the Caroní River: the giant complex at Guri (one of the largest in the world) and the two smaller plants at Caruachi and Macagua. He knew them as well as anybody did. Juan Carlos listened to his friend's appeal. When the friend was done, he said, in the polite, measured manner that was typical for him, that he was sorry but he wouldn't be able to help. Later that Sunday a second friend from the utility knocked on his door. This friend told Juan Carlos that his name had come up during a meeting with Delcy Rodríguez, the vice president, who had flown in to supervise the recovery of the electrical system. Again, Juan Carlos politely declined.

Juan Carlos wanted to help—but not if it meant working again for Luis Motta Domínguez.

Maduro had appointed Motta Domínguez as president of Corpoelec and minister of electrical energy in 2015. Motta Domínguez had no experience in the electrical sector; he was a former general in the national guard. Maduro needed to shore up his support in the military and he was handing out sinecures to generals, regardless of their qualifications. Motta Domínguez also checked another box: he was close to Tareck El Aissami, a powerful governor who controlled an important faction within Chavismo. Corpoelec, even in its reduced state, was a juicy plum: there were patronage jobs to hand out and millions of dollars in contracts to assign.

A few months after Motta Domínguez arrived at Corpoelec, a problem occurred at the Guri Dam that caused the water level in the reservoir to fall precipitously, in a way that could have imperiled power generation. The incident drew concern at the utility, and Motta Domínguez wanted someone to blame. He summoned Juan Carlos to a meeting of company managers and ministry officials and, with intelligence agents standing by, threatened to have him arrested, accusing him of being a saboteur. "That's his favorite word," Juan Carlos told me.

There was an investigation and Juan Carlos was cleared, but he'd seen enough of Motta Domínguez. Juan Carlos had worked his entire career for the utility. He was a member of Chávez's socialist party. He'd once met Chávez and felt a deep personal connection. Juan Carlos had even volunteered to teach classes about socialism to his fellow workers. Motta Domínguez was as incompetent as he was authoritarian. He represented the worst that had come out of Chavismo. In 2017, Juan Carlos retired, after three decades on the job.

Now, with the lights out across the country, when Juan Carlos told his friends that he couldn't help, what he meant was that as long as Motta Domínguez was in charge, he wasn't going anywhere near Corpoelec. It wasn't just personal animosity. He'd already been falsely accused of sabotage once; what was to stop Motta Domínguez or someone else from scapegoating him again?

Finally, that Sunday evening, as darkness settled over Guayana City, Juan Carlos received a phone call. It was another friend at the utility, a top manager. He told Juan Carlos that if he didn't come in on his own, then they would have to send someone to bring him in. Juan Carlos understood what that meant: the Sebin secret police or the DGCIM, military intelligence. This time he said: *Okay. I'll come.*

* * *

WHEN HE ARRIVED at Corpoelec headquarters Sunday night, he found some familiar faces. There was Antonio Martini, a former manager of the Guri complex; Francois Morillo, who had been a regional manager in charge of the three hydroelectric plants; and Luis Dimas, another former manager with long experience.

They were all friends. If you added up their careers, they equaled more than a century of experience working in the utility. They had something else in common too: they'd all been driven out of the company by Motta Domínguez.

Antonio Martini says that Motta Domínguez fired him without explanation almost as soon as the minister took over Corpoelec. Francois Morillo, like Juan Carlos, said that Motta Domínguez accused him of sabotage; he said that his photograph was posted inside a guard booth at Corpoelec headquarters with the word saboteur splashed across it. Luis Dimas was also fired; he had appealed the firing, but in the meantime there was an order barring him from Corpoelec facilities.

They'd all been pushed out by Motta Domínguez. And now they'd all been called back into service.

They were escorted into the building, where they met with Delcy Rodríguez, the vice president. She impressed the four men with her quick grasp of the problems that the utility faced. She appealed to their patriotism and told them that the country needed their expertise and their loyalty. Delcy suspected that many of the workers at the disabled power plants favored the opposition and were in no hurry to help out a government they hated by turning the power back on. She told them that during a visit to one of the plants she had shaken the hand of a technician, a woman. Afterward Delcy noticed that the woman had wiped her hand on her pants as though shaking the vice president's hand had made it unclean.

There was one other thing that Delcy said. She guaranteed that she would keep Motta Domínguez away from them.

The men agreed to go to work. They decided that the key to bringing power back was the hydroelectric plant called Caruachi. It was the smallest of the three plants, in terms of generating capacity. But the tur-bines there were of a type that could respond more quickly to varia-tions in supply and demand within the power grid, making it crucial for maintaining the equilibrium of the entire system. "If we could keep Caruachi stabilized, then from that point on the job of bringing back the system would get much easier," Juan Carlos told me.

The men had all been away from Corpoelec for a few years, and when they arrived at Caruachi that night they were appalled by what they found. One of the plant's twelve generators had been leaking oil, appar-ently for weeks; it was surrounded by a lake of oil that no one had both-ered to clean up. Basic maintenance had been neglected. Spare parts were exhausted. Radios didn't work. Burned-out lightbulbs hadn't been replaced. That grabbed Juan Carlos's attention: burned-out lightbulbs in a power plant.

Like the generator spewing oil, Corpoelec had been leaking human beings. People had deserted the company because they could no longer afford to live on wages that had once guaranteed a middle-class lifestyle and now provided for a starvation existence. Many experienced work-ers had left the country. Caruachi, in the middle of an emergency, had about half the workers who would have been assigned to a normal shift a few years earlier. In the coming weeks the men would visit the other two hydroelectric plants and find the same math—half the personnel needed for normal operations. And those who were left were working extended shifts, sometimes of sixteen hours or more.

Caruachi had a reputation for being a pro-opposition workplace. It was here that the woman had wiped her hand after shaking hands with Delcy. When Juan Carlos and the others arrived, the small comple-ment of workers on duty stood around waiting for orders, acting as though they had no idea what to do. Luis Dimas and Antonio Martini said that it appeared to them that workers at the plant had been drag-ging their feet, deliberately stalling. "There are different types of sabo-tage," Antonio told me. "There is sabotage that comes from an action that you take, and there is another kind, which is sabotage by omission. By not doing something, you can commit sabotage as well."

Luis Dimas said that they took the plant manager aside. "Let's work on this together," they told him. "We're not here to make trouble for any-one, but we're going to do what we have to do."

The plant was at zero, producing no electricity. They set to work, eval-uating each generator in turn. They found no significant mechanical problems. Antonio said that they didn't even pick up a tool. It was a matter of proceeding methodically, bringing the generators online one by one. Nothing was damaged. "We'd say, adjust this setting here, adjust this there and let's start it up. Let's connect it to the system. It's gener-ating energy. Okay, now let's look at the next one and the next one. There was a fluctuation and the units adjusted their velocity and didn't disconnect and we asked ourselves: 'So how come it's working now and it wasn't before?'"

Antonio and Luis weren't suggesting that the workers at the plant had caused the blackout. But no one seemed to be in any hurry to resume operations. I pressed Antonio on the question of sabotage. The plant em-ployees had been working shorthanded for long hours, under a huge amount of pressure. And I pointed out what others had told me—in the intensely politicized atmosphere at Corpoelec, where even top manag-ers like Juan Carlos were falsely accused of sabotage, people had devel-oped a defense mechanism whereby they would rather do nothing than take an action that someone could point to later in order to blame them for what went wrong. The plant workers were paid next to nothing, and the utility was falling apart around them. Antonio said that was all true. "People were dispirited, demoralized."

By 4:00 A.M. they had five generators in operation. The lights had come back on in parts of Guayana City.

"That gave us some hope," Francois Morillo told me. "Finally you see the light!"

At 4:30 A.M. they went home. They slept a few hours and went back to work. By the next day they had eleven of the twelve generators at Caruachi producing power. The restoration of generating capacity at Caruachi allowed the other two plants, Guri and Macagua, to gradu-ally increase generation so that by Tuesday virtually all of the country had electricity.

That night, March 12, they went home thinking their job was finished.

* * *

ON THE AFTERNOON of March 25 an explosion caused a fire in a group of transformers at the Guri hydroelectric plant, and the lights went out again across the country.

Once again, Juan Carlos and the others were summoned back to work. It was the first time that Antonio had been back to Guri since he was sent into exile by Motta Domínguez. It was an emotional return for him, and he was shocked to see the deterioration of the plant where he had spent so many years. Everything was run-down; morale was low. It was like going home to your old house and finding that the plumbing was leaking, the roof had holes in it and there were mice in the walls. The damage from the explosion was extensive and it took several days to fully reconnect the plant. The four of them came and went together, and at some point someone made a joke: *Here come the Cuatro Fantásticos* (the Fantastic Four). The crippled transformers sat at the junction between the hydroelectric plants on the Caroní River and the main artery of high voltage lines that carried power to the rest of the country. When the transformers blew, the link was broken and the country went dark. During the first blackout, the plants themselves had not been damaged. This time the physical destruction made the task of recovery more difficult. Two large transformers had exploded and started a fire that had impaired adjoining transformers and the cables that connected them. The disruption in power flow also caused damage to equipment inside the generating plant. American sanctions had cut off the country from financial and commercial markets, and as a result, the government couldn't easily go out and buy new equipment. So they cannibalized what they had. They pulled backup transformers from other substations, allowing them to patch up Guri but creating new vulnerabilities in the system.

After two days they were able to resume power transmission to the center of the country.

By now the grid was highly unstable and power was barely restored when another massive blackout occurred on March 29. The men told Delcy that unless significant steps were taken to stabilize the system, it would continue to crash.

Three days later, Maduro removed Motta Domínguez as president of Corpoelec and minister of electrical energy and replaced him with a longtime manager at the utility, Igor Gavidia, who was friendly with Juan Carlos and the others. Gavidia lasted barely two months. In June he too was replaced.

The public explanation was that Gavidia had left for health reasons. But inside the company it was believed that he'd been shoved aside for insisting on too much independence.

Corpoelec had a system of state and regional managers. When Gavidia came in, he wanted to make sure that the people in place had the necessary experience and expertise. This was particularly true in some crucial states, like Bolívar, where the three big hydroelectric plants were located, and Carabobo, a central state that had an important thermal generating plant. Luis Dimas told me that Gavidia had complained to him that some of his choices for regional managers had been blocked. In both Bolívar and Carabobo, the governors overruled Gavidia's choice. Gavidia had fought to appoint his own people and had been overruled by the politicians. It wasn't long before he was replaced by someone who had a better idea of how to play the game.

The story fascinated me because of what it said about the fragmentation of power in post-Chávez Venezuela. The central government, after the death of Chávez, was made up of competing circles of power. The most important one was centered on Maduro. Diosdado Cabello, the socialist party enforcer, controlled another; Tareck El Aissami, another; Vladimir Padrino López, the defense minister, another; and so on. At times different factions worked together against other factions, but at all times they each worked for their own survival and to maximize their access to both power and graft. Governors in some states also controlled important quotas of power. The governor of Bolívar was a former general whose territory included a vast gold mining region that had become increasingly important to the government in Caracas as a source of revenue. By removing Motta Domínguez, who was close to El Aissami, Maduro had already upset the balance. And then Gavidia had the temerity to try to run the utility his own way.

Even during a national emergency—when you might think that the highest priority was the recovery of the electrical system, which would require having the most qualified people in place—politics and the division of spoils took precedence. When Luis told me about this, he'd used a phrase that I put quotes around in my notebook to emphasize the words: "*el mío.*" Even in the midst of a crisis, Luis said, the most important thing for so many people remained the same: to get "mine."

Venezuela still represented a giant piñata for those in a position to swing a stick at it. Less than four months after the massive blackouts, U.S. prosecutors in Miami indicted Motta Domínguez and Corpoelec's former head of procurement, for allegedly taking millions of dollars in bribes to steer contracts to friendly businessmen at inflated prices.

* * *

WHAT CAUSED THE power to go out?

I asked Juan Carlos and Antonio about the government's claims about cyberattacks and electromagnetic pulse attacks and snipers firing on transformers. Yes, they said, the computer systems at the Guri generating plant might have been vulnerable. The technology for an electromagnetic pulse attack existed. Antonio said that a company official at Guri claimed to have found the bullet fired by the sniper.

Any of those things were possible, they said. But that didn't mean they'd happened.

"We were able to confirm that the failure didn't occur in the generating plants," Juan Carlos said. "It occurred in the transmission network. The sequence of events allows you to draw that conclusion. I was in all the plants. I inspected the machines. I saw that the machines had not failed. The machines disconnected because there were fluctuations in the power grid beyond the plant."

A person involved in the investigation of the first blackout confirmed to Juan Carlos what most independent experts had expected—the outage was triggered by a fire under one of the high voltage power lines (the investigators had visited the site of the fire).

But a brush fire alone was not enough to produce such an extensive blackout.

Power transmission lines are divided into segments that can be isolated in case of problems, such as a brush fire that causes a surge of current in one area. In that case, there are devices that operate like circuit breakers. A current spike triggers the circuit breakers, which then isolate the problem. But in this instance, the circuit breakers didn't break. Maintenance and inspections had been deferred, parts were not replaced, and the circuit breakers failed to function. A fire would have caused a surge of current that would have cascaded through the system because it wasn't isolated as it should have been. In response, the generators at the hydroelectric plants shut down, as they were designed to do.

"What caused the system to break down?" Juan Carlos said. "The deterioration of the system."

Regarding the second blackout—which the government said was caused by a sniper firing on transformers—Juan Carlos said that he saw data from Guri showing that prior to the transformer explosion, there had been a voltage spike in the transmission system. Three generating units at Guri shut down in response to the surge, before the transformer blew up. The voltage spike had caused the explosion, which caused the fire. He said that two other transformers in other areas of the country were damaged in the same incident.

The third blackout, he said, was caused by a sudden fluctuation in power demand in the center of the country. With Guri still operating below capacity, the generating plants weren't able to respond adequately and the system crashed again.

What bothered me in all this was a crucial disconnect here between the public explanation and the real cause. You can't fix a problem if you insist on pretending that the cause is something that it's not—a fiction, a conspiracy theory. If you really believe that saboteurs and snipers and electromagnetic pulse weapons are wreaking havoc with your electrical grid, then you'd better go out and figure out ways to stop them. But if what's really happening is that years of mismanagement have weakened the system to the point where small disruptions cause it to collapse, then you'd better come up with a maintenance plan and start fixing what's broken.

I'd seen news stories where workers at the hydroelectric plants talked ominously about an "external" cause of the blackouts. Did these technicians believe the propaganda or were they afraid to diverge from the official line?

I asked Juan Carlos if the people in positions of power who talked about snipers and electromagnetic pulses expected the workers at Corpoelec to spend their time trying to safeguard the system against saboteurs and mystery weapons.

"In very closed technical circles, we speak clearly," he said. "The official discourse is something else."

Kidnapped

José Vicente Haro had dropped off his older daughter at an evening math class in Caracas and was returning home in his car, an eleven-year-old brown Mitsubishi sedan, when he was stopped at a checkpoint manned by the Special Action Force. The FAES, as it is known, is a police force that was created by Maduro in 2017. It was proposed as an elite anti-crime squad, but it became clear early on that it had a different purpose.[1]

The FAES is designed to intimidate. FAES agents dress in black, with black body armor, and they often wear black balaclavas to hide their faces. They drive black pickup trucks without license plates and carry assault weapons and automatic pistols. The symbol of the FAES is a death's-head, which agents wear in patches on their uniforms.

The FAES would carry out sweeps in poor neighborhoods, often resulting in a high body count. The dead would be identified afterward as criminal suspects who were killed while resisting arrest. A 2019 report by the UN High Commissioner for Human Rights documented many cases of extrajudicial killings of young men by the FAES in slum neighborhoods. After the killings, the FAES would plant weapons or drugs on the bodies of their victims, according to the report. In some cases, the killings occurred after the victims had attended anti-government protests. The government classified such killings as cases of "resistance to authority." In 2018, the government recorded 5,287 cases of killings due to "resistance to authority." The UN report called this amount "unusually high" and noted that Venezuelan human rights groups had reported an even greater number. In its cautious, bureaucratic style, the report said that the Office of the High Commissioner for Human Rights was "concerned" that the government was using the FAES and other security forces "as an instrument to instill fear in the population and to maintain social control."[2]

At the FAES checkpoint, José Vicente, seated in his car, handed over his identification. It was about 7:40 P.M. on October 3, 2018.

José Vicente is a lawyer who specializes in constitutional law. In 2014 he started receiving death threats for his work defending political prisoners, including jailed politicians and people arrested during protests. His phone would ring, and on the other end of the line would be someone telling him that they were going to cut off his testicles and stuff them into his mouth and dump him in the Guaire River, the fetid waterway that runs in a concrete channel through the center of Caracas. Or he would receive photographs of bloody corpses, sent from social media accounts. In 2015 the Inter-American Commission on Human Rights petitioned the Venezuelan government to guarantee José Vicente's safety. The government did not respond.[3]

On this occasion, José Vicente waited at the checkpoint for the agents to return his identification. He had work on his mind and wasn't paying much attention. Finally they handed back his ID and waved him on.

Minutes after he drove away, an SUV swerved in front of him and he slammed on the brakes. Another car pulled up behind. Immediately, his car was surrounded by men with automatic weapons. A man with a gun like an Uzi jumped on the hood of the car. The driver's side window shattered, and the car door flew open. A man whose face was hidden behind a balaclava yanked him from the car. José Vicente was wearing a cotton sweater, and the man pulled it up and over José Vicente's head, covering his face and knocking off his glasses. ("I'm very nearsighted," José Vicente told me as he related the incident. "I'm Mr. Magoo . . . That makes me very anxious because without glasses I feel outside my safety zone.") Someone hit him across the back of the head several times with the butt of a weapon. Then he was shoved into the back of a vehicle, men crammed in on either side of him, doors slammed, and they sped off. He still had his sweater pulled over his head and now one of the men placed a hood or a balaclava on top of that. The hood smelled like plastic. He couldn't see and it was hard to breathe. The men told him that they were with the FAES. "If you keep resisting, we'll kill you right here," one of them said. They hit him again with the butts of their weapons. He could feel blood seeping down the back of his head.

They drove for a long time, perhaps an hour or more. Finally the car stopped. José Vicente was ordered out of the car. They took his shoes and wallet and keys. They led him down a spiral staircase, into what he sensed was a basement room, and they sat him down on a sofa and began to interrogate him. They asked him about his work on human rights cases. "So you think there's torture in Venezuela?" one of the men shouted, and then he beat José Vicente over the head with the butt of a pistol. They kept asking him about the National Assembly, which was controlled by the opposition. Did he work for the assembly? (He didn't.) Why had he made certain public statements about the assembly? (He was an expert on the constitution and was often called on to offer an opinion.) They asked who had paid him to make these statements. (No one.) They asked what political party he belonged to. (None.) One of the men hit him over and over across the knees with a pistol butt. This went on for a long time.

Finally they took a break. It must have been very late, but José Vicente was afraid to go to sleep. He forced himself to stay awake, sitting on the sofa, trying to breathe through the fear and the pain and the thick fabric of the hood. He was short of breath. He felt like he was being asphyxiated. Once, during the interrogation, he asked for water. They gave him a glass of water and let him lift the bottom of the hood just enough to take a drink. That allowed him to draw a few unimpeded breaths. That simple act was a tremendous relief. "Perhaps one of the most anxiety-producing elements of the whole captivity was trying to breathe under that hood during all those hours," he said. "If you said to me, 'What was the hardest part, between the violence, the torture, the interrogations?'—the hardest part for me was being able to breathe."

José Vicente tried to visualize himself somewhere else, somewhere out of doors, far away. He pictured himself as a young man, during a summer he spent in Spain, a particular day he remembered as being one of unequaled happiness. He also focused his thoughts on his two daughters, who were nine and seventeen.

"In my mind I drew a triangle. At the top I put God. And on the bottom were my two daughters. And the only thing I thought was 'You have to resist, because if you don't, they're not going to be okay. You have to hold out. You don't have any other option. You can't lose control, you can't overreact, you have to stay calm.'" He feared what his daughters would go through if he were killed or imprisoned for months or years, as so many of his clients had been. He'd watched so many families go through the ordeal of having a loved one "disappeared" or held in an endless limbo of illegal imprisonment. He didn't want to put his daughters through that. "I could tell you that I held out because I'm strong or because I'm brave or because I have courage or because I'm tenacious. But no. None of those. I held out because of something spiritual, because of the eternal love and affection that I have for my two daughters and my belief that God couldn't have created such a terrible destiny for me."

Time was elastic. He forced himself to remain alert. He became aware of activity again. There was talk of coffee, food. He could hear movement, the sound of doors opening or closing, the chiming sound that Windows makes when a computer is turned on. There was talk of calling for instructions. He came to identify seven different voices. The men all used nicknames for one another. One was called Muñeca (Doll). Another was called El Míster. The people they called to receive instructions were referred to as the Director, the Doctor, and the Engineer.

The second interrogation began. It was much more aggressive and violent than the first one. They asked him repeatedly about some statements that he'd made at a news conference about Diosdado Cabello. At the time Cabello was the head of the Constituent Assembly that Maduro had created to act as a parallel legislature to the opposition-controlled National Assembly. Cabello was one of the most powerful and feared figures in Chavismo, and he had close ties with the security forces. José Vicente's interrogators battered him with the butts of their weapons on the back of his neck, his knees, his ribs. They kept asking him about Cabello and said: "Don't you know who you're messing with?" Every once in a while he would ask them for water and they would give him a glass with enough for a few swallows and the hood would come up just a little and he would breathe. He was like a prisoner scratching marks on a cell wall: during all the hours of captivity he counted thirteen glasses of water. The questioning went on and on and then there was a crescendo of violence as the men rained blows on him, as though they were trying to outdo one another. "I told them, 'I've answered all your questions,'" he said. "'What else do you want?'"

One of the men responded: "You know we're going to kill you."

They made him stand up and walk, still hooded, to another room. They made him lie on the floor. The floor was cold and seemed to be made of tiles. They yanked off his pants and his underwear. Someone grabbed the hood from behind and smashed his face into the floor. Then he felt the end of a wooden stick or a pole as it was dragged across his back. He knew what was coming because he'd had clients who had been through this kind of torture. José Vicente focused on the triangle in his mind. God at the top, his daughters at the other corners.

"Do you feel that?" one of the men said as the stick moved along his back. "Is this what you call torture? Is this what you've been denouncing?"

At times an odd, almost comical propriety comes over Venezuelans of a certain generation or upbringing. José Vicente said, "Basically, in certain words, they told me they were going to place it in my anus." I asked him to tell me what they said, using their language. He apologized for using a vulgarity. "'Now we're going to stick it up your . . .'"—he hesitated—"'up your asshole. So you know what it feels like.' In those exact words."

They were holding his arms pinioned out, so that he was like a man on a cross. He stayed focused on the triangle and said nothing. "I don't know how I did it," he said, "but in my mind I was able to take myself out of that room."

Then all of a sudden, his torturer raised the stick and brought it down with immense force on his back. The pain was intense. "Why don't you say something?" someone yelled at him. "Why don't you beg?"

He responded: "Because I'm already dead. You told me that I'm a dead man. What else do you want? You're talking to a corpse."

Later, recalling the incident, José Vicente reflected on what he'd just told me, and he gave a weak laugh. "Right then I was being as honest as I could be," he said. "That was the most spontaneous part of me talking, the least calculating, the most human, the most instinctive. 'You're talking to a corpse.'"

They told him to get dressed.

There was another trip to the couch. Another glass of water. More waiting. And then *"Te llegó tu hora."* "Your time has come." They led him back up the spiral staircase, put him back in the car. They drove a short distance and pushed him out. Now he sensed the sea, smelled it or heard it. There was sand underfoot. They pushed him down to the ground, onto a large rock. When he told me the story, José Vicente got down on his hands and knees and showed me how he had crouched on all fours, hugging the rock. The hood was still on his head. All this time he'd seen nothing; he never saw the face of any of his torturers. Someone held a pistol to the back of his head. "This is as far as you go," the man said. "We told you we were going to kill you."

José Vicente heard a voice saying that they needed to get confirmation. There was discussion about who to call, the Director or the Engineer. But not the Doctor, he was always putting up obstacles, creating delays. Time went by. José Vicente hugged the rock. The gun was at the back of his head. "Are we ready?"

And then: "No. No. No. Abort the procedure."

Someone grabbed him, stood him up, told him that he was lucky. For now.

Back in the car. Back to the basement. Back on the sofa. And then another interrogation, this one less vehement, as if their hearts weren't in it anymore. It was almost as if they were trying to understand him now. What is it you do? Why do you defend the protesters? So you're an *esquálido* (it had been one of Chávez's favorite put-downs), one of the squalid ones? They could almost have been a group of puzzled Republicans trying to understand a Democrat: *You voted for Hillary? Really? How could you?*

Hours passed. By now it must have been late at night. They gave him back his shoes and his wallet. José Vicente asked for water. They gave it to him, another breath: the thirteenth glass. The most aggressive of his interrogators said, "Now we're going to kill you for sure." Once again they pushed him up the spiral stairs and shoved him into the car. They drove for a long time.

Finally the car stopped. They took him out and threw him to the ground: "This is the end of the line." José Vicente was facedown on the ground. Again he felt the barrel of a gun on the back of his neck. Someone yanked off the hood. The sweater was still pulled over his head and he couldn't see. He heard the men walk away. Doors slammed and the car drove off. He lay on the ground for a long time, without moving, straining to hear. Was it a trick? Were they waiting nearby? Were they waiting to shoot him as he ran away?

"After a while I dared to pull the sweater off of my head," he said, "and I looked from side to side and there was no one there. There was no one there. And finally I saw the light."

"What light?" I asked.

"No, no, no. I saw the light of the darkness." We'd been talking for close to three hours and he let out a frayed scrap of laughter. It was all too absurd and too mundane at the same time. He meant that it was dark, but now he could see, and what he saw was the darkness. "I saw something waaaaaaaay far away, a light up above, like there was a highway there or something."

He started walking.

José Vicente made it to the highway and eventually he reached a National Guard post, where he was able to call a colleague, who came to pick him up. He wasn't sure what time it was when he arrived home. Perhaps 5:00 A.M., about thirty-three hours after he'd been taken hostage.

But his ordeal wasn't over yet.

He rested for a few hours, cleaned up, and went to a doctor. He had what the doctor called cerebral edema, a buildup of fluid, or swelling, on the brain. The rest of his body was a catalog of bruises.

Later that day he went to an office of the CICPC, the Venezuelan equivalent of the FBI. He met with an investigator who wore a red shirt and red hat with the *4F* logo used to commemorate the anniversary of Chávez's February 4 coup. The message was clear: no one is neutral here.

"In Venezuela anything can happen," the investigator told him. "A person can be here one day and disappear the next. One day he could be walking along and the next day he could be found in the Guaire."

José Vicente left and at last went to see his daughters.

But José Vicente has a stubborn streak. He continued to insist on an investigation. He made an appointment to see a police doctor, but the doctor refused to examine him. "I don't want problems," the doctor told him.

Finally, José Vicente was able to schedule an appointment with a prosecutor.

"She was very frank," he said. "She told me, 'Don't ask about this again. Don't investigate anymore. Don't push. There's nothing to be done.'"

After the kidnapping, José Vicente thought about his life and his priorities. He decided that he wanted to spend more time with his daughters. For a while at least, he decided not to take on any new cases. In all, he had represented 371 people who had been detained because of their political activities. Every one of them had been freed. All but three had left Venezuela.

* * *

THE 2019 REPORT on Venezuela by the UN High Commissioner for Human Rights said that United Nations investigators had collected detailed information on 135 cases of people detained for political reasons. These included what the report called "enforced disappearances," where the whereabouts of detainees were not revealed to family members or lawyers until days or weeks after their arrests. In most cases, people were held for exercising basic rights of free speech or political activity, and the detentions "often had no legal basis." It found that people were repeatedly denied the right to a fair trial. In most cases, detainees were subjected to torture and other forms of cruel or degrading treatment. These included beatings, suffocation, waterboarding, and sexual violence. Women reported being dragged by their hair, forced to strip naked, groped, and threatened with rape. The cases investigated by the High Commissioner were a small sample of a much larger universe.

The report cited the Venezuelan human rights group Foro Penal, which keeps a running count of people that it believes have been detained for political reasons. The group said that 15,045 people had been arrested and held for political reasons between January 2014 and May 2019.

The authoritarian turn was Maduro's. With Chávez, there was protest but also money and good times. There were political prisoners, but not many—a judge who defied Chávez in a case, a general who went from ally to foe. Armed motorcycle gangs called *colectivos* were used to intimidate or deliver a beating, but these were most effective as a threat, in the potential for violence that they represented rather than the potency of violence they unleashed. Maduro's back was to the wall. He had little money and less margin for error. In the transactional relationship between the Venezuelan state and society, he had fewer plums to dole out, so instead he doled out violence and repression.

A subsequent United Nations report, released in late 2020, said that investigators had reviewed nearly 3,000 allegations of human rights abuses. The report concluded that they were part of "a widespread and systematic attack directed against a civilian population" and that they constituted crimes against humanity.[4]

I've talked to dozens of people who, like José Vicente, were beaten or tortured by security forces. Many of them were ordinary people, rounded up during protests. One woman stands out. Her name was Keyla Brito. In 2014, in the city of Barquisimeto, she was out grocery shopping with her teenage daughter. There was a protest going on nearby, but they did not take part. Soldiers made a sweep through the neighborhood and Keyla and her daughter were detained with several other women. They were taken to a National Guard post and handed over to a group of female soldiers, who taunted them, saying: "The fresh meat is here." They beat them with fists and riot helmets and kicked them and threatened to kill them or to hand them over to male soldiers to be raped. They dumped the contents of the women's purses on the ground and crushed them under their boots. Keyla wore her hair down to her waist. The soldiers cut it off, hacking at it with a small scissors. They did the same to her daughter and the other women. The abuse went on for hours. What shocked Keyla the most was the hatred that she felt from the soldiers.

They saw the world split in two, the people versus the enemy. Venezuelans weren't like that, Keyla told me. That kind of hatred was something that they had to be taught. After the ordeal, Keyla went to a salon to have the ragged edges of her hair trimmed. I talked to her a few weeks later. She told me that she still avoided looking in the mirror. And she agonized over not having been able to protect her daughter from the soldiers. Why couldn't she have thrown herself on top of her daughter and taken the blows instead? Keyla was just under five feet tall.

* * *

WHEN JOSÉ VICENTE told me the story of his kidnapping,[5] we were sitting in a friend's Caracas apartment. Behind José Vicente was a window with a view of the Ávila mountain. The sun poked in and out of clouds. It rained on and off, and once, with the sun shining, I thought, *There must be a rainbow somewhere.* There was another window behind me, and the changeable sky was reflected in José Vicente's glasses. It occurred to me that, since his glasses had been knocked off during the kidnapping, this must be a new pair. The frames were tortoiseshell.

Jose Vicente told me that he hadn't talked to very many people about what he'd been through. He'd observed a pattern over the years. There were people who became stuck in their victimhood. What had happened to them—the beatings, the feelings of anger and guilt—came to define their identity. He didn't want to give his torturers that kind of power. His ordeal had changed him, and the biggest change was in the way that he saw things—how he understood now, more keenly than before, what was valuable and meaningful.

I'd known José Vicente since the days that I'd lived in Caracas as a correspondent and would sometimes interview him about legal issues or human rights. He had a pale Clark Kent face with thin lips and lank dark hair. We'd met for lunch some weeks earlier, and it was then that I'd noticed an occasional tremble in his lower lip that hadn't been there before.

"My conclusion," he said, "is that this could happen to anyone. Lots of people go through this. Some survive and others don't." The experience had swept back the curtain to reveal a brutality that even he wasn't prepared for.

"It's pure power," he said. "There is no constitution. There are no limits."

At the end of our conversation José Vicente pointed out that it was July 24, Bolívar's birthday. The eternal present of Venezuela. His voice had become deeply weary; the effort of telling his story had drained him.

Outside, the light turned golden in the falling day, and I mentioned how beautiful the Ávila was after the rain. José Vicente turned his head and looked out the window at the mountain. His thin lips made a rueful smile that said: Even this most familiar of sights looks different now.

"*El consuelo nuestro,*" he said. "Our consolation."

Blackout

The sack of the Hotel Brisas del Norte in Maracaibo started on the sixth day of the blackout, when power was already coming back on. It was Tuesday, March 12. Two days later, on Thursday, Margelis Romero returned to the hotel, where she had worked for the last three years. She came with a few of her coworkers—a driver, the head of maintenance, and some others. The men took pipes and sticks and chased out the last of the looters. When Margelis saw them using the pipes and sticks to hit the stragglers, she told them to stop. She was afraid that if one of the looters got hurt, they might go to the police and bring charges, and the hotel would be liable. As absurd as that sounds, the fear of it was in her brain. There was no law. During two days of looting, no authority had come to stop it. But now that the looting was over, maybe the law would protect the looters. No law at all or the law upside down.

It wasn't until after the last of the looters were gone that Margelis noticed the Virgin.

She walked around the ruins of the hotel. It was hard for her to register what she was seeing, to take it all in and believe that it was real. It was like the hotel had been turned over and shaken violently before being set right side up again. Almost every window was broken. All the doors were gone from all the rooms. Everything of the least value had been stripped away: the pipes, the wires, every fork and spoon.

Eventually Margelis wandered over to the entrance to the hotel driveway, where the metal gates had been removed by looters and carted off.

On the low stucco wall by the entrance was a ceramic tile image of the Virgen del Carmen, about a foot high. It's the kind of thing that over time you see and don't see, it becomes so familiar to the eye. The Virgin, wearing a gold crown, with a ring of gold stars around her head, was dressed in coffee-colored robes. She stood barefoot on a bank of dark blue clouds, in front of an azure background. She cradled the baby Jesus in the crook of her left arm, and in her right hand she held a scapular—a small garment consisting of two squares of cloth suspended from thin straps, which is typically worn over the shoulders by Catholic devotees and is emblematic of the Carmelite Order, of which the Virgen del Carmen is the patroness. The baby Jesus was also holding scapulars, one in each tiny hand. Hanging from their straps, the scapulars looked like miniature shopping bags.

What Margelis saw now was that during the looting someone had taken a tool or a rock and poked a hole in the tile, gouging out the Virgin's face. Margelis didn't know why someone would do that, but it was clear that it was done for a reason. Venezuelans are Mary worshippers. The church would say instead that they venerate the Virgin Mary (a practice called hyperdulia), worship being reserved for God and Jesus. But the religion of Venezuelans tends toward the syncretic, especially among the popular classes, and few would slight her the use of the verb: the Virgin is held in the highest esteem. She is a powerful symbol, and in Venezuela, the Virgen del Carmen is one of her most revered forms. The Virgen del Carmen is the patroness of the army and of drivers, especially those who drive for a living, like taxi drivers. At first Margelis thought that maybe the person who poked out the Virgin's face had been looking for treasure—it was said that people sometimes hid valuables behind a religious ornament. But that didn't really make sense. The hole was small, about an inch across, occupying only the space where the Virgin's face had been. You could still see a bit of her crown, and the face of the baby Jesus wasn't touched. Maybe whoever did it was ashamed. He didn't want the Mother of God to witness his sin, to see him as he stole—what? A flat-screen TV? A mattress? Some copper wire?

Or maybe it was something else entirely: an act of pity. The vandal wanted to spare the Virgin from witnessing what had become of Venezuela.

"How did we lose all of this?" Margelis said on the day she showed me around the hotel and took me to see the faceless Virgin. We walked around the ruins and then sat down on a curb in the driveway, facing the hotel building, its tan facade punctured at regular intervals by empty window frames. Margelis wore a blue-and-white-striped polo shirt, blue jeans, and burgundy shoes that matched her handbag. Sometimes when she talked about what had happened, a crease of worry would form between her eyes. Her black hair was pulled back and fastened with a plastic clip the vivid blue of swimming pools. "I wish that I could wake up and it would turn out to have all been a nightmare, something like that, and we could go back to how it was before. We were happy here. We were happy. Even though it was a job, we were happy. We were like a family, always watching out for each other. From one day to the next, they took all that away from us. Everything that you had. It's not just the paycheck. It's that you felt useful, you had a job, you had an income, your coworkers were like a family. And then all of a sudden it's over. Now we have nothing. We'd like to start over, but where do you start? Where? How are you going to buy the air-conditioning units? Where? How are we going to get another vehicle? How are you going to wire all this again and bring in electricity? How?" Margelis stared at the gutted building. "Look at it," she said.

From the outside, you could almost pretend that the damage wasn't so bad. Inside was a different story. The looters had been thorough. There was nothing left. "The first floor is just like the second, the third, the fourth, the fifth. They're all the same."

*　*　*

MARGELIS GREW UP in Machiques, a town of 80,000 people a two-hour drive southwest of Maracaibo. Her family and her friends call her Marge, which is pronounced *MAR-hay* and sounds a bit like Margie to American ears. They also call her Negra, for her brown skin, or Gorda, which means Fatty, which is funny, because she's sapling slender. But she was chubby as a kid. That's how it is. People still see you how they saw you years ago. Beginnings count for so much. Margelis's mother worked as a domestic, cleaning and cooking in other people's houses. When she was ten, Margelis started working too. Sometimes on weekends her mother took on extra work, and when she couldn't do it all, she would send Margelis in her place. Margelis would cook and clean just as her mother did. She liked chipping in, making money, doing her part. Her mother worked hard, and she wanted to be like her mother. Not like her father, who drank too much and didn't seem to care whether the family had nice things or not. For him it was always enough to live day to day. Margelis liked going to the middle-class homes where she worked. It was like traveling to another world. A world with new refrigerators and appliances and furniture. Her mother would give her a little bit of money from what Margelis had earned. She would go to the park with friends and buy a shaved ice or some candy.

Margelis was born in 1976, the year the country nationalized the oil industry, when Venezuela was intoxicated with the promise of a new era of abundance.

The price of oil had soared in the early part of the decade, and most of the oil that Venezuela produced back then came from Zulia state and the area around Lake Maracaibo. But by the time Margelis was ten, everything had changed. The price of oil had started to fall, and Venezuela went into a long decline.

The family lived in a small house with a zinc roof, built by the government with oil money. It was an era of cookie-cutter houses, every family with an identical house. Her father worked off and on, as a ranch hand and then as a taxi driver. He could barely read and write. Her mother had gone to school through the fourth grade. Margelis had two older sisters. As a teenager, Margelis liked going to parties and taking trips. Someone would say that there was a party in Maracaibo and she was the first to respond: *Let's go!* She never drank—her father's excessive drinking horrified her—but she could dance all night. Margelis was restless too. Machiques was a small town, and she wondered what else was out there. She didn't want to be poor anymore, to live wanting things she couldn't have. She dreamed of having a house like the ones that she worked in, of having nice things, of buying a new table and chairs when the old ones wore out and were scuffed and dented with age.

When she was nineteen, Margelis went to Maracaibo to study at the university. She stayed with her grandmother. Tuition was free, but she had to pay for transportation and food. To pay her expenses, Margelis's mother had to borrow from moneylenders in Machiques, who charged 20 percent a week. Her mother had to take on more and more work to make the payments. Margelis didn't want to put her mother through that, so after two semesters she quit school and came home. A technical school had opened an extension in Machiques and Margelis started taking classes in business administration. She cleaned houses and took in sewing to make money. After she graduated, she landed a job in a call center in Machiques. Before long she was promoted to manager. That's how it went with Margelis. She rose up fast.

Now that she could support herself, she was ready to put Machiques behind her. She found an office job in Maracaibo. After that, she was hired to be the manager of an electronics store in a shopping mall. Her grandmother died, and her father received a small inheritance. Before he could drink it all, some relatives intervened and the money went to buy a small house in Maracaibo for Margelis to live in. Margelis was happy. She was an independent woman. She gave money to her parents. She bought them a new bed—they'd been sleeping on the same bed for thirty-five years. (The way she tells the story, she bought *her mother* a new bed; her father never cared one way or the other.) Margelis felt like she was achieving what she'd always wanted.

In 2016 an uncle recommended her to the owners of the Hotel Brisas del Norte. They gave her a job managing what they called "the cabañas," a group of trailers converted into guest rooms. A year later they made her business manager. Often she would supervise operations on the weekends. (What could go wrong? Her first weekend a pipe burst and flooded the restaurant and lobby.)

Brisas del Norte. Northern Breezes. The hotel takes its name from the neighborhood where it is located, which despite the found poetry of the name is a mean slum of rutted dirt streets and concrete block houses, mechanic shops, chickens in the roadway, barefoot children. Mostly Wayuu Indians live there, the women in their floor-length gowns in bright blue or red, a bit of embroidery on the edges, trudging through the blast of the Maracaibo heat.

The hotel had modest beginnings. It opened in 1992, the same year that Chávez staged his coup and was jailed. The owners were two friends who worked at PDVSA. The hotel started out as a lovers' motel, with just the cabañas, a few trailers divided into rooms. It was near the highway, so it was a handy stop for truck drivers. In 1998, when Chávez was first elected president, they built a banquet hall. They added a swimming pool, and then in 2010, they erected the five-story main building, with 105 rooms, a bar, and a restaurant.

The hotel became a success. Business travelers stopped there, students lived there while studying at a private university nearby, and it was a popular venue for the weddings and parties of Maracaibo's middle class. It had about sixty employees. Some of them lived in the slum beside the hotel.

* * *

THE BLACKOUT STARTED on a Thursday. By the weekend, there were almost no guests left in the hotel, because the hotel had no backup generator. The last guest, a businessman who had trouble departing because his flight had been canceled, left Monday morning.

The back of the hotel abuts a concrete-lined cañada, or drainage channel, with a little black water flowing between heaps of trash. There is a cinder-block wall at the back of the hotel grounds, and just beyond it, a road that runs along the top of the cañada's embankment. On the other side of the cañada, there is a Pepsi warehouse and a Makro store, the Venezuelan equivalent of Costco. On Sunday, looters cleaned out the Pepsi warehouse. On Monday, they looted Makro. On Tuesday morning the first looters showed up at the hotel. They broke a hole through the cinder-block wall at the back, by the cañada. They backed up a flatbed truck and started loading it up. They knew what they were doing. A crew of looters went to the roof and removed the hotel's four large air-conditioning units. Each one weighed hundreds of pounds. They lowered them to the ground and put them on the truck. Word started to get around: *They're looting the hotel!* More and more people showed up.

The few hotel employees who had been able to make it to work that day fled before the wave of looters. One of them was Odalis Vergara, who had been a manager at the hotel for more than twenty years. She went to a local National Guard post and begged an officer to send troops to stop the looters. He told her that a patrol had been dispatched that morning to the Makro store, on the other side of the cañada. She went to the Makro and found a platoon of soldiers in riot gear. By then, of course, there were no looters at the Makro—they were all at the hotel. Odalis found the general in command and asked him to take his soldiers to the hotel and stop the looting. He told her to calm down. Eventually, a group of soldiers and an armored vehicle ventured out, but they stopped at a small metal bridge that crossed the cañada. From the bridge you could see into the hotel grounds. A soldier could have thrown a rock from the bridge and beaned one of the looters. The soldiers stayed on the bridge for a while and then retreated back the way they'd come. At one point a police helicopter buzzed low over the hotel roof and flew away. That was it. No authority ever showed up again.

Margelis hadn't been able to make it to work that morning because there was no way for her to get there. There was no public transportation during the blackout. And there were no taxis, either: without power the gas stations couldn't pump gas. She finally arrived at the hotel in the afternoon. One of the owners was worried about a car that had been left parked at the hotel, and Margelis and a coworker volunteered to try to rescue it. A cousin of Margelis gave them a ride to the hotel. He was afraid to drive too close, so he dropped them off at the bottom of the street and they continued on foot.

When Margelis came to the hotel entrance, there were so many people inside that she just kept going. She was afraid at first to even look. She worried that someone might recognize her as an employee of the hotel. People were swarming over the hotel building, the grounds, the outbuildings, the cabañas, like ants on an anthill. People were running every which way. It was bedlam. She saw a man whacking with an axe at an electrical transformer mounted on a concrete pad. He hit it again and again, with great swings of the axe, until he broke through the steel shell and oil spurted out. She heard the explosion of windows being smashed. From the upper stories, men shoved mattresses out the windows and let them fall to the ground. Cars drove out loaded with loot. Others drove in to take their place.

Later on, when people asked her to tell the story, she would say that she didn't know what words to use. She said that it was the ugliest thing that she'd ever seen.

What took twenty-seven years of hard work to build was disappearing in a day. The chaos, the violence, and the frenzy of the looters frightened her. At the same time, in the midst of all that mayhem, people were acting like everything was normal. Looters went in and out, as casually as guests. Cars drove by on the main road, not fast, not slow, as though this were just another day—cars, a road, people, a hotel, destruction. It turned out that the car that they had come to rescue had already been removed and was parked at the home of a man who lived nearby. Margelis found it there, and she and her coworker drove it back to the owner's house. As they passed the hotel, she took another look. One of the things that disturbed her most was the age of the looters. So many of them were young. Men in their twenties. Teenagers.

Margelis and everyone else from the hotel stayed home on Wednesday. The sack of the hotel went on through the night and into a second day, and there was nothing they could do. Finally on Thursday she returned. After her coworkers had chased out the last of the looters, she picked her way among the ruins.

The cabañas were stripped down to the studs. The roofs were gone, the doors, the windows, every toilet and sink and plumbing fixture, every inch of pipe, all the furniture, the wiring, the light switches. Gone.

That was only a prelude to the devastation in the main building. Every piece of equipment was gone from the restaurant: freezers, refrigerators, stoves, ovens, a fryer, dishwashers. The granite countertops from the bar had been pried up, the tables and chairs carted off. "They didn't leave so much as a spoon. You can look. You won't find even a spoon." The furniture was taken from the lobby. The computers were stolen from the front desk and the office, and everything else too, down to the staplers and the paper clips. The elevator doors were forced open. In one of the cars the mirrored walls were shattered, the floor covered with silvered splinters reflecting the daylight.

She went upstairs. Up there, if possible, it was even worse. The carpets were pulled up and the ceilings pulled down. All the copper wiring and the copper pipe was stripped away, as well as anything made from aluminum. The floor was littered with chunks of plaster and broken ceiling tiles. Ductwork and conduits hung down through great gashes in the ceiling. The looters had taken the doors from the rooms and the closets and the bathrooms, and when they couldn't open a room, they broke the door down with an axe. Inside the rooms, all the furniture was gone—beds, mattresses, tables, chairs, lamps. All the fixtures were missing—sinks, shower heads, even the toilets. What they couldn't take, they broke: windows, mirrors. Room after room, floor after floor. The Presidential Suite was denuded of everything but the potted palm on the terrace. They'd pulled the motor and the wiring out of the Jacuzzi. The tan wallpaper, painted with white dogwoods, was scarred with holes where they'd pulled out the electrical sockets and the light switches. The debris crunched underfoot. You looked down: a *Do Not Disturb* door hanger, a mangled Gideon Bible, a shard of mirror reflecting your face. In places there was dried blood on the walls, probably from a looter who cut himself on broken glass or a jagged edge of metal.

"How can you go out and destroy something that isn't yours?" Margelis said. "Something that never did you any harm? I mean, okay, you need a bed, take the bed. You need a TV? Take the TV. Okay. But don't come and destroy what someone has built with his own sacrifice. This here, all this took time, dedication, years. This here is day after day, working, struggling. So it's hard . . . it's very hard to understand: What happened here? Why did this happen to us? I don't know what to call this. This is ugly. This is horrible. That very day I wondered: *My God, how are we going to help ourselves now?* I cried. I said, 'How are we going to help ourselves now?' With what? There's nothing left. They left us nothing. It was horrible. There's not even anything here to start over with. Really, I don't know. I say, my God, if you're going to steal, okay, come on in, take a lightbulb—if you need it, take it. But so much destruction. I think that the worst harm that has occurred in this country is to society. No one cares. This is a new generation. This isn't my generation. No way. There were lots of young people here, children, with their fathers, taking whatever they could get. Look at the elevator. It was beautiful. And they broke it."

* * *

FOR A WHILE the owners paid Margelis and a few other employees a reduced salary. But with the hotel closed, they had no money coming in, so that didn't last long. A man Margelis knew from Machiques had a business making cheese, and he hired her to take care of sales in Maracaibo. He'd drive to town with the cheese and they'd spend a couple of days making deliveries.

Margelis lives on a cul-de-sac with five modest houses. When she moved in, all the houses were occupied. Now the other families have moved away, two to Argentina and two to Chile.

Margelis moved into the house after her older sister, Marisol, died of cancer. Marisol, who lived in Machiques, was fifty years old. She was diagnosed with cancer, and two weeks later she died. People in Margelis's family don't like to go to the doctor. For a long time, Marisol had ignored the warning signs. When she finally went for help, it was too late. Marisol had three daughters: a fifteen-year-old and thirteen-year-old twins. Suddenly they were Margelis's responsibility. She went from being an aunt to being a surrogate mother. Those were hard times. The family's meager savings had all been spent on Marisol's brief treatment and the funeral. Then they went into debt. All they had to eat was lentils, for breakfast, lunch, and dinner. Her parents were in their seventies and Margelis decided to bring them and the three girls to live with her in Maracaibo. She moved out of the little house that had been bought with the money left by her grandmother and found the house on the cul-de-sac, which was big enough for all of them. The rent was $40 a month (paid in dollars). Working at the hotel, she could afford it. But after the looting she was making a fraction of what she made before. Her parents each received a monthly pension that was barely enough to buy a carton of eggs.

Now Margelis thinks about leaving Maracaibo—following so many others to Colombia or some other country (her other sister, Maylibeth, had gone to Peru), or perhaps moving to another city in Venezuela that wasn't so hard hit by the crisis. Somewhere where there was electricity, at least. She thinks of those things, but she knows that she's not going anywhere. Her parents are too old and her nieces are too young for her to leave them behind.

"I feel worn out," Margelis told me. "Just recently I had a migraine. I vomited and vomited. Because I was so worried. I was thinking about everything so much that I started to throw up. I vomited, my head hurt, I vomited. My God. I threw up everything inside me. I get all worried and I get overwhelmed. I don't know. The truth is that I just don't know. I threw up and then it went away. My head hurt so much. Someone would say something to me and I'd say, 'Please, don't talk, don't talk.' I felt so bad, so bad."

Means Without Production

It is commonplace to say that Hugo Chávez had charisma and that this was the key to his success as a politician. And he certainly did have an ability to connect with people, especially those who had felt shut out for so long, pushed to the margins of Venezuelan political and economic life, the slum dwellers and the ranch hands and those left behind in the small towns.

But more than charisma, what Chávez really had was the steadily rising price of oil. Put another way: oil at $100 a barrel is a lot of charisma.

In 1998, the year Chávez was elected, Venezuelan crude sold for less than $8 a barrel, close to a historic low. Fueled by economic growth in China, world oil prices rose for most of the time that Chávez was in office, averaging more than $100 a barrel in 2011 and 2012.[1]

The $768 billion in total oil sales from 1999 to 2013 was almost double the total value of petroleum exports, adjusted for inflation, during the historic oil boom that lasted from 1974 to 1985. In 2012 alone, Venezuelan oil sales were more than $93 billion.[2]

As it had during the previous boom, all that money brought a stampede of willing lenders. Venezuela's public sector foreign debt during the Chávez years increased almost fourfold, to $112 billion in 2013, up from $29 billion in 1999.[3]

At the same time that prices were going up, so were the country's proven oil reserves. By 2011 Venezuela was declared to have the largest oil reserves in the world, surpassing those of Saudi Arabia.

* * *

THE FIRST ROAD trip I took inside Venezuela, a couple of weeks after I arrived in January 2012, was to Maracay, a medium-sized city west of Caracas. We drove along the Central Highway, past farm fields and palm trees and a rum distillery. There was a wonderful freshness to the day, the blue, washed Caribbean sky, the cleansing light so unique to Venezuela, the adventure of seeing a new country for the first time. As we drew closer to Maracay, I noticed some construction workers building a rail line beside the highway. It turned out that I was looking at one of the great white elephants of Chavismo. The project had been going on for years, at a cost of hundreds of millions of dollars. I would drive along the same highway many times after that, and now and then I'd see a crew working along the line. Great stretches of it would seem to be abandoned, but then I'd see sparks falling from a section of elevated track where some welders were at work. There would be a scissor lift and a few men standing around with orange vests. We'd drive along and there'd be no one else working.

In 2000, the year after he took office, Chávez had announced a National Rail Plan, which later would be renamed the Socialist Railway Development Plan. It was also sometimes called the Simón Bolívar National Railway System. The plan called for tens of billions of dollars to build or rehabilitate fifteen rail lines with about 5,300 miles of track. The only part of it that was ever finished was a short commuter line connecting Caracas to a town called Cúa. The line covered twenty-five miles and had four stations. When it was finished in 2006, the government said that it had cost $3 billion.[4]

What struck me about the rail line beside the highway is that it was out in plain sight, for everyone to see. And what you saw was waste. And futility. There was a shamelessness about it, as though merely beginning were enough. As though promising something was all that was needed, and actually delivering on the promise was not what counted.

Of course, promising and not delivering wasn't something invented by Chávez. Building a train to connect Caracas to the central cities of Maracay and, further west, Valencia, had been talked about for decades. The difference with Chávez was the scale of the waste. He had more money than any of his predecessors to squander on miles of concrete and steel, on trains to nowhere.

A few years later I was in Barinas, the state where Chávez was born, and where his older brother was governor. (Their father had been governor before him—a few years on and a younger brother would fill the seat; it was a family sinecure.) This was Chávez country, by definition. On television Chávez would rhapsodize about his childhood in Barinas. He idealized the place, held it up as the heart and soul of Venezuela.

But now it was December 2015 and there was discontent in the land. Chávez was dead and Maduro was floundering. The economy was bad, there were shortages and high inflation, and people had soured on the eternal leader's eternal revolution—like the rail line, it had gone nowhere. In an election earlier that month the opposition had won an overwhelming majority in the National Assembly. Among the results: Chávez's party had been trounced in Barinas. I wanted to go see how that had happened. I found that people there were just as fed up as they were everywhere else.

Driving around the state capital, which is also called Barinas, I chanced upon a stalled construction site with one of the big signs out front that governments everywhere put up to take credit for public works. It was supposed to have been a state-of-the-art cancer hospital. Chávez had announced the project on an *Aló Presidente* in 2007.[5] He'd climbed onto an earthmover and moved some earth, the kind of thing he got a kick out of. That was eight years ago. Now, behind a cement block wall, there was the skeleton of a building, three stories of bare concrete, like a broken toy discarded in a sandbox. A scrawny white cow, its skin stretched like an unpainted canvas over bones, grazed in what was to have been a parking lot. The project had been left derelict, but somehow there was still a watchman. His name was Silvano Berrio. He was thirty-four but looked much older. There was a skinny kid with him, Kevin Ramírez, who was twenty. Like the cow, they hadn't had enough to eat. "I'm a Chavista, but Chávez isn't here anymore," Kevin said. Chávez's family had been in charge in the state for years, and what was there to show for it? "They didn't do anything. If they'd done something, this would be finished." Silvano talked about how you couldn't buy rice, couldn't buy medicine, how the stores were empty and there wasn't enough money. "We'll see," he said, "if there's a future up ahead."

Barinas, the city, sits on the edge of the enormous plains that extend across Venezuela, backed up against the bulwark of the Andes. It was one of those days when you become aware of the dome of the sky, a great overarching powder-blue sphere that keeps going beyond the horizon, dotted with clouds like the putti on a cathedral ceiling. And beneath it all, the weed-choked lot, the cement wall, two skinny watchmen, a journalist, the skeletal cow, and the unfinished hospital that was supposed to have treated patients suffering from the same disease that killed the president who moved the earth. The big faded sign promised 200 beds, an intensive care unit, and a heliport.

The Chavistas like to look back at what they call the Fourth Republic (the four decades of democracy between the Pérez Jiménez dictatorship and Chávez) and claim that everything then was bad and corrupt and cruel, that the poor were oppressed and hungry and humiliated by nasty, greedy capitalists and a yanqui-loving, anti-patriotic elite. The opposition looks back on the same period as a dreamy, gauzy wonderland of plenty, when people were happy and well fed, when the classes got along, when wine and honey flowed. The fact is that Chavismo was born of what came before it. Chávez's greatest talent wasn't inventing something new. It was just repackaging the old and pretending that he'd come up with it himself. The democratic governments in the four decades before Chávez had had their share of corruption and their share of wasted money. The Chavistas had either the good luck or the great misfortune to have been in power when the spigot was turned on all the way. You think of what could have been accomplished with all that money—how the country could have taken a different road, arrived at a different place. That is perhaps the greatest tragedy of Chavismo.

How do you measure the waste?

The day Chávez announced the hospital in Barinas, he said that work was also starting on five other new hospitals around the country, each with a medical specialty: maternity, gastroenterology, urology, cardiology, and another cancer center. He said that the following year construction would start on nine more hospitals. All of them were to be completed within three years. The total cost was to be nearly $12 billion.[6]

Chávez was correct about one thing: work did start on the six hospitals in the first round. None of them were ever finished. Every few years, a government official would announce plans to restart the stalled projects. And then the partially built structures would sit there weathering and rusting for a while longer. The great advantage of not finishing things was that you could come back every few years and announce them again: *New Hospital Coming Soon!* It was like a person who knows only one joke and keeps telling it over and over. And laughing each time. At one point, prosecutors began a corruption investigation of a former health minister, relating to construction contracts for the unfinished hospitals. There was some noise and then silence. Neither the hospitals nor the legal case progressed any further.[7]

There were so many avenues for waste. A paper plant sucked in more than $800 million and never produced a single roll of paper. An aluminum rolling mill was announced with an initial investment of $210 million. A few years on, Chávez complained about delays in construction and announced that he had approved an additional $500 million. In 2019, Maduro dredged up the rolling mill project again—more than a decade after its first announcement—and said that he was installing a new manager. On television, he wagged a finger at the man and said, "Get it done!" Six months later, the construction site for the project was quietly shut down.[8]

In 2006 Chávez announced plans to build the country's third bridge across the Orinoco River. He said it was one of Venezuela's biggest engineering projects ever. Pilings were built, approach roadways were constructed. In 2012, the government said that it had spent nearly $900 million. In 2013, the transportation minister said the budget had increased to $2.8 billion. In 2014, he said that the project would be completed in 2017. Today there still is no bridge—the pilings stand like enormous traffic bollards in the brown water.[9]

The landscape is littered with unfinished projects. If you were a giant striding across Venezuela, you would have to watch where you stepped. You would stub your toe on an unfinished hospital here; you would howl in pain when you stepped on the pilings of an unfinished bridge over there. The exposed and rusting rebar poking up from half-built factories would be like splinters in the soles of your feet.

The waste was large and small, profligate and petty.

How much did it cost to fly Hilda and her colleagues to Argentina to be trained to work in a dairy plant that was never built? Much less than a bridge across the Orinoco. And what did that spending produce except votes in the next election and failed expectations and disappointment down the road? As the Venezuelans say, bread for today, hunger for tomorrow.

*   *   *

IN 2005, CHÁVEZ declared his intention to make Venezuela a socialist country. He said that the nation would create a new kind of socialism that he called twenty-first-century socialism.[10] No one ever knew what that meant. It wasn't an ideology—it was a brand. The one thing that everyone knew about socialism was that the workers should control the means of production. Talking about socialism, then, meant making a show of acquiring the means of production for the working class. So Chávez embarked on a campaign of nationalizations. There was nothing new about that. In the 1960s and 1970s the fashion among Latin American governments was to create (or acquire) state-controlled companies. But fashions in government come and go. By the 1990s, it had become fashionable to sell off government-owned properties. But Chavismo is always about nostalgia. It is rooted in the ideological struggles of the 1960s almost as much as in its yearning for the golden age of Bolívar. His pockets stuffed with oil money, Chávez started buying back the privatized companies and went on a spree of expropriations and nationalizations.

The national telephone company, CANTV, had been privatized in the 1990s. In 2007, Chávez bought it back, paying $572 million to Verizon, the largest shareholder. He paid about $1 billion for several privately owned power companies in order to create the single electrical utility that he christened Corpoelec (the former owners included the American companies AES and CMS Energy). In 2009, Chávez paid $1 billion for Banco de Venezuela, one of the country's largest banks, which was owned by Spain's Grupo Santander. Chávez paid $2 billion to a multinational corporation for a steel mill that had been privatized a decade earlier.[11]

Now, you can make an argument that certain industries or certain types of companies might be better under public control. Many countries have public utilities and banks. But if you're going to go out and buy up private companies and put them under government control, you ought to make an effort to run them well—to invest in them and to hire competent administrators. Chávez didn't do those things. He put loyalists in charge and did almost nothing to prevent corruption. He starved his newly acquired companies of investment. The steel mill wasn't for making steel, it was for making Chávez look like a socialist. He failed to read the full sentence. Chávez's socialism was all means and no production. It was *showcialismo*. He created a single national electrical company and insisted on charging low rates—to protect the buying power of the poor and to buy support from the middle class at election time. But he didn't provide the financing that would allow the company to perform maintenance and invest and grow. It's fine if you believe as a matter of policy that Corpoelec should charge next to nothing for the only thing that it has to sell—electricity. But Corpoelec still needs money from somewhere to operate adequately. That wasn't in the plan. It was magical math: 2 minus 1 equals 4. It couldn't last, and it didn't. That became clear on March 7, 2019, when the lights went out.

When Chávez wasn't able to negotiate the purchase of a company, he would expropriate it, deferring the payment until a price could be fixed by an international arbitration panel. But that process took years, and the bills came due when Venezuela could least afford to pay.

Chávez expropriated a large gold mining project from the Canadian mining company Crystallex International in 2011. In 2016, an arbitration panel ruled that Venezuela must pay the company $1.2 billion. Another Canadian company, Rusoro Mining, won a judgment of $1.2 billion for another gold mine. Chávez seized the Venezuelan assets of ConocoPhillips, the American oil company, in 2007. Arbitration panels ruled that Venezuela must pay the company more than $10 billion.[12]

Once Chávez had the properties, what did he do with them? Nothing. The gold mines were never developed. The oil ventures languished without sufficient investment.

*   *   *

CHÁVEZ CREATED A national development fund, called Fonden, in which he deposited billions of dollars in oil money. The fund was under his direct control—a slush fund, pure and simple. (While Fonden had a board of Chávez loyalists who could have blocked the president's spending decisions, it did not.) He spent the money on large industrial or infrastructure projects or anything else he felt like supporting. From 2005 through 2014, Fonden received $142 billion from PDVSA and the Central Bank. That equals a fifth of oil exports during that period—under the sole control of the president, with no independent oversight and no consistent follow-up.[13]

Chávez (and Maduro after him) also borrowed heavily, often using future oil revenue as collateral. Chávez established a series of off-budget development accounts with loans from China and investment from PDVSA. Between 2007 and 2014, these so-called Chinese Funds received a total of $62 billion, including more than $50 billion from China. As with Fonden, this money was under the president's control.[14]

In a television broadcast in early 2012, Chávez announced a flurry of projects that he said were financed by Fonden. He plowed through it all so fast you couldn't keep track. It added up to billions. A cement plant. A paper mill. A metalworking plant. A group of sawmills. Operating money for Corpoelec and the Caracas subway. "A bourgeois government would eliminate all this," Chávez said, "money for the bourgeoisie, hunger and lead for the people. That's what history teaches us."[15]

*   *   *

IN A TELEVISED pre–May Day celebration on April 30, 2008, Chávez announced to a theater full of workers that he was going to nationalize the country's largest steelmaker, a company called Sidor. "We're going to transform Sidor into a socialist company owned by the socialist state and the socialist workers, to move forward with the Bolivarian revolution," he said. The workers cheered.[16]

So that no one would miss the message, Chávez said the words *socialist* or *socialism* forty-one times during the speech, which was repeatedly interrupted by applause and shouts of *Viva!* He said the words *revolution* or *revolutionary* thirty-eight times and he named Bolívar or used the word *Bolivarian* twenty-five times. The following year he agreed to pay $2 billion to the Luxembourg-based company Ternium for its majority stake in Sidor.

Sidor was originally built by the government, starting operations in the 1960s, and then was privatized in 1997. In 2007, Sidor produced a record of 4.3 million tons of liquid steel. After the government takeover, production fell every year but one. In 2019, the company produced no steel at all. Zero.[17]

* * *

WHEN CHÁVEZ NATIONALIZED Sidor, the company had 5,600 employees. The total payroll eventually grew to more than 14,000 workers.[18] It kept adding employees even as production fell. At the same time, the union came under control of the government and was effectively neutered. To be a unionist meant being a revolutionary, and that meant supporting the government, which was now the boss. Under Maduro, union leaders who asserted independence were jailed.[19] Management was chosen based on loyalty rather than expertise. Corruption was commonplace.

I visited Sidor, in Guayana City, near where the big hydroelectric plants are located, in 2013. By then some of the workers had revolted and gone on strike, demanding bonuses and benefits that they claimed had gone unpaid for years. The strike had started as a grassroots walkout by rank-and-file workers. The timid union leaders were slow to get behind the movement but eventually came on board. At the same time, a pro-government faction was trying to force an end to the strike. The strikers were labeled counterrevolutionaries and saboteurs. Maduro said that the gringos were behind the walkout.[20]

The Sidor plant was as big as a town, a labyrinth of streets and buildings with a lacework of power lines overhead and vast empty areas of rust and weeds, brown on tan. The two factions had called rallies at the plant on the same day. They set up dueling banks of speakers, with hundreds of gritty, hard-faced laboring men milling in between. The leaders on both sides took microphones and shouted harangues, demands, pleas, accusations, drowning each other out. I talked to a worker named Hugo Navarro, who stood in the middle. "You can't understand any of it," he said. "One speaker on this side, the other on that side. The factory is paralyzed."

I returned to Guayana City in 2019. As the plane made its approach, we flew over Sidor. You could see the slant-roofed structures of the big plants, the smokestacks, the miles of roads and railroad tracks. Everything was stained with rust on the rust-colored earth on the banks of the brown river. In all that great expanse, nothing moved. No truck or car or human being. No whiff of smoke or steam rose from a chimney. Everything was shut down, stopped.

18

Piñata

In 2012, a tip called into the U.S. Department of Immigration and Customs Enforcement led investigators in Houston and Miami to focus on a pair of Venezuelan businessmen living in the United States who had made millions of dollars selling equipment and supplies to PDVSA, Venezuela's government-run oil company. Banking records revealed that the two men, Roberto Rincón and Abraham Shiera, had made large payments to employees of a U.S.-based procurement subsidiary of PDVSA. Investigators determined that Rincón and Shiera had been paying bribes to receive contracts that allowed them to sell items such as pipe or drilling equipment at hugely inflated prices. The high prices provided for outsize profits for the two businessmen and also covered the cost of the kickbacks.[1]

The feds indicted Rincón and Shiera on bribery and other charges; the two men pled guilty in 2016.[2] The investigation led to the indictment of at least sixteen other people. Investigators would knock on the door of someone who took bribes from Rincón or Shiera. That person would spill his guts and the investigators would ask: Who else did you take bribes from? They would name another PDVSA supplier, and the investigators would drive across town and knock on that person's door. The supplier would then name other PDVSA workers who had taken bribes. And on and on.

It was like contact tracing for a virus. Each person with the disease infected multiple others. Reading the indictments, I got the impression that they were describing a natural process, something as unremarkable as drawing a breath, exhaling, spreading a sickness. Squeezing money out of PDVSA was what Venezuelans did. The oil money belonged to everyone, so it was just a question of getting your hands on your share.

Investigators estimated that over a period of five years, Rincón and Shiera received contracts worth more than $1 billion. Their scam went along smoothly until PDVSA experienced a cash crunch, which caused it to delay payments to its suppliers. But adversity breeds opportunity. A Venezuelan lawyer approached Rincón and Shiera with an offer. He said that he represented high-level officials at PDVSA who could de-cide which suppliers were paid and which were not. These officials would make sure that Rincón and Shiera were paid on time, the lawyer said, if the businessmen kicked back to them 10 percent of everything that PDVSA paid them. They would also make sure that Rincón and Shi-era continued to receive lucrative contracts. Rincón and Shiera said yes and began to funnel tens of millions of dollars in bribes to the officials, which prosecutors said included PDVSA's head of security, the general manager of the company's procurement subsidiary, and a former vice minister of energy.[3] There was a poetic symmetry to the shakedown: pay to get paid. In any case, the bribes could always be factored into the next contract.

* * *

IN EARLY 2020, U.S. prosecutors in Miami filed charges against a Ven-ezuelan businessman named Leonardo Santilli. Like Rincón and Shiera, Santilli, who had companies in Florida and Venezuela, was accused of paying bribes to secure PDVSA contracts. One relatively modest transac-tion caught my eye: Santilli had sold PDVSA a consignment of 55-gallon drums for $9.2 million. Nothing could be more mundane: selling oil barrels to an oil company. But investigators said that the drums were actually worth just $2 million. In other words, Santilli was charging a markup of 360 percent. According to court documents, that was typical of Santilli's transactions with PDVSA.[4]

The barrel sale occurred in October 2015, when the price of oil was

in free fall and PDVSA could hardly afford to pay a $7 million premium
for metal barrels. The sale was made to a PDVSA subsidiary in what is
known as the Orinoco heavy oil belt, the location of the massive reserves
that gave Venezuela the distinction of having more oil in the ground than
any other country.

At the end of 2015, Venezuela was producing about 2.4 million barrels of oil a day. Soon production would start to decline, and by 2020,
it had dropped below 400,000 barrels a day.[5] Venezuela was becoming
an oil-producing country that could barely produce oil. There are many
reasons that production fell. American sanctions cut off the country from
oil markets and from financing. PDVSA was badly managed. It failed
to make necessary investments and maintain its facilities. Maduro had
installed a general with no oil experience to run the company, and he
put his wife's nephew in charge of its finances. And always there was corruption, sowing inefficiency and waste. The indictment doesn't identify
the PDVSA procurement manager in the heavy oil belt who allegedly
pocketed a bribe to buy Santilli's drums at nearly four times the market
price, but whoever it was, that person was giving PDVSA one small
shove toward the cliff edge.

I took a trip to El Tigre, the city at the center of the heavy oil belt, in
2018. Maybe I saw some of Santilli's 55-gallon drums lying around. By
then, PDVSA wasn't an oil company anymore. It was a junkyard. Thousands of employees had stopped going to work or fled the country
because the wages PDVSA paid had become worthless. All the installations I visited were in ruins. Thieves stole the motors from pumpjacks
and tore transformers off poles to remove the copper inside. Workers
had no tools. Vehicles were broken down. The company had stopped giving workers the meals required by their contracts. At one storage facil-
ity, a leaking tank spewed a lake of black crude.

"This was a golden cup," said a PDVSA employee who had worked
for more than twenty years in the oil fields around El Tigre. "Not silver.
Gold. Now it's a plastic cup."

On that trip I saw one of the most astonishing things I ever saw in
Venezuela. Shortages of food and other basic items were extreme. People
would stand in line for hours to enter supermarkets where they would
buy whatever was on the shelves. Outside a large supermarket in El

Tigre, I came upon a line of hundreds of people. They stood pressed one against the other, front to back. Stranger against stranger. They said that it was to keep people from cutting in line. There was something horribly dehumanizing about it, the way every person was squeezed between the person behind and the person in front. The desperation of it, the willingness to go along with any sort of humiliation in order to get a bit of food for your family. And the distrust—that someone might take your place in line and buy the last item before you could get to it. There was a bone-tiredness to people's faces. I met a man there dressed in red PDVSA coveralls. He used to work in the oil fields. Now he was selling loosies—single cigarettes—to people in the line.

A manager for one of the foreign oil companies that worked with PD-VSA in the heavy oil belt told me that the looting of the oil fields was done by the workers themselves. They would steal copper wire or tools and sell them for a few bolivars to buy food. I thought of that when I read about the hundreds of millions of dollars stripped from PDVSA in bogus contracts and bribes.

* * *

THERE WERE SO many ways to steal.

In 2017, Alejandro Andrade, a former national treasurer of Venezuela, pled guilty to bribery charges in federal court in Florida.[6] Andrade had been Chávez's bodyguard before being elevated to treasurer for the nation. His only qualification was loyalty. In court he admitted taking hundreds of millions of dollars from a Venezuelan businessman named Raúl Gorrín. The bribes included private jets, a yacht, show horses, fancy cars and watches, and real estate. Andrade said that Gorrín had been paying him for near-exclusive rights to handle billions of dollars in lucrative currency exchange transactions with the Treasury.

The transactions allowed Gorrín to take advantage of the spread between the official and black-market exchange rates, often doubling his money, just like the Venezuelan importers who would over-invoice to get their hands on cheap dollars. In this case, the transactions were legal; it was the alleged bribery and subsequent money laundering that drew the attention of investigators.

Gorrín grew rich. He bought an insurance company and, in 2013, after Maduro took over as president, a TV station called Globovisión. Gorrín was close to the Chavista elite, including the first lady, Cilia Flores. Globovisión was the last major TV station in the country with a pro-opposition stance. After Gorrín bought it, the station steered clear of politics, and pro-opposition shows were canceled. Gorrín had reaped enormous profits thanks to his government connections; with the muzzling of Globovisión, the government got something in return.

If it's worth doing, it's worth overdoing.

In 2015, Gorrín was allegedly involved in another currency operation, this time with PDVSA. It was essentially the same as what Gorrín had done with the Treasury department: buying cheap dollars from the government and profiting off the spread between the official and black-market exchange rates. But now, because the bolivar had lost so much value against the dollar on the black market, the profits were exorbitant. Although it was dressed up with bells and whistles, the deal amounted to a simple currency exchange: PDVSA was selling dollars and receiving bolivars (the company needed bolivars to pay expenses that it incurred in the national currency, such as wages). In this case, according to U.S. court documents, PDVSA handed over $600 million to Gorrín and his partners and received 7.2 billion bolivars in return. The trick was that Gorrín and his partners had bought the bolivars on the black market for just $43 million. In other words, they turned $43 million into $600 million in a single transaction.[7]

It was a killing.

Three years later, U.S. prosecutors indicted several people, including the scion of a prominent Caracas family and a former PDVSA finance director, on money laundering and racketeering charges, in connection with the PDVSA deal. Gorrín was not charged but he was referred to in the indictment and other court papers as "Conspirator 7," whom the documents identified as the billionaire owner of a Venezuelan television network (a person with knowledge of the case confirmed that Conspirator 7 was Gorrín).[8] The court papers said that Gorrín (as Conspirator 7) received about $265 million from the deal (the split was done in euros, so the dollar amounts are approximate) and that he passed along about $186 million from his share to the three sons of Cilia Flores, Maduro's wife. The papers described a meeting in Gorrín's office in Caracas, where he told an associate that Flores's sons, who were known as Los Chamos, or the Boys, helped him "solve issues" with their powerful mother.[9]

Federal prosecutors in Miami eventually indicted Gorrín, in 2018, on bribery and money laundering charges in relation to the Treasury business with Andrade.[10] The feds alleged that Gorrín was moving so much illicit money around that he bought his own bank in the Dominican Republic to make it easier to pay bribes and launder money. (Since his indictment, Gorrín has remained in Venezuela and out of the reach of U.S. authorities.)

* * *

RAFAEL RAMÍREZ, A close confidant of Chávez, was the head of PDVSA for more than a decade. Although Maduro had pushed him out of the company by the time of the $600 million score by Gorrín and his partners, Ramírez had been president of PDVSA while millions of dollars flowed out the door through inflated contracts purchased with bribes.

"An atmosphere was created that was conducive to all of this," Ramírez told me when I asked him about corruption at PDVSA. I'd talked to several former Chávez ministers, and I noticed that they had a way of slipping into the passive voice when discussing the failings of the comandante's government. Ramírez denied ever having taken a bribe or a kickback, and he has never been publicly charged by U.S. prosecutors. (Venezuelan authorities accused him of corruption, but that came after he began criticizing the government.) Since breaking with Maduro, Ramírez had been living in Rome, which is where I interviewed him. Just before my visit, a group of Venezuelan legislators had accused him of living like a prince in an Italian castle. He told me that he lived in an ordinary apartment (he was vague about its whereabouts, and we met in the lobby of a hotel near the Piazza del Popolo—there was a cloak-and-dagger element to the meeting that suggested that he didn't want his enemies in the government and the opposition to know where he lived, although it seemed that it would be easy enough to track him down). He said that someday, on another trip, he would invite me to his apartment for lunch, where I could see for myself that it was no castle. I pointed out that even if he had not lined his own pockets, he had presided for years over a company that had an immense corruption problem. Even the small number of cases that had found their way to the U.S. courts showed that, at all levels of the company, there were PDVSA officials on the take.

"It wasn't a PDVSA problem, it was a problem with the whole government," Ramírez said.

Okay, but you were in charge of PDVSA.

"True, but let's put things in context. It's not like PDVSA was a corrupt organization in the middle of a country without problems. There was a problem of corruption in the whole country, in all of the ministries, and it wasn't just a Chávez government problem, it was a Carlos Andrés [Pérez] problem too, and the rest. It has to do with a country that receives an immense quantity of money in dollars that is not the product of anyone's labor, but it comes from the sale of oil. It's the problem of an oil-producing country."

Ramírez told me that PDVSA had strict controls in place to prevent corruption and catch it when it occurred. He sounded like an American finance executive the week before Lehman Brothers collapsed, talking about how Wall Street was so heavily regulated that nothing could possibly go wrong. "Everyone was watching PDVSA. If there were acts of corruption, as there were, well, it was an exception. It's not like PDVSA was a spiral of corruption."

Under Venezuelan law, Ramírez said, corruption is an individual act, a question of personal responsibility. "Take Chávez, for instance. He was president and in charge of the public purse, but Chávez had nothing to do with what Andrade did, and Andrade was his treasurer." Government had worked, had done its job—the president and his ministers had delegated responsibility, as was proper. "It's not a new problem for us," he said. "It's a permanent problem for Venezuela."

* * *

IN THE SPRING of 2020, when much of the world was shut down because of the Covid-19 pandemic, I spoke by phone with my friend Patricia about corruption in Venezuela. I had been reading through piles of court documents and was feeling overwhelmed at the enormous scale of the pilfering. I was in New York City. Patricia was in Caracas, in a country without gasoline, without drinking water, without medicines. Patricia said that she'd read a news story online about the U.S. government giving $35 million to a company to work on a coronavirus vaccine. What occurred to her when she read the article was this: in Venezuela, there was no money for public health, but there had been plenty of money to steal—any idiot could have stolen $35 million from the government. Could have and did. It made her think about how the country had gone down the tubes because its own people robbed the place blind, stripped the place of everything of value. It was like the looted hotel in Maracaibo, Las Brisas del Norte. But imagine that the hotel is an entire country. And while everyone was living in it, they were stripping out the copper wire, the mattresses, the sinks and toilets, the tables and silverware in the restaurant, the stoves and refrigerators in the kitchen, the air-conditioning units from the roof, the computers in the office. Before long all that's left is the wreck of a hotel. The wreck of a country.

The whole country, Patricia said, became corrupt. After Chávez put in place currency controls, just about everyone got involved in gaming the system. It wasn't just the Chavistas or unscrupulous importers or financiers. It was everyone. One of the first groups to take advantage was the middle class. In fact, the currency controls were Chávez's way of buying off the middle class. Cheap dollars made it possible to take trips to Madrid, Rome, Miami, Houston, New York. That was perfectly legal. But then people started selling their travel quotas to operators who came up with ways that let them extract money from the system without ever leaving the country. There was also an internet allowance, through which the government provided cheap dollars to buy stuff online. Maids from the barrios would sell their internet allowance to their well-off employers. Another program provided cheap dollars to pay tuition and living expenses to attend universities abroad. As with everything else, you'd obtain the dollars cheap from the government and sell part of them on the black market, and before junior had graduated, you might actually be turning a profit. How many brown-eyed Venezuelan youths who went off to Yale or Chicago or Wharton—at a discount!—came home and promptly set to work defrauding the country of millions more?

The nation was an all-you-can-eat buffet and everyone was pushing to the front to fill their pockets with delicacies before they ran out.

It was everyone in the pool or no one. It destroys your sense of right and wrong, Patricia said. It destroys your sense of belonging to a society, something that matters and has value. It destroys the idea of being a citizen. Everyone becomes complicit. Anyone who didn't drink from the overflowing cup before it was empty and cracked, anyone who didn't grab his fistful of dollars while he could was just stupid and to be pitied—no, not pitied: scorned.

And that's how the corrupt want it. The corrupt man can't stand the honest citizen. He wants everyone to be swimming in the dirty water together. The honest man is a repudiation, a reminder of what the corrupt man used to be, of what he could have been. And that above all is something that he cannot abide, cannot allow to exist.

19

Blackout

Night falls.

Santa Teresita is a small middle-class neighborhood in Maracaibo, just off the main road to the airport. Little more than a cul-de-sac, one long, curving dead-end street with a couple of other dead-end streets branching off it. Tonight the residents have thrown tree branches across the airport road to keep traffic from going through. For them it's another night without electricity and they're fed up. Everyone out to protest! Block the street! Build a barricade! No one goes through until we get electricity!

Their location is strategic.

But the strategy has a flaw.

Since there are almost no flights coming in or going out (and none at night), and since there is a shortage of gasoline, there isn't much traffic to block.

The crisis frustrates people's ability to protest it. What does it mean to block a road that has no traffic?

It is May 2019. Power went out here, in this neighborhood, this circuit of the larger grid, three days ago. After a day and a half, it came back on briefly and then went out again. That was yesterday at midday, and the lights haven't come back on since. Within the general uncertainty of blackouts and power rationing, the residents of Santa Teresita feel as though they've been singled out for an additional portion—one humiliation too many.

When I arrived there around eight P.M. about forty people were at the roadblock. Every once in a while a car pulled up. The driver would lean out the window and argue with the protesters. After a while the car would turn around and drive away. The residents of Santa Teresita were angry and afraid. They were afraid of the police and they were more afraid that the police would send the *colectivos*—the armed motorcycle gangs that served as the government's shock troops. They were afraid that the colectivos would come and that there would be violence.

People crowded around me. They saw that I was an American, a journalist. "When are the Marines going to come and overthrow Maduro?" someone said, a voice in the darkness. "You tell Trump we're waiting for him," said another.

Invasions come with casualties, I said. They don't always go as planned.

People are dying anyway, a man said. That's right! A woman jumped into the conversation and they talked over one another: People are dying from hunger, being shot in protests, dying for want of medical care.

Those are deaths, the man said, that nobody sees.

A woman said, "We don't have money, we don't have water, we don't have electricity."

It was too dark for me to write in my notebook, so I used a recorder. It preserved a jumble of desperate, overlapping voices. The only light came from the floodlights, powered by a generator, in the parking lot of a hotel on the airport road. It was called Hotel Aeropuerto. The parking lot was empty, a black rectangle under a black sky: no flights, no guests.

A woman told me that she'd just returned from a trip to Colombia, and at the border, Venezuelan National Guard soldiers stole the medicine she was bringing home: antibiotics, and drugs for high blood pressure and diabetes.

There was a lot of shouting. A white pickup truck pulled up and some policemen in uniform got out. They were very young. They talked in a nonconfrontational way to a few of the protesters, climbed into the truck, backed up, and drove away.

I spoke with a man named Alejandro Delgado. He was a criminal lawyer. Between cases he drove a taxi. "You feel powerless," he said. He was talking about the disruptions to their lives, the arbitrariness of electricity's coming and going, of the uncertain water supply. It robbed you of your sleep. That was the worst. Normally you slept with the air conditioner on. But without power, in the heat of Maracaibo, you had to leave the windows open or sleep outside, and the mosquitoes wouldn't leave you alone. You could wrap yourself up in a sheet, but then you felt like you were suffocating and still you couldn't sleep. On top of all that, you were on edge all the time. You were worried about your family, your neighbors. And you were always ready to wake up in the middle of the night if the lights came on or the water came on. If you finally fell asleep, it was like you were sleeping with one eye open. "This is not a life with dignity," Alejandro said.

A man listening to us broke in: "We're the walking dead here!"

"They're killing us slowly," Alejandro said.

"We're like zombies!" said a short, wiry woman with thin bare arms. Her words came out in angry, repetitive bursts. "They're killing us! No food! No electricity! We're going to disappear! Any day now! Look! Sometimes you get up and your stomach is flat against your spine." Maybe you could afford to buy some rice, but nothing to go with it. Or maybe some corn flour, but then you make arepas and there's nothing to put in them. "They're starving us to death! So what does that make us? Zombies! Zombies! Zombies! Here! Here! Here! No one is obese here. We're all skinny. We're all skinny. Skinny."

Alejandro said, "You get up from the table and you're already thinking about tomorrow. *What am I going to eat tomorrow?*"

The agitated woman who talked about zombies was named Xiomara Jaime. "You're having your arepa for breakfast," she said, "and you're already thinking, *What am I going to make for lunch?* You've got rice, because you bought some, okay, and what about meat? Or chicken? Salad? Soup?"

"Chicken, salad, cheese," Alejandro said. They were like old people remembering the names of vanished artifacts of their childhood. "Nothing. Nothing."

Xiomara said that she'd always been with the opposition, always against Chávez and now against Maduro.

Alejandro had a soft, thoughtful voice and he spoke slowly. "I don't consider myself on one side or the other," he said. "I applaud the good things and criticize the bad things."

Alejandro had always voted for Chávez. But he stopped voting after Chávez died. Now he believed that the elections were rigged.

We took a walk through the neighborhood. They all knew one another, greeted one another. The houses were modestly middle class, the homes of government workers, professionals, office workers. Nothing fancy, but you could see, even in the dark, that life had been good here, in an unpretentious, hardworking way. Some houses had torches burning in front: crooked sticks with a black can on the end, containing a rag soaked in diesel fuel, with a flame leaping out. They gave off a fluttering mothlike light. Alejandro said that the streaky black smoke helped keep away the mosquitoes, which came in swarms from a creek behind the houses. At the end of the street there was a gray cinder-block wall. It was too high to see over, but on the other side was the hotel that I'd noticed from the barricade. The glow of light produced by its generators crowned the wall like an aurora, like the glow of a distant city that you might see while driving across the plains at night. It gave off light, but it didn't illuminate.

The people here took care of one another. One woman had a mastectomy last week. Another suffered a stroke. Their neighbors checked in to see how they were doing. One family had two children with special needs. The woman who'd had the medicine stolen was bringing some back for a neighbor. But the neighborhood was emptying out. Alejandro took the inventory of the block: "That house is empty. That other one is empty. That one there is empty. There are lots of empty houses. These two here are empty. This one is empty." One family had left two days ago, for Medellín. Another was leaving later in the week. "Those folks over there went to Ecuador. The ones next door went to Peru."

"We'll be next," said a woman who lived a few doors from Alejandro. She was an architect. Her husband was a graphic designer. Their three-year-old daughter needed an operation for a congenital heart problem. They'd been told that in Caracas it would cost $10,000. More than they could afford. They were looking at emigrating to Argentina or Ecuador. They hoped they could find treatment for their daughter there. "We've gone backward," the woman said. "To before the Second World War. To 1910. We've gone so far backward."

The orange light of the torches flickered across her face. Inky smoke melted into the black sky burning with stars. You could feel the darkness like a curtain all around us, just beyond the torchlight and the diffuse aurora of the hotel behind its wall.

Alejandro walked with me back to the main road. The tree branches were still there, blocking the way. People were milling about, still angry, restless, without power, without light, without future. The only power they had was to say no. The street was blocked. The people were blocked. The whole city felt blocked, without a way forward, stymied. Emptying out.

PART THREE

Not Anymore

On May 26, 2018, Tom Shannon was a month away from retirement, after more than three decades at the State Department. Shannon, who held the title of Career Ambassador, was at the time the highest-ranking member of the Foreign Service. He'd served as the acting secretary of state at the start of the Trump administration, during the twelve days in January and February 2017 between the exit of the outgoing secretary, John Kerry, and the arrival of his replacement, Rex Tillerson. Shannon had started his diplomatic career in 1984, with a posting to Guatemala, and in 1996 he became the political counselor of the American embassy in Caracas, staying through the start of Chávez's presidency. That began more than two decades of engagement with Venezuela. For many years, Shannon was considered the person in the U.S. government who best understood what was happening in Venezuela. It was Shannon who set the tone of American policy toward the Chávez government.

Shannon counseled moderation. When Chávez went to the United Nations and said that President George W. Bush was the devil, it was Shannon who advised the president not to respond in kind. And the president listened.

All that had changed sharply under Donald Trump, who favored a more confrontational approach. But on this day, as his retirement neared, Shannon could feel some satisfaction and some vindication. For two years he had been working quietly to win the release of Joshua Holt, a young American who had been arrested in Venezuela and was being held by the Maduro government as a bargaining chip. Holt had traveled from his home in Utah to Caracas in June 2016 to marry a woman he'd met on the internet. About three weeks after his arrival, security forces arrested Holt and his new wife, Thamy, claiming to have found a grenade and an assault rifle in their apartment. Holt said the weapons were planted by police. That began a long ordeal for the couple and intensive efforts by American officials to secure their release. Holt was held at the Caracas prison of the Sebin, the intelligence police. Government officials said that he was a terrorist stockpiling weapons for an attack; later they claimed that he was the head of CIA operations in the region. Holt was twenty-four years old.

In September 2016, three months after Holt's arrest, Secretary of State John Kerry met with Maduro on the sidelines of a ceremony in Cartagena, Colombia, to celebrate the signing of a peace agreement between the Colombian government and the country's largest rebel group, the Revolutionary Armed Forces of Colombia.[1] The Obama administration had shown limited interest in Latin America until the president's second term, when the United States, in 2014, negotiated a momentous rapprochement with Cuba, and then became directly involved in the Colombian peace talks.[2] Administration officials hoped that the Cuba thaw would mean improved attitudes toward Washington across the region, but relations with Venezuela had remained tense and the U.S. approach had changed little since the Bush years—ignore provocations and keep the temperature low. It was in that context that Kerry sat down with Maduro in Cartagena, both men dressed, like the other regional leaders who attended the ceremony, in white shirts meant to symbolize peace. Kerry told Maduro that he was interested in making an official visit to Caracas. It was a significant gesture designed to appeal to Maduro—no U.S. secretary of state had set foot in Venezuela since Madeleine Albright in 1998. Maduro could claim a visit by Kerry as a sign of recognition by the highest levels of the U.S. government.

But Kerry set a condition: he would make the trip only if he could take Holt home with him.

The Venezuelans appeared eager for Kerry to visit, but they ultimately refused to hand over Holt. Shannon, who was with Kerry on the trip, saw this as a sign of the fragmentation of Venezuela's power structure. Maduro was president but controlled only certain parts of the government. He essentially shared power with other important figures who had their own circles of influence. These included Diosdado Cabello, who was believed to control the Sebin intelligence police. Some of these figures were Maduro's allies and some his rivals. Some Chavista leaders might have welcomed Kerry's visit as an acknowledgment of Maduro's legitimacy, while others might have been against it for the same reason.

"Kerry was very clear," Shannon said. "'I get Holt or I don't go.' And for me that was indicative of the fact that Maduro didn't control Holt. He was being controlled at Sebin, and he was probably in the hands of the Cubans or Diosdado or people who were not prepared to release him and probably people who didn't want to see Kerry in Caracas anyway. So that's when it became apparent that we were dealing with a hostage-taking that revealed the complexities of Maduro's government."

The standoff continued for two years. For a time, Venezuelan officials sought to trade Holt for two nephews of Venezuelan first lady Cilia Flores, who had been convicted in New York on drug trafficking charges. This time it was the Americans who said no.

Holt's release finally came about through the intervention of Senator Bob Corker of Tennessee, the Republican chairman of the Senate foreign relations committee. Corker had an aide, Caleb McCarry, who had maintained good relations with Venezuelan officials since the early 2000s, when a group of Venezuelan legislators, including Maduro, had visited the United States.

McCarry was in contact with a Chavista state governor named Rafael Lacava, who favored more cordial relations between the two countries. (Lacava was flamboyant and eccentric; he called himself Dracula and became known for attaching his nickname to government programs in his state, such as a bus system he called TransDrácula.) After Maduro's reelection in May 2018, Lacava told McCarry that he thought that Maduro could be persuaded to release Holt. From Shannon and McCarry's perspective, the timing seemed favorable. Maduro didn't want to appear as though he were caving in to American pressure, but now he could cast Holt's release as an overture to improve relations, made from a position of strength. It might have seemed like a contradictory sign, but two days after the election Maduro expelled the top two U.S. diplomats from Caracas, accusing them of conspiring against his government. That could give Maduro cover to release Holt—an act of aggressiveness followed by an act of benevolence. McCarry told Shannon that he thought he had a deal and that Corker was prepared to fly to Caracas to retrieve Holt.

But Shannon was now dealing with the same kind of fractured power structure in Washington that he had perceived on the Venezuelan side when Maduro rejected Kerry's offer in Cartagena. Just as there were factions in Caracas that didn't want improved relations with Washington, there were hard-liners in the United States who didn't want a thaw with the Venezuelans. By now the Trump White House was in the midst of a maximum pressure campaign against Maduro—steered by National Security Advisor John Bolton and backed by hawkish legislators like Senator Marco Rubio of Florida.

As McCarry negotiated, Shannon said that he refrained from reporting the progress to the White House or Secretary of State Mike Pompeo, who had been appointed less than a month earlier. "While all this is going on and Caleb and I are talking, I'm keeping it to myself," Shannon said, "because I'm just not convinced that the people that I'm dealing with at the White House are prepared for his release. And I'm very concerned that if Caleb's progress was spread broadly across the U.S. government, and especially into the Senate, that somebody would try to undo it." No one was opposed to Holt's going free. "It's just that they hated the idea of us negotiating with Maduro and his gang."

On May 24, on the sidelines of a foreign relations committee hearing, Corker told Pompeo that he was planning to fly to Caracas to negotiate Holt's release. According to McCarry, Corker asked Pompeo to hold off telling the White House. The next day Corker and McCarry flew to Caracas, where they met with Lacava and Maduro, who finally agreed to let Holt go.

It was McCarry's second trip that year to Caracas to try to obtain

Holt's freedom. He'd met with Maduro there in January, and after returning home to the United States, McCarry had an unusual dream. He
dreamed that he talked with Chávez, who spoke approvingly of a real-
life conversation that McCarry had with Maduro during his visit a day
or two earlier. Now, on seeing Maduro again, McCarry told him about
the dream. "I said, 'Soñé con Chávez, con el comandante. I dreamed
about Chávez.'" Maduro became emotional. "He teared up and he said,
'Estas cosas son reales. These things are real.'"

That night Corker, McCarry, and Lacava had dinner together. Corker
called Trump and told him that he expected to bring Holt home the next
day and suggested that Trump receive Holt in the Oval Office to celebrate
his return. Then he told Trump about the key role Lacava had played.
"Corker said, 'If you want to thank the guy who actually got this done,
here's Governor Lacava.'" McCarry said that Trump and Lacava (who
studied at Rutgers and speaks English) had a cordial conversation that
lasted several minutes.

On May 26, Corker and McCarry flew back to Washington with Holt,
his wife, and one of her daughters (another daughter was already living
with Holt's family in Utah). Holt was reunited with his parents, who had
flown in to meet him, and then they all headed over to the White House
for the welcome home ceremony with the president.

Once the travelers were safely on the ground, Shannon received a call
from his chief of staff telling him that he was "on the manifest" for the
Oval Office ceremony that evening. Shannon was interested in meeting Holt and looked forward to seeing Holt's parents; he had been in
frequent contact with them and was pleased that the family was being
reunited at last.

At the appointed time, Shannon went to the southwest gate of the
White House and handed the guard his credentials, as he had done
countless times before. As he was waiting to be passed through, the
phone rang in the guard booth. "He picks up the phone," Shannon
said of the guard, "and then he says, 'Well, one of those gentlemen is
here right now—Mr. Shannon.' And he goes, 'Uh-huh, okay, thank you
very much.' And he hangs up the phone and then he hands me back
my credential. And then he says, 'I'm very sorry, sir, but I can't give

you access to the compound.' And I said, 'Well, I believe I'm on the manifest for an Oval Office meeting.' And he said, 'I'm very sorry, sir, but not anymore.'"

No one ever told Shannon why he was suddenly barred from the White House. He suspected that the National Security Council, which, under Bolton, was staunchly against negotiating with the Maduro government, might have been to blame.

Whatever the motive, when the guard handed him back his credentials and said *not anymore,* it was a symbolic end to the period in which Shannon's approach had defined America's policy toward Venezuela.

"I thought it showed very clearly that you can talk to these people," Shannon said of Holt's release. "And you can negotiate with them. And that you can get stuff from them if they're approached in the right way and if the circumstances are right."

* * *

SHANNON ARRIVED IN Caracas for the first time in 1996. The economy was stagnant, inflation was over 100 percent, and street protests sparked by deteriorating living standards were common.

Despite all that, Shannon said, Venezuela "had a reputation for being one of South America's longest-running democracies, and a model to which we turned when talking about democracy in the hemisphere." But as he made the rounds, talking to politicians, businessmen, and labor leaders, he developed a different impression. "It became apparent to me that something was terribly wrong, that Venezuela was a kind of Universal Studios. You know, in Universal Studios, you walk down the street, and you think you're in a town, but if you open up a door, there's nothing behind it. And that was Venezuelan democracy in 1996. Once you got into the Congress, once you got into the political parties, you realized that this was a political system that had become narrowly clientelistic and corrupt and was not representative of much of anything except for some very established interests and that it was very vulnerable to somebody such as Chávez."

Shannon and I met in an antiseptic conference room at the

Washington law firm where he'd gone to work after leaving the State Department. Shannon's blue eyes matched his blue suit. His dress shirt was open at the collar. After all those years at State, now he could get by without a tie. But he retained the ambassadorial demeanor. He spoke in a soft voice, with many pauses as he considered his words. And he spoke without using his hands. Sometimes he tapped the table to emphasize a point, but mostly he kept them still, resting in his lap.

In 1999, shortly after Chávez's inauguration, Shannon moved to Washington and was posted to the National Security Council. In December, at the end of Chávez's first year as president, heavy rains caused catastrophic landslides along the coast near Caracas. Hundreds were killed, towns were buried.[3] The Venezuelan military was struggling to reach the victims. Long sections of the coastal highway were knocked out, making the rescue effort more difficult. The United States offered to lend a hand. At that point it was still unclear what direction relations would take under Chávez, and Washington saw an opportunity to show goodwill. Officials worked out a plan with the Venezuelan defense minister: U.S. naval ships would take troops and earthmoving equipment to the eastern end of the disaster zone. They would work their way westward, clearing the highway, while Venezuelan troops, starting at the other end, worked in the opposite direction. They would meet in the middle, Shannon said, "in some kind of joyous moment of cooperation and collaboration.

"The U.S. mobilizes ships and engineering battalions, bulldozers and you name it, and put them all on board vessels and sent them south," Shannon said. "And as they're steaming, Fidel Castro calls up Chávez and says, 'You cannot do this. You cannot allow American troops to land in Venezuela because they won't leave and you'll be finished. This is all a trick.' And so Chávez calls it off."

I asked Shannon how he knew what Fidel had told Chávez on the phone call. "Because we listened to it," Shannon said.[4] "That's when it became apparent that Chávez did not see us as a friendly or even a neutral force, but as a potentially hostile force, and that he still viewed himself as vulnerable to us."

The definitive break in the relationship came with the coup that pushed Chávez from power for two days in April 2002—a change that, while it lasted, was celebrated by the Bush administration. Chávez was convinced that the United States had, at a minimum, given its approval in advance. (Documents released subsequently showed that the Central Intelligence Agency knew that Chávez's opponents were plotting a coup—and that the White House had been briefed on the topic.[5]) But Shannon said that he wasn't aware of any direct U.S. involvement in the putsch.

What might be thought of as the Shannon Approach to Venezuela emerged after Condoleezza Rice became secretary of state in 2005 and installed Shannon as assistant secretary of state for Western Hemisphere Affairs. By then the United States had troops in Iraq and Afghanistan and was waging a global war on terror. Rice told Shannon that she didn't want to take on any more fights. Shannon's proposal was to engage with those Latin American countries willing to work with the United States, regardless of ideology (Brazil, under the leftist Workers' Party, for instance), and avoid open conflict with the rest.

"We had determined that Chávez was feeding off of confrontation with us, that it energized him and it gave him stature in the region and that therefore, we had to take that away from him," Shannon said. "And we were going to take it away from him by not confronting him. And I was able to convince the president never to mention Chávez's name. Don't talk about him at all."

A U.S. diplomat who worked in Latin America for many years told me: "Tom's view was that there will be an inevitable tendency to take a maximum pressure approach and that will fail. As in Cuba, it will unite the rest of Latin America against us."

At the same time, U.S. diplomats stationed in Venezuela were encouraged to speak out against Chávez's undermining of democratic checks and balances, and they offered support to opposition parties.

Over time, however, Shannon's methods began to draw fire from critics who said that the United States should be more aggressive in countering the erosion of democracy in Venezuela and Chávez's regional influence. It was a difficult policy to defend because there was no clear line of cause and effect. How could you measure to what degree ignoring Chávez's provocations had given the United States more room to pursue its broader agenda in the region? Criticism mounted, including within the Obama administration, after Maduro took over and began to step up repressive measures, while his mismanagement of the economy pushed the nation deeper into crisis.

The change of course under Trump was partly a reflection of an ideological shift and partly the product of a growing frustration that policy makers in the Obama White House had shared.

"Because of a lack of results, what you're seeing is the vision of a group that believes we were too soft on them for a long time and what's needed is a crackdown, maximum pressure," the diplomat said. "It fits in with the Trump vision."

By the time he retired, eighteen months into Trump's presidency, the one man in the U.S. government who knew the most about Venezuela had been largely shut out of discussions about the country.

"One of the challenges that I faced in dealing with issues related to Venezuela and especially with people who were pushing for a much more aggressive approach is that, at least from my point of view, they didn't understand Chavismo," Shannon said. "And they didn't understand the rooted nature of Chavismo in Venezuela. And they still don't. And there's this belief that grows with time, especially after Chávez takes ill and then dies, that Venezuela is run by a very small group of criminally oriented, ideologically driven politicians who are dependent on Cuban intelligence officers and security officials and Chinese and Russian money to stay in power. And that if these things were to be taken away from them, they would be swept out to sea immediately and Venezuela would become this tabula rasa for whatever political leadership would present itself. I think that's foolish, quite frankly. I don't think it's true."

We were talking in 2019, the year that the young opposition leader Juan Guaidó had mounted a challenge to Maduro by declaring himself interim president of Venezuela, with fervent support from the Trump White House. "Chavismo in Venezuela is like Peronism in Argentina," Shannon said. "It's now a lasting feature of the Venezuelan political landscape. And given the fact that it is a political movement and now a party that has dominated Venezuela for twenty years, dominated the Venezuelan state, dominated the Venezuelan security services, the armed forces, that even if you had a magical moment tomorrow where Juan Guaidó were to suddenly find himself in Miraflores palace wearing the sash of the presidency, what would he control? He would be sitting on a Chavista state. And so there's a whole political challenge that I don't think is understood or accepted by those who are driving U.S. policy right now or by those who think that this is an easy thing to do."

Maximum Pressure

Two days before Craig Deare became one of the first people fired from the Trump White House, he was sitting in the Oval Office waiting for the president to speak by phone with President Mauricio Macri of Argentina, a wealthy businessman whom Trump had known for years. Deare was the director of Latin America policy at the National Security Council, and someone mentioned that Deare's wife was Argentine. "He looks over at me," Deare said, referring to the president, "and he goes, 'Oh, Argentina, beautiful women.'" Then Trump brought up Macri. "He said, 'Yeah, we used to chase girls together in New York.'"

During the four weeks in early 2017 that Deare worked at the White House, that was the only exchange he had with the president. But he watched up close as Trump developed his unique approach to foreign relations. "A conclusion that I reached at some point, which has been reinforced a million times over, is that the president doesn't think about foreign policy per se," Deare said. "He's not thinking about, 'Well, what are the foreign policy issues at stake?' It's all, 'What does the base think?'" Deare went on: "Venezuela? Oh, that's Florida. Mexico? That's the southwest border. Canada? That's timber and dairy farmers. It's all domestic politics."

Deare was hired by Trump's first national security advisor, Michael Flynn, who was forced out in February 2017 for lying about his contacts with the Russian ambassador. Deare was fired, the same week as Flynn, for speaking the truth. He gave a talk at the Woodrow Wilson Center in Washington in which he was bracingly frank about dysfunction in the administration. Word got back to the White House and Deare was shown the door.

* * *

THE NEW NATIONAL security advisor was H. R. McMaster, a retired army general. To head up Western Hemisphere Affairs at the council, McMaster brought in Juan Cruz, the chief of the CIA's Latin America division, a veteran agent with decades of experience in Venezuela, Colombia, and other countries in the region.

The first order of business was to reverse Obama's opening with Cuba. Next, they turned their attention to Venezuela.

Cruz had been stationed with Tom Shannon in Caracas in the mid-1990s. Cruz respected Shannon's experience but thought that Shannon's approach had ultimately been ineffective. "I felt that in the eighteen years of Chavismo we had gotten it wrong," Cruz said. "We'd tried benign neglect. The only thing we hadn't tried was head-on confrontation, and everything we did, they kept head-butting us. Everything we did they saw as a sign of weakness." Cruz and I met in Washington, at the restaurant at the back of Kramers Books, off Dupont Circle. He is short and round, with a disarming frankness and bonhomie. He wore a blue suit, and a blue patterned dress shirt with no tie, a white undershirt visible at the collar.

Working with officials from across the government—the State Department, Defense, the CIA, DEA, Justice, Treasury—Cruz started to implement a new direction for Venezuela policy.

First, the policy makers at the National Security Council looked at the electoral calendar in Venezuela. There were elections for governor scheduled for later in the year and a presidential election in 2018. A little more than a year before Trump was sworn in as president, the Venezuelan opposition had won an overwhelming majority in elections for the National Assembly. Given that precedent, and with conditions deteriorating badly in Venezuela, it was conceivable that, if it had a level playing field and stayed unified (two very big ifs), the opposition could win several governorships and then take the presidency in 2018. The goal was to keep up the pressure on Maduro to allow fair elections.

The strategy that Cruz's team at the NSC developed had two main pillars. One was to work with other countries, in the region and in Europe, to apply broad international pressure on Maduro. The other was economic sanctions.

There were two types of sanctions at their disposal. Individual sanctions could be aimed at important figures in the Maduro government who were involved in repressive or anti-democratic activities or corruption. Broader sanctions would seek to disrupt the overall economy or specific sectors, like the oil industry.

"For most of my life, I haven't been impressed by sanctions," Cruz said. "Sanctions by themselves often were a poor substitute for policy and bigger decision-making." It can often take a long time for the full effect of sanctions to be felt, he said, and if you get results, it's hard to know if it was because of the sanctions or other factors. Too often sanctions were something that policy makers did just so that they could say that they'd done something.

Nonetheless, the NSC was under pressure from hard-liners like "the Cuban Americans and the Rubio-ites" to "go full monty," Cruz said. "They want us to sanction everybody."

But the McMaster team resisted. "When you do that, you remove this hard-hitting effect," Cruz said. "What we wanted to do was, like, really pinpoint, send a message by who we did." They wanted to roll out sanctions little by little, targeting high-level officials and the corrupt businessmen who supported them in "onesies and twosies," rather than large groups of people all at once. "We wanted that to be part of the lesson, to be dissuasive, you know: 'Don't do that kind of stuff, because you'll get sanctioned.' People always think of sanctions as punitive, but they're actually designed to change behavior. So the idea was, we really wanted a case where we could say, this person changed behavior, they're off the sanctions list."

The result was what they called the escalatory road map, made up of a series of carefully targeted sanctions. Rather than sanction the whole oil sector, for instance, they envisioned targeting segments one at a time: shipping, insurance, the additives needed to produce products like gasoline. "We salami-sliced the sanctions," Cruz said. He made a motion with his hand like he was shaving off fine slices of salami. "It was going to be slivers."

The idea was to ratchet up the pressure little by little in the hope of forcing Maduro to engage in negotiations that could lead to an even playing field for the opposition in the presidential election scheduled for 2018. The McMaster team did not believe that sanctions alone would force Maduro from power.

"You don't bring about regime change through sanctions," said Fernando Cutz, a rare holdover from the Obama White House in the Trump administration, who helped develop the new Venezuela policy at the NSC. "Our goal was to create enough pressure on Maduro to force a real negotiation to happen. Our only ask was free and fair elections." The road map, as they envisioned it, included "off-ramps." "We were prepared to de-escalate."

At the very end of the road map was a sort of doomsday sanction that Cutz referred to as an oil embargo. That sanction would bar Venezuelan oil sales to the United States and more broadly restrict the country's ability to sell its oil anywhere. "We never intended to use it," Cutz said. "There was discussion of if we would do more harm to the Venezuelan people." They worried that shutting off all oil sales, and therefore virtually all of the country's income, would simply push the country further into chaos and exacerbate the misery of ordinary Venezuelans. It was a break-glass-in-case-of-emergency sanction. "If we felt the regime was about to collapse and it just needed one more push, that's when you do that and it collapses and then you undo it," Cutz said. "If we do it and the regime doesn't collapse, then we're setting ourselves up for another Cuba."

In February 2017, the Treasury Department announced the first Trump sanction on Venezuela, directed at an influential Chavista named Tareck El Aissami, whom the United States accused of being involved in drug trafficking. The sanction barred Americans from doing business with El Aissami, who was Maduro's vice president at the time, and froze any assets he might have had in the United States.

The move got rave reviews from Republicans and Democrats in Congress and showed that Venezuela policy was one area—perhaps the only one—where the Trump administration could find bipartisan support. "The Trump administration developed a kind of Pavlovian response to sanctioning Venezuelans," said a former administration official. "Politically there was a lot of upside and very little downside, and it was different from every other thing the administration was pursuing."

* * *

LILIAN TINTORI, THE wife of the jailed Venezuelan opposition leader, Leopoldo López, was in Washington the week that the El Aissami sanction dropped. Tintori had been traveling widely, advocating for the release of her husband and other political prisoners. Two days after the sanction announcement, Senator Marco Rubio accompanied Tintori to a meeting with Vice President Mike Pence at the White House.

It turned into much more. Pence greeted Tintori warmly and then led her and Rubio to the Oval Office, where he introduced her to Trump. It was the typical chaos of the early Trump White House: aides and hangers-on lurking around the Oval Office, frequent interruptions. Jared Kushner looked Tintori up on his smartphone and announced to the room: "She has more than a million followers on Twitter! This is amazing!"

Tintori told Trump about her husband, who had been sentenced to more than thirteen years in prison on spurious charges of inciting violence during demonstrations in 2014. Trump responded: "Wow! Thirteen years! That's a lot!" After a while, Trump asked if he should write about the meeting on Twitter and Rubio said yes. Trump, Tintori, Pence, and Rubio posed for a photograph in front of the portrait of Andrew Jackson in the Oval Office. Tintori is petite, with long blond hair. Standing between Trump and Pence, she wore a white lacy blouse with peasant sleeves. The president made a thumbs-up sign. Trump took the telephone and wrote that López should be freed immediately. He pressed send.

The tweet, with the Oval Office photograph, caused a sensation in Venezuela. It showed that Trump had taken a personal interest.

It also provided a glimpse of what would become a key alliance in shaping American policy toward Venezuela. Mike Pence and Marco Rubio had much in common. Pence was born a Catholic and then became an evangelical Christian. Rubio was a Catholic who became an evangelical and then returned to the Catholic Church. Both men had made their faith a centerpiece of their political persona.

Pence was Trump's bridge to the most conservative elements of the Republican Party and the religious right and a liaison to the influential Koch brothers,[1] who were important backers of both Pence and Rubio. Like other Republicans who had been Trump's opponents during the 2016 primary, Rubio had reason to resent Trump (who ridiculed him as Little Marco) and Pence appeared to make it his mission to heal any lingering wounds.

The Trump team had hardly walked into the White House when they began looking ahead to the next presidential election, in 2020, and they were keenly aware of the need to fortify their position in Florida, a pivotal state with twenty-nine electoral votes. The 2018 midterm elections in Florida loomed large in this scenario. Democratic senator Bill Nelson would be running for reelection and he was vulnerable. The governor's race was also going to be competitive. Success in Florida in the midterms would be crucial to influencing the outcome of the next presidential election in the state. And Rubio's support was important. Rubio, the son of Cuban immigrants, was a hard-liner on Cuba policy, and reversing the Obama rapprochement with Cuba was one of his priorities.

Increasingly, American policy toward Venezuela and Cuba was becoming intertwined. Cuba hard-liners believed that Chávez had saved the Castro regime by offering it a lifeline of cheap oil. That assistance continued under Maduro. Now, with both Chávez and Fidel Castro gone (Castro died the same month Trump was elected), an idea took hold that the road to regime change in Cuba went through Venezuela. The Cuban American lobby believed that if it could force a change of government in Venezuela, then Cuba's source of oil would dry up and Cuba would fall too. The same applied to Nicaragua, with its leftist Sandinista government, which also received generous support from Caracas. The result was a reverse domino theory. Instead of Southeast Asian governments falling like dominoes to communist revolutions, as theorists had posited in the 1950s, there would be a domino cascade in the Americas, where leftist governments would fall one after another. And the domino that would start the chain reaction was Venezuela.

This convergence of Cuba and Venezuela policy meant influence for Rubio. The Cuban American voting bloc in Florida wasn't as cohesive as it had once been, but it could be decisive in a close election. Trump didn't seem interested in the particulars of his policy; he simply wanted a policy that would make him look tough and would appeal to Hispanic voters motivated by Cuban American–style anticommunism. Over the next two years, Trump would name Cuban American allies of Rubio's to fill important positions at the National Security Council, the Organization of American States, and the Inter-American Development Bank.[2] Little Marco wasn't so little anymore.

After the Twitter photo was taken, Tintori thanked the president and said goodbye. Rubio stayed on to have dinner with Trump.

* * *

MEANWHILE, MCMASTER'S TEAM set about shaving off slices of salami.

In May the Treasury Department sanctioned eight members of the Venezuelan Supreme Court, including the chief justice, Maikel Moreno. In July, it sanctioned the head of the National Electoral Council and a dozen other prominent Chavista figures.

Then it sanctioned Maduro.

Ever since the opposition took over the National Assembly in 2016, Maduro had sought ways to block the assembly's ability to exercise its legislative powers. He had used the Supreme Court to invalidate virtually every piece of legislation approved by the assembly. Then in mid-2017, Maduro called an election to install a Constituent Assembly. In theory it was created to consider changes to the constitution, but it was designed to act as a parallel legislature with broad powers to neutralize the National Assembly even further.

The opposition boycotted the election. Officials at the NSC felt a strong response was needed. The day after the Constituent Assembly was elected with a full slate of Chavista candidates, McMaster held a news conference in Washington. "Maduro is not just a bad leader, he is now a dictator," McMaster said. The sanctions against Maduro were announced at the same time.

But Trump was growing impatient. While on vacation that August at his Bedminster, New Jersey, golf club, he told reporters that he was considering military action against Venezuela. "We have many options for Venezuela, including a possible military option, if necessary," he said.[3]

McMaster was never a good match for Trump, and neither was Secretary of State Rex Tillerson, a former chief executive of ExxonMobil who argued against oil sanctions targeting Venezuela. Now a shake-up was coming that would empower the most radical elements in Venezuela policy. In April 2018, the ultra-hawkish John Bolton became national security advisor and Pompeo became secretary of state.

"The Bolton era could be defined as 'throw the strategy out the window,'" Cutz said.

Cruz told me: "The sanctions that were remaining, instead of salami-slicing it, they just used a mallet." Cutz departed with McMaster, and Cruz left a few months later.

The new approach was maximum pressure.

In September 2018, Bolton hired Mauricio Claver-Carone, a hard-right Cuban American ideologue, to take Cruz's job as the head of Western Hemisphere Affairs at the NSC.

Claver-Carone was the director of a political action committee that donated money to anti-Castro, pro-embargo candidates like Marco Rubio. Although his portfolio at the security council covered the hemisphere, his interests seemed to focus primarily on Cuba and the ways that other countries in the region related to Cuba.[4]

Bolton also had a long history of hard-line views toward Cuba.

Increasingly, the U.S. stance toward Venezuela obeyed imperatives that had nothing to do with the well-being of Venezuelans. Instead, Venezuela policy became part of a Florida electoral strategy and a Cuba geopolitical strategy.

In the fall of 2018, as the U.S. midterm elections approached, Trump began to wield Venezuela as a cudgel against Democrats. In late October, he tweeted that Andrew Gillum, the Democrat who was running against the Republican Ron DeSantis for governor of Florida, would "make Florida the next Venezuela" if he won.

On November 1, Bolton went to Miami and gave a speech warning of a "troika of tyranny" in the hemisphere, vowing that the Trump administration would bring down the leftist governments in Venezuela, Cuba, and Nicaragua. It was an overtly political speech for a national security advisor days before a major election.

The Democrats made big gains in the midterms but not so much in Florida. By a narrow margin, DeSantis defeated Gillum for governor. In another close race, Rick Scott, a Republican, won the Senate seat. The victory in the governor's race was particularly important to giving Trump and the Republican Party the ability to shape the conditions of the 2020 presidential election in the state.

Trump's revamped Venezuela policy had so far failed to force any changes in Venezuela. But it had achieved one objective: victory in Florida.

Exodus

In December 2015, the Venezuelan opposition won an overwhelming majority in the National Assembly. It was a stunning repudiation of Maduro and Chavismo. The opposition parties had mostly set aside their traditional bickering and stayed united within the coalition that they called Democratic Unity.[1] For the first time in years, the opposition seemed to have the momentum.

The opposition alliance was always a difficult one. Political parties in Venezuela tend to be less about issues and more about the personality of the party leader. "They were created simply as platforms so that their leaders could at some point become president," said Chúo Torrealba, who headed the opposition coalition at the time of the 2015 legislative victory. Chúo was picked to run the coalition because he wasn't a politician; he was an activist who hosted TV and radio shows. As coalition leader, he tried to be an arbiter of the clashing egos.

The base of the coalition consisted of the four largest parties. Democratic Action was the old-line party that had once dominated Venezuelan politics and seemed to presume, arrogantly, that it still did. The parties Justice First and Popular Will were the upstarts, led by two rising stars, Henrique Capriles and Leopoldo López. Capriles was a state governor who had run strong campaigns for president against Chávez and Maduro. López, who had been in jail since the protests in 2014, was the Harvard-educated son of a wealthy family that traced its lineage back to one of Bolívar's sisters.[2] The rivalry between Capriles and López was intense. A fourth party, A New Era, played peacemaker or kingmaker among the other three.

Even before the new legislators took their seats in January 2016, a fight broke out over which party would hold the assembly presidency, similar to the speakership of the U.S. House of Representatives. Justice First had won the most seats, but the other parties, keen to keep a rival from gaining momentum and ascendancy, ganged up to give the leadership to Democratic Action instead. Bitterness lingered, and for several months the parties stopped meeting under the auspices of the unity coalition that had engineered the electoral victory. "The country didn't deserve that absurd level of irresponsibility," Chúo said. Momentum was lost.

At the same time, there was disagreement about next steps.

Some wanted to focus on the electoral route, organizing for upcoming governor elections and eventually, in 2018, the presidential race. Others were less patient—why wait, they said, when, with their newfound strength, they could simply force out Maduro now? The most radical advocated massive street demonstrations to drive him out. Others argued in favor of a recall referendum to remove Maduro at the ballot box. That was a risky course; the opposition would have to collect millions of signatures on a petition to place the referendum on the ballot and it would depend on the Maduro-controlled National Electoral Council to validate the signatures and schedule an election. Nevertheless, the recall emerged as a kind of lowest common denominator—it included an electoral component and it aimed at the quick removal of Maduro— and that was the option that the parties finally agreed to pursue.

Predictably, it was a failure. After months of creating obstacles to the petition drive, the electoral council simply suspended the entire process. Many Venezuelans saw the derailment of the recall referendum as the point when the Maduro government crossed the line into a full-blown dictatorship.

Throughout 2016 the government used the Supreme Court to strip the assembly of its powers. In 2017, Maduro held his controversial vote for the Constituent Assembly, another breaking point. The Constituent

Assembly acted as a parallel legislature, with unlimited powers to bully and negate the opposition-controlled National Assembly.

With presidential elections approaching in 2018, the opposition was in disarray. But there was still reason to hope. The "Son of Chávez" aura that had carried Maduro to the presidency in 2013 had faded. The economy was in free fall. A united opposition might still be able to pull off a victory.

The opposition and the government held negotiations to discuss conditions for the upcoming election. The government showed little interest in providing guarantees. At the same time, the opposition ripped itself apart. Popular Will, Leopoldo López's party, pulled out of the talks. On social media, radical factions lacerated the remaining negotiators. The mere willingness to speak with the government had become an act of betrayal.

To no one's surprise, the talks broke down.

Presidential elections were usually held in December. This time the government scheduled the election for May. The two most popular opposition figures, Capriles and López, were banned from running, and several parties and the unity coalition were barred from participating. Maduro and his advisors appeared to understand that the only way that he could win reelection was if no one ran against him. They seemed intent on baiting the opposition to pull out. And that's what it did. Labeling the planned election a farce, opposition leaders said that they would not field a candidate and called on voters to boycott the election.

Despite that, a former governor named Henri Falcón declared that he would take on Maduro. Falcón was a leftist who had split with Chávez years earlier and joined the opposition. Falcón argued that despite the difficulties, the opposition had a now-or-never chance to beat Maduro. But the other party leaders refused. At best, they said, Falcón would legitimize an inevitable Maduro victory; at worst, he was a Chavista stalking horse. In the end, voters heeded the call to abstain, turnout was extremely low, and Maduro won by a wide margin.

The United States, the European Union, and many Latin American countries condemned the election as undemocratic. Washington announced a new round of sanctions. But none of that could change the blunt fact of Maduro's reelection. Neither McMaster's escalatory road map nor Bolton's mallet-like use of sanctions had succeeded in pressuring Maduro to accept the conditions for free and fair elections. The policy had failed to meet its goal.

*　*　*

WHILE THE OPPOSITION squabbled and the government became more repressive, ordinary Venezuelans experienced a rising level of misery.

Many responded by fleeing the country.

Oil prices started to fall in the second half of 2014. That year, according to data compiled by Colombian immigration authorities, there were fewer than 24,000 Venezuelan citizens living in Colombia. In subsequent years, as conditions worsened, the number of Venezuelans who had abandoned their homes and took refuge in the neighboring country increased, gradually at first and then in surges. In 2016, Colombian authorities counted nearly 54,000 Venezuelans in the country. Maduro had partly shut down the border in mid-2015; seeking to deflect blame for the country's economic problems, he accused Colombian smugglers of causing product shortages and high prices in Venezuela.[3] When the border reopened in August 2016, the exodus started in earnest. In 2017, Colombian authorities estimated that there were more than 400,000 Venezuelans in the country. In earlier years the immigration numbers often reflected Venezuelans who had gone to Colombia to take a job or to live with family there; but now circumstances had changed. These migrants were refugees, fleeing chaos and hunger. In 2018, the number of Venezuelans in Colombia was almost 1.2 million. By 2019, it was nearly 1.8 million.[4]

The most compelling data of all speaks to the number of Venezuelans who entered Colombia and in their desperation kept going, crossing the country and moving on to Ecuador. Perhaps they hadn't found the work or sanctuary they'd hoped for in Colombia or perhaps they'd always meant to continue on, heading south across the continent. Many of these people traveled by bus or car. Thousands made the trip on foot, 900 miles or more. Eventually their journey took them along the Pan-American Highway to the main Colombia-Ecuador border crossing at the Rumichaca International Bridge. Nearly a hundred years earlier,

Bolívar and his liberating army had crossed into Ecuador at more or less the same spot.[5]

In 2012, Rumichaca was a sleepy outpost; on average, 263 Venezuelans a month crossed the bridge into Ecuador from Colombia, according to Ecuadorian immigration records. By the end of 2016, the number was almost 6,000 a month; by the end of 2017, it was 41,000 a month. The human flood reached its desperate peak in October 2018, when 80,262 Venezuelans crossed into Ecuador at Rumichaca.[6] Some of the refugees stayed in Ecuador. Many of them drifted on, to Peru, Chile, Bolivia and other destinations.[7]

These people were fleeing economic hardship. Inflation reached 130,060 percent in 2018; the Venezuelan economy contracted about 17 percent a year from 2016 through 2018.

But they were also fleeing because of political events.

The inflation rate tells you about the evaporation of the buying power of the money in a person's hand. The immigration numbers tell you about the evaporation of hope in a person's heart.

On three key occasions in those years Maduro trampled on the constitution and choked off space for political activity, crushing expectations that conditions might improve. Each of these coincided with a significant jump in refugees.

The exodus surged in late 2016, around the time that the electoral council blocked the recall referendum (the increase also coincided with the reopening of the border crossings with Colombia). It jumped again, roughly doubling in volume, in July 2017,[8] when Maduro created the Constituent Assembly. And it soared in 2018 as Maduro locked in his reelection. Leaving the country was the absolute form of voter abstention.

It was a human river, defying gravity, weaving up and over the Andes, a river of hunger and misery. By 2020, the United Nations estimated that 5.4 million Venezuelans had left their home country, almost a fifth of the pre-crisis population.[9]

The only country bleeding more refugees was Syria, which was in the midst of a civil war. The thread that linked both countries was Russia, which had become Maduro's staunchest ally. Russian support for Syrian president Bashar al-Assad and the Russian bombing of rebel areas in Syria's civil war had catalyzed the Syrian refugee crisis. The flood of Syrian refugees into Europe heightened political stress there and energized the right-wing nationalist parties that were friendly to Russia. In Venezuela, there was no need to drop bombs. All Russia had to do was stand by Maduro while he ravaged the economy and the White House piled on sanctions that multiplied the country's economic distress. Venezuela even bought weapons from Russia and gave it lucrative participation in its oil fields.

The pattern was the same: more chaos. The massive outflow of Venezuelan refugees destabilized neighboring countries and fed the same currents of nationalism as in Europe. There were riots or protests against Venezuelan refugees in Brazil, Colombia, Ecuador, Panama, Peru, and other countries. Colombia, the top U.S. ally in Latin America, had taken in more than 1.6 million Venezuelan refugees by 2020, an influx that far outpaced the country's ability to respond. All of this forced Washington to pay greater attention to affairs in Latin America, creating potential distractions from U.S. commitments elsewhere. Venezuela was at the center of a great power contest, and refugees and unrest were its new export commodities.

23

Swearing In

As 2018 wound down, the Venezuelan opposition considered how to respond to the challenge of a second Maduro term. There were a few points of agreement. The May election was illegitimate and so was Maduro's victory. Come January 10, when the new presidential term started, the National Assembly would be the last remnant of Venezuelan democracy.[1]

But what could be done?

Some pointed to Article 233 of the constitution, which said that if a president-elect was unable to take office, for reasons such as resignation or death, then the head of the National Assembly would become a caretaker president until a new election was held, within thirty days. This wasn't a perfect fit, partly because the opposition insisted that there was no president-elect at all. But, to some, it seemed to be the closest the constitution came to providing a remedy.

Others proposed that the assembly, as a body, should lead a transition back to democracy. The constitution said that any actions taken by someone who had usurped power were invalid, and that it was the duty of all Venezuelans to reestablish the constitutional order if it should be broken. They reasoned that if Maduro was declared a usurper, that could justify the assembly's exercising power in his place.

Yet it was like arguing about how many angels could dance on the head of a pin. No matter what they did, they'd still be standing outside the presidential palace while Maduro was on the inside.

And all of this was tied up with the familiar tensions within the opposition. The parties had agreed to a power-sharing arrangement in which they rotated the assembly leadership every year, and, in January 2019, it would be the turn of Leopoldo López's Popular Will party to hold the legislature's top post. López was distrusted by other opposition leaders, who saw him as a radical and a hothead who put his own interests above those of the coalition. Although López was under house arrest,[2] he still controlled his party and was determined to seize the opportunity. He assured his peers that this time he would be a team player.

López and his lieutenants studied their options. Maduro was deeply unpopular. All over the map, spontaneous protests were breaking out. The opposition had the street—it could call a march and people would turn out. And it had international support. More than forty countries had condemned Maduro's bogus reelection.

But these things were not enough to push Maduro from power.

The group around López concluded that the military was the key. As 2018 drew to a close, their discussions kept returning to what they called *el quiebre militar*, a break in the military.[3] They knew that there was discontent in the armed forces. A soldier's wages were just as worthless as everyone else's. Top officers sanctioned by the United States might be persuaded to come over in exchange for having the sanctions lifted. Mid-level officers and the rank and file might simply be waiting for the right opportunity to switch sides.

There was precedent. In 1958 a military coup attempt sparked a popular uprising that led to the removal of the dictator Pérez Jiménez and cleared the way for electoral democracy.

Bólivar was said to have described the idiosyncrasies of the far-flung regions that made up his Gran Colombia this way: Bogotá was a university, Quito a convent, and Caracas a barracks. Venezuelans respected the uniform; they swooned for a general on a horse. Venezuelan soldiers had liberated half of South America. Now they would liberate Venezuela from Maduro. All that was needed was a spark.

Another urgent question was which of the Popular Will legislators would take the role of assembly president. The party's ranks were depleted. López was under house arrest. His top lieutenant had gone into exile, another had sought asylum in the Chilean ambassador's residence, and still another had been expelled from the party after falling out with López. Next in line was a skinny, long-limbed, thirty-five-year-old legislator, largely unknown outside his party, named Juan Guaidó.

Guaidó grew up in a middle-class family. His father was a pilot, his mother a teacher. In college he studied engineering, became a student leader, and took part in protests against the Chávez government. When López started his party in 2009, Guaidó was among the founding members. In 2015, Guaidó was elected to the National Assembly. For three years he'd managed not to draw much attention to himself.

The early election in 2018 had given the opposition time to come up with a plan for how it was going to respond to the challenge of a new presidential term for Maduro. It had also given it abundant opportunity to argue. When the new year arrived, it was still arguing.

On January 5, the new session of the assembly began, and Guaidó was formally installed as assembly president. In his acceptance speech, Guaidó promised that the assembly would "create an organ of transition to restore constitutional order." Behind the scenes, opposition leaders still weren't sure what that meant.

* * *

THE OPPOSITION'S ALLIES in Washington were watching it all unfold with concern.

The year before, Keith Mines, the State Department's director of Andean affairs, had designed a Venezuela strategy that he had summed up on a PowerPoint slide. It included pressure tactics, like sanctions, support for the opposition, and what he called off-ramps for Maduro and other top government figures, to give them a way out if they chose to take it. That was all on the left side of the slide. On the right side, he put transitional government, economic recovery, and elections. In between there was a gap, which Mines called "the canyon." "A bit of a void," Mines told me. "Something happens. And that something was undefined because we couldn't define it."

Mines expressed his frustration in notes that he wrote on January 2, 2019. "We are kind of stuck," he wrote. "I haven't heard a good new idea lately." That changed a few days later when López and a small circle of allies began reaching out to State Department officials with a novel proposal: now that Guaidó was the leader of the National Assembly, he could invoke Article 233 of the constitution to become interim president. The United States and other countries would recognize Guaidó as Venezuela's legitimate head of state. That would galvanize the opposition and supercharge the effort to remove Maduro.

Secretary of State Pompeo warmed to the idea, but others were skeptical.

"There was a fierce debate in the American government whether this was a good idea or not," Mines said. "And there was a number of us that thought it was not a good idea because we just didn't think it was going to work and we thought it was going to get Guaidó killed. It was as simple as that."

On January 10, Maduro was sworn in for a second term. The same day Pompeo called Guaidó and assured him that he had the support of the U.S. government.[4]

The next two weeks were marked by rising anticipation and confusion. Guaidó gave a speech on January 11, in which he mentioned Article 233 of the constitution and talked about assuming the obligations of the presidency, but it came out garbled. He seemed unsure of himself and it was impossible to know what he meant. On January 15, the assembly passed a measure declaring that Maduro was a usurper who was illegally occupying the presidency. The measure laid out the assembly's vision for reestablishing the constitutional order and reflected the mutual distrust within the opposition. There was no mention of Guaidó becoming interim president. Instead it asserted that there was "no express solution in the constitution" for the country's "current situation" and called for the assembly to take on the powers of the executive branch.[5]

While all this was going on, López and Guaidó were performing a balancing act. Even as they worked with the State Department to lay the groundwork for Guaidó to declare himself interim president, they concealed their intention from others in the opposition who they feared would seek to block the maneuver. Guaidó's public statements were vague, but they hinted at greater possibilities. López later told me that the goal was to generate grassroots pressure for Guaidó to be sworn in as president, which would overwhelm the doubters.

Meanwhile, in Washington, Mines sent a memo to his bosses on January 20, titled "Guaidó Presidential Declaration Decision." Summarizing discussions that had been going on inside the State Department, Mines laid out various scenarios for Guaidó to declare himself president at a public event in Caracas on January 23, the anniversary of the start of Venezuelan democracy. Mines's evaluation revealed the intense expectations that had been generated within the U.S. government—and it was wildly optimistic. "This alone," Mines wrote, "could have the impact of causing the regime to crumble in the face of widespread and overwhelming public support." Mines speculated that it might take several weeks to negotiate the details of an exit for Maduro and other top figures. "The end is closer," he concluded, "but this will be the tricky part."

On January 22, John Bolton, the national security advisor, met with cabinet officials to discuss Guaidó's swearing in and the U.S. response; later in the day, Marco Rubio and other members of Congress met at the White House with Trump, who said that he intended to recognize Guaidó as president, according to Bolton's memoir *The Room Where It Happened*. That evening, Vice President Pence called Guaidó to assure him of U.S. support. Bolton, who sat with Pence during the call, wrote that Guaidó pledged to "work hand in hand with us, given the risks we were taking." It was a strange observation: it would seem that Guaidó was the one taking all the risks. When the call ended, Bolton told Pence, "This is a historic moment."[6]

At that point, it's likely that more people in Washington than in Venezuela knew what was going to happen the next day in Caracas.

* * *

AT ABOUT SEVEN A.M. on January 23, in a house in an upscale Caracas neighborhood on the skirts of the Ávila mountain, Guaidó met with Stalin González,[7] an opposition legislator who was the second vice president of the National Assembly.[8] González was about Guaidó's age and a member of the party called A New Era. Guaidó told González that he planned to formally swear himself in as the interim and legitimate president of Venezuela at the opposition rally that was to take place later that day.

González was stunned. This was not what the parties had agreed on. And it was being done without coordination or preparation. Guaidó reassured him: he'd talked to Mike Pence and the Americans were on board. After Guaidó and González talked, they joined several other leaders from the main opposition parties who had arrived to discuss the day's program. In the meeting, Guaidó said nothing about the swearing in.

A few hours later, Guaidó strode onto an outdoor stage, in front of a sea of supporters. There are countless videos of the event posted online. Wearing an open-collared white shirt and a blue sport coat, Guaidó stands behind a lucite podium with the national seal on it. To his left is Stalin González. To his right is Edgar Zambrano, the assembly's first vice president, who was a member of the Democratic Action party. Guaidó is holding up his right hand as he takes the oath of office. All around him, people are raising their right hands to match Guaidó. "I swear," Guaidó shouts as people cheer, "to formally assume the competencies of the national executive as the interim president of Venezuela." The atmosphere is celebratory, giddy. Everyone has their hand raised except González and Zambrano. González has his arms down, hands at his sides. Zambrano's hands are clasped in front of him. They both have troubled looks on their faces. Everyone else is smiling.

Just off camera, Enrique Márquez, an assembly member from Zulia state, stood with a group of other lawmakers. They were taken by surprise and Márquez quickly left the stage. Why hadn't the swearing in been discussed and approved in advance by the full assembly? Why was it done on the fly, in the street instead of in the legislature? "It showed a lack of respect," Márquez said, "to take on that role without the support of the National Assembly."

Within minutes of Guaidó's swearing himself in, the White House issued a statement from President Trump, recognizing Guaidó as interim president. President Iván Duque of Colombia, President Jair Bolsonaro of Brazil, and Chrystia Freeland, the Canadian foreign minister, were at the World Economic Forum in Davos, Switzerland; they called an impromptu news conference and, together, recognized Guaidó as Venezuela's president.

Canada, Colombia, and Brazil were part of a group of countries that had been working for more than a year to seek a solution to the stalemate in Venezuela. Called the Lima Group (because it first met in that city), they had condemned Maduro's slide to authoritarianism and advocated for democratic change. It was hoped that, by leaving the United States out of the group, more progress could be made, without the irritant of the ill will between Washington and Caracas. Given that history, it might have made sense for the Lima Group countries to be the first to recognize Guaidó.

But Washington wanted to be first. By doing so it stamped a *Made in America* label on the day's events.

"That's where the U.S. jumps the gun," said Pedro Mario Burelli, a Venezuelan émigré who had been in frequent contact with American officials on behalf of López and Guaidó. "Washington appeared to take ownership of something that had originated with the Venezuelan opposition. Where I got really angry is, why, if it was not your strategy, do you then try to make it seem like it was your strategy? The fucking arrogance." That was the start, Burelli said, of the White House "running this in a very superficial way, without an understanding of Venezuela."

A South American diplomat told me that Washington's insistence on going first put its Latin American allies in a bind, exposing them to criticism that they were doing the White House's bidding when they recognized Guaidó. The diplomat said: "People are going to say that they led us by the nose."[9]

Guaidó would later assert that he was obligated by Article 233 to become interim president. "This is why the oath I took on Jan. 23 cannot be considered a 'self-proclamation,'" Guaidó wrote in an op-ed in *The New York Times* a week later. "It was not of my own accord that I assumed the function of president that day, but in adherence to the Constitution." But that argument failed to acknowledge the intense debate within the opposition about what to do and that there were other options under consideration. Article 233 gave it the look of legitimacy, but Guaidó's swearing in was a political decision.[10]

* * *

MADURO RESPONDED BY breaking diplomatic relations with the United States, giving its diplomats seventy-two hours to leave the country.

"I am the only president of Venezuela," Maduro said. "We do not want to return to the twentieth century of gringo interventions and coups d'état."

The United States said that since Maduro wasn't president, he couldn't order its diplomats to leave. (The U.S. had made no preparations to safeguard embassy personnel—a noteworthy omission, given Pompeo's history. As a member of the House of Representatives, he had been the driving force behind a lengthy investigation into security lapses at the U.S. diplomatic mission and a CIA compound in Benghazi, Libya, where four Americans were killed when Hillary Clinton was secretary of state.)

For several weeks the United States tried to carry on the pretense that it had diplomatic relations with a Guaidó government that didn't exist in anything but name, while it mostly ignored the orders of a Maduro government that could have taken retaliatory measures against its personnel. Jimmy Story, the U.S. chargé d'affaires, took to sleeping on a cot in his embassy office. In early March, Venezuela's foreign minister, Jorge Arreaza, informed Story that he had a duty to warn him that his life was in danger. Arreaza said that fringe elements in the opposition planned to assassinate Story so that his death would be blamed on the Maduro government and provoke a U.S. invasion. U.S. officials were skeptical of the details but could not ignore the warning. On March 11, the U.S. announced that it was shuttering the embassy in Caracas.

Mines said that the move was necessary for security reasons but that it made the task more difficult. "You've lost your eyes and ears and you've lost the on-the-ground support for the opposition," he said.

Juan Cruz, the former CIA agent and security council staffer, had been watching events unfold with skepticism. When his Venezuelan opposition friends had told him that the unknown Guaidó was going to declare himself president, he said to himself, *Jesus Christ, you can't fucking drive and you want to fly a plane? It's, like, good luck with that shit.* He told them it was a bad idea. "I said, 'I don't like it. I think it's a Hail Mary.' And I said, 'To me, it's desperation. It reeks of desperation, and if you fail, you're going to fail big.'"

Avalanche

The days after Guaidó's swearing in were heady ones. The streets filled with people, by the tens of thousands, calling on Maduro to leave. In the poor barrios and in the rich enclaves, there was a sense that something big had happened, that the country was balanced on a pin. Maduro fulminated in the presidential palace, but so much noise seemed to be a sign of weakness rather than strength. Let him go on—now we've got our own president, we've got Juan Guaidó.

Guaidó's greatest assets were his anonymity and his youth. He wasn't associated with the old pre-Chávez parties—Democratic Action and COPEI—or even very much, in the public mind, with the new ones. It's true that he belonged to Leopoldo López's party, Popular Will, but López was out of sight, under house arrest. Guaidó was handsome and full of energy; he would stride about, a little goofy, with long legs and gangly arms and a big grin. Guaidó stood for one thing only: getting rid of Maduro. Before long, more than fifty countries had recognized Guaidó as the legitimate president of Venezuela.

Some people warned against raising expectations too high, but they were drowned out by the many who said: We've waited long enough! Now is the time!

In a news conference two days after the swearing in, Guaidó said that Venezuela had woken up from a nightmare. He told the millions of Venezuelans who had fled the country: "Get ready to come home very soon!" A couple of days after that, Guaidó went online with a live video feed. Wearing a dark gray suit and a dark tie, he sat at a desk, with the Venezuelan flag to his right and a bust of Bolívar behind him to his left—just as Chávez used to do. "We're doing great!" he said. "We've recovered our sense of hope. Our country has recovered its ability to dream. We're doing great! We've taken giant steps forward." On the desk in front of him was a blotter and two red and gold volumes of the *Gran enciclopedia de Venezuela*. "Very soon we're going to achieve freedom for Venezuela!" "*Vamos bien*," he said. "We're doing great!" It became his tag line: *Vamos bien!*

* * *

GUAIDÓ'S PUBLIC SWEARING in had come as a surprise to other leaders in the opposition, but once he started to take on the look of a winner, they were all in. They didn't want to be left behind. And yet there wasn't much that you could call a strategy or a plan. There was just the hope that the military would see which way the wind was blowing and throw its support to Guaidó, that it was merely waiting for the right moment to switch sides.

Guaidó had called on Maduro to allow outside groups to bring in shipments of food and medicine. It was a tactic that emphasized the privations of Venezuelans and the intransigence of the Maduro government, which insisted that the country's problems were caused by the United States and that, in any case, Venezuela could fend for itself.

Guaidó was also eager to find a way to show that his interim government could actually do some governing—that there was more to it than an improvised stage set of a desk with a bust of the Liberator and two volumes of the encyclopedia.

To bring all those pieces together, Guaidó declared that his government would act on its own to bring humanitarian aid to the Venezuelan people. He announced that the United States and other countries were donating tons of food and medical supplies that his government would bring into the country on February 23, the one-month anniversary of his new mandate. And that bold act, it was hoped, would prompt the military to break ranks. It would force officers and soldiers to choose:

their stomachs, their families, and their country—or the dictator? The choice seemed obvious.

* * *

As THE STAGING area for what he promised would be an "avalanche" of aid, Guaidó picked Cúcuta, a shapeless Colombian border city that sits across the Táchira River from Venezuela. Several bridges connect the two countries there, and, to counter Guaidó, Maduro had them blockaded with shipping containers and other barriers and had stationed troops and police on the Venezuelan side.

On the Colombian side, the shipments started to arrive in Cúcuta: crates of corn flour, powdered milk, and surgical gloves and masks. The Colombian government provided a customs warehouse to store it in. Young Venezuelans sent by Guaidó showed up to take charge of the aid and prepare for the big day.

They looked at the barricaded bridges and discussed how to move the aid across. They talked about having a crowd of people surround each aid truck as it crossed into Venezuela, where more supporters would be waiting. They talked of daring the army to fire on unarmed marchers escorting shipments of food. Or they envisioned a joyous scene where soldiers dropped their guns and embraced protesters, and the aid flowed through in a great convoy that stretched all the way to Caracas. Guaidó predicted that 600,000 Venezuelans would show up to carry the supplies across the border.

"There was a lot of irrational exuberance," said a U.S. official who was in Cúcuta. "There was a real sense that it was going to be this before-and-after moment. Just to put it in the baldest terms, it's that these tractor trailers were going to get going and they were going to burst through the barricade and they were going to drive to Caracas, and it was going to be a big party, everything was going to work out, it's going to work out great. What there *wasn't* was a lot of careful planning and thinking."

Five days before the aid avalanche was set to take place, President Trump gave a speech in Miami. He warned Venezuelan soldiers not to block the aid. If they continued to support Maduro, he said, "You will

find no safe harbor, no easy exit, no way out. You will lose everything."
He predicted a rapid victory. "We seek a peaceful transition of power,
but all options are open."

The United States flew enormous battleship-gray military cargo planes
loaded with food into the small Cucutá airport.[1] The mixing of military
might and humanitarian aid was intentional and it made some observers uneasy. There were established rules for distributing humanitarian
aid. It was meant to be neutral—help for people who needed it, often
desperately—delivered without political content. This was different. It
was aid as spearhead, intimidation.

The night before the aid was supposed to move, the billionaire Richard Branson hosted a charity concert in Cúcuta, called Venezuela Aid
Live. Gritty Cúcuta had never seen so much star power: the Colombian
singer Juanes, the Mexican rock band Maná, the Venezuelan actress Patricia Velásquez, who starred in the *Mummy* movies. Colombian president Iván Duque was in town, along with the presidents of Chile and
Paraguay, Sebastián Piñera and Mario Abdo. Maduro had issued an order barring Guaidó from leaving the country, but Guaidó snuck across
the border and appeared on the concert stage to a joyous reception. The
other presidents stood with him—four presidents together, from Chile,
Colombia, Paraguay, and Venezuela. A clear message: Guaidó was a
president too. They waved to the crowd.

* * *

THE NEXT DAY hope was replaced by violence and chaos. The bridges
were sealed and nothing crossed over. Venezuelan soldiers fired tear gas
as demonstrators coming from the Colombian side tried to cross the
bridges. The demonstrators threw rocks and Molotov cocktails at the
soldiers. It was the kind of pointless, seesaw street battle that had been
going on for years between protesters and security forces in Caracas
and other Venezuelan cities. Explosions and fury. A standoff. Never any
change.

There was no mass defection of soldiers. Some waded across the river,
in ones or twos, to surrender on the Colombian side. Guaidó had called
on the armed forces to back him up, to become the force that carried

him to the presidential palace. What turned up was a few dozen mostly low-ranking soldiers who handed their weapons over to their Colombian counterparts in the hope of receiving something to eat. At the end of the day the Colombian government said that about sixty had come across.[2]

Near the aid warehouse, Guaidó, in a white shirt, stood on the step of a tractor-trailer truck and posed for news photographers and cameramen. It was as close as he came to the action. His Colombian hosts ordered him not to go onto the bridges where violent confrontations were taking place. They considered it too dangerous.[3]

Meanwhile, on a two-lane bridge connecting Cúcuta to the Venezuelan town of Ureña, four tractor-trailer rigs crept forward, hauling boxes of food. The trucks stopped near the far side of the bridge, blocked by a line of Venezuelan soldiers. Here again was the familiar surge of anger, followed by rocks and tear gas. And then one of the trucks caught fire, apparently touched off by an errant Molotov cocktail. Black smoke billowed into a blue sky with cotton-ball clouds.

The standoff at Cúcuta reminded Tom Shannon, the retired diplomat, of the ancient battle of Thermopylae, where a small Spartan force held off the Persian army by making its stand in a narrow mountain pass that gave it a tactical advantage. "All the regime has to do is secure the bridge," Shannon said. "And how easy is that?"

* * *

THERE WAS NO avalanche of aid, just violence and disarray.

"It was an abortion," said Juan Cruz. And it set the tone for what was to come. "You got a snapshot of the promises not kept and unable to be kept by the opposition. The overselling, the underdelivering."

When we spoke about Cúcuta, Keith Mines sighed heavily. He said that it was the first of "a whole series of these, what I call the forty-eight-hour operations, to try to swing the whole country in a single weekend." Another sigh. "And really not comprehensively designed."

There had been no break in the military. There had been no groundswell of hundreds of thousands of supporters. And now Guaidó shifted gears. "We must have all options open to achieve the liberation of our country," he tweeted, echoing Trump's talk of a military option.[4]

Julio Borges, one of Guaidó's senior diplomatic envoys, went further. "We will demand an escalation in diplomatic pressure and in the use of force against the dictatorship of Nicolás Maduro," he tweeted from Cúcuta.

But Guaidó's international allies not named Donald Trump acted fast to quash any thought of military action. Peru's assistant foreign minister, Hugo de Zela Martínez, said that the use of force was "unacceptable." Canada's foreign minister, Chrystia Freeland, said that Venezuela's transition must come "without the use of force."[5]

Overnight, the opposition went from the euphoria of the benefit concert—when it seemed that the whole world was lined up behind the cause of a free Venezuela—to the deflation of having nothing to show for its efforts. Even the concert fell short. Branson projected it would bring in $100 million in donations. Venezuela Aid Live raised $2 million.[6]

Bubble

Armando Briquet, a Venezuelan political consultant, told me that Guaidó had three "theses" of how to achieve the goal of removing Maduro. One was a military coup. Another was what Venezuelans call a social explosion—a massive popular upwelling of protest or rioting. The third was foreign intervention.

The question became how to light the fuse.

One way was the bold stroke. Guaidó and his advisors had hoped that the mere swearing in of Guaidó and the rush of countries to recognize him would be enough to spark a popular revolt or a rupture in the military.

Next they tried the humanitarian aid push in Cúcuta.

There were more bold strokes in the offing, but there was another card that they were playing at the same time. That card was sanctions.

The objective of the broad economic sanctions increasingly deployed by the Trump White House was to starve the Maduro government of the cash that kept it going. The thinking was that the government survived only because it could continue to dole out graft to top-level Chavistas and military officers. And if the graft dried up, then the people that propped up the government, especially in the military, would stop doing so.

The first of the broader sanctions was enacted in August 2017. This was a few weeks after the election of the Constituent Assembly, McMaster's declaration that Maduro was a dictator, and Trump's musing, at his New Jersey golf course, about a military option for Venezuela. The sanction barred most financing to PDVSA and the Venezuelan government. While the order applied only to U.S. residents and companies and transactions carried out in the United States, because of the global dominance of the U.S. financial system, its effects were much broader. It was followed by a warning by the Treasury Department of a high risk of corruption and money laundering associated with Venezuelan government agencies and corporations like PDVSA. Banks were also concerned that if they lent money to the Maduro government, the debt might not be honored if the opposition eventually came to power. The economist Francisco Rodríguez said that those things combined to make Venezuela toxic in financial markets. Even if a bank was willing to lend money—why take on the headaches and the risk?

And that had a profound effect on the Venezuelan economy. It kept Venezuela from renegotiating its foreign debt and prevented foreign oil companies from financing joint ventures with PDVSA.

Rodríguez believed that the financial sanctions in August 2017 had a particularly strong impact on PDVSA. Venezuelan oil production—the amount of oil pumped from the ground—had begun to fall in 2016, but it went off a cliff the following year, after the financial sanctions went into effect.[1]

There were many reasons for oil production to decline. There were years of corruption, mismanagement, and underinvestment. At the end of 2014, Maduro put his wife's nephew in charge of PDVSA's finances, and in late 2017 he installed a former general with no experience in the oil industry as head of the company. Under the guise of a corruption investigation that had the appearance of a political housecleaning, the government jailed dozens of PDVSA executives.[2] Once the economic crisis started pushing Venezuelans to leave the country, the exodus included many experienced PDVSA managers and workers. The theft of equipment also affected operations—thieves even stole the motors from the pumps on oil wells. Rodríguez considered that, coming on top of those factors, the loss of access to financing due to sanctions was decisive.

Finally, in January 2019, after Guaidó's swearing in as interim president, the White House enacted the sanction that barred U.S. companies from doing business with PDVSA, effectively banning Venezuelan oil sales to the United States. This was the sanction that the National Security Council under McMaster had placed at the far end of the road map, to be used only if it was clear that the Maduro government was about to crumble. In his memoir, Bolton said he pushed for the oil embargo by arguing: "Why don't we go for a win here?"[3] But there was no win. Maduro endured. And the United States continued to add more sanctions.

A strange debate was going on as this occurred. On the one hand, Rodríguez and a few other economists argued that the sanctions had an adverse impact on PDVSA's ability to produce and sell oil—and therefore on the Venezuelan economy and the living standards of ordinary Venezuelans. On the other side were economists and politicians who argued that Maduro's policy mistakes should be seen almost exclusively as the cause of the drop in oil production, the country's economic collapse, and therefore the suffering of Venezuelans. The sanctions, they said, were needed to put pressure on the Maduro regime and take away the resources that it used to oppress the Venezuelan people.[4]

Paradoxically, some of the same people who had been calling for broad economic sanctions now argued that they had only a collateral effect on the overall economy. They wanted to believe that the negative effects of the sanctions were felt primarily by Maduro and his inner circle.

It seemed an absurd, and typically Venezuelan, dispute. Yes, there were many factors contributing to the decline in oil production. Yes, Maduro, more than anyone else, was responsible for disastrous economic policies that had created pain and suffering. And yes, sanctions were a factor too.

The Trump administration was less squeamish. When Bolton announced the sanction on oil sales, he estimated that it would result in more than $11 billion in lost export revenues over the next year.[5] That was almost the full value of goods imported by Venezuela in 2018. In other words, the sanctions would mean a significant drop in imports, more empty shelves, and higher prices. That's what the sanctions were designed to do—to wipe out a large portion of the country's economic activity.

Guaidó applauded the U.S. sanctions, and he urged the European Union to enact its own. "We need additional sanctions from the E.U.," he told the German newspaper *Bild*. "More and more people are being murdered. It is also clear that the regime is absolutely corrupt."[6]

In general, the sanctions made exceptions for the sale of food and medicine to Venezuela. But most companies were leery of any transaction with the country, lest they fall afoul of American law. The result was that Venezuela remained largely cut off.

There was something deeply disingenuous and cynical in the debate around sanctions.

Other than a foreign invasion, Guaidó was proposing two methods for removing Maduro: military revolt or popular unrest that would be so explosive that it would force Maduro to step down or force the military to remove him. And one way to provoke either of those things was to increase the pressure on ordinary people. At what point would people become so miserable—lacking food, medicine, hope—that they would rise up? At what point would military officers say, *The country can't take it anymore and neither can we?*

Fernando Cutz, the former McMaster aide, told me that the security council had brought together a team of government economists to evaluate the impact of proposed sanctions. Those who designed the sanctions had no illusion that their negative effects would be felt only in the upper levels of the regime. "A full-blown oil embargo would have been very, very consequential to Maduro and to the government of Venezuela and, potentially, would be the final straw for them," Cutz said. "But everybody also thought it was going to be very devastating from a humanitarian perspective."

Sanctions also had a political dimension. Maduro had been saying for years that the country was under attack in an economic war waged by the United States. Playing the victim was always a Chavista fallback—the nation's woes were always someone else's fault. After twenty years in government, Chavismo still tried to pretend that it was the valiant outsider fighting the evil establishment. In this case, it was also a way of deflecting responsibility for bad economic policy. And it was a fantasy—until Trump made it a reality. What are sanctions if not economic warfare? Every day, on television, radio, social media, the government hammered away at the message: Venezuela was the victim of an economic war by the United States.

In 2019, I talked with a man named Hermes Albino, who worked at an arepa stall in the market in Petare, the Caracas slum. The stall used to sell hundreds of arepas a day. Now it sold none. Customers couldn't afford to buy arepas anymore. Instead, the stall sold empanadas, which were cheaper, but not very many of those.

On the wall was a big sign, with the different arepa fillings the store used to sell, painted in red block letters. Shredded Beef. Grilled Tuna. Cooked Tuna. Scrambled Eggs. Chicken. Chorizo. Chicharrón. Fish Filet. Ham. Mixed Grill. Reina Pepiada (a kind of chicken salad). Octopus and Clams Vinaigrette. Surf and Turf. Ham Salad. Pot Roast. Shark. Squid Vinaigrette. Shrimp Vinaigrette. Garlic Shrimp. Smoked Ham. Ham and Cheese. Liver. Grilled Pork Shoulder. Smoked Pork Shoulder. Chicken Gizzard. Quail Eggs. There were three different kinds of cheese to choose from, and you could also order a *mixta*— two or more fillings in one arepa. All that and quail eggs in a tiny shop in a public market in one of the poorest sections of Caracas in one of the biggest slums on the continent.

"Anyone who's conscious can see that things aren't good, but neither are *they* making things good," Hermes said. "I'm talking about the Americans. They're putting on all these sanctions. And who are they putting the sanctions on? The people. Because the big shots, Maduro and Guaidó, they've got food to eat. So who do the sanctions hurt? The people. Us, the people. Prices are high, we can't get food, that's the situation."

Hermes had voted for Chávez and then Maduro, but now he said that he was fed up with politicians on all sides. "I'm never going to vote again," he said, "not for any of them."

* * *

Sanctions were a regular source of tension between the State and Treasury Departments, on the one hand, and Bolton's National Security Council, on the other.

Kimberly Breier, the assistant secretary of state for Western Hemisphere Affairs, was at the meeting of the National Security Council Principals Committee in the White House Situation Room, where Bolton pressed for the oil sanction. "He pounds the table and says, 'Let's go for the win,' as if using the ultimate sanction . . . was somehow going to perpetuate the outcome that he wanted, which was a path towards an election and a transition in Venezuela," Breier said. "And there was absolutely no evidence to support that theory, and he and Mauricio [Claver-Carone] set the expectation that somehow this was magically going to occur."

In an email to senior State Department officials, Breier outlined her misgivings. Would the sanction put Guaidó in greater danger? Would Maduro target U.S. embassy personnel or seize the assets of American oil companies? How would the military react? Instead of getting officers to flip, would the sanction unite them behind Maduro? What would the humanitarian impact be and how would the loss of oil income affect food imports? What was the diplomatic strategy of the U.S. to dissuade other countries from buying Venezuelan crude? None of these questions had been adequately addressed. In another email she wrote: "From tomorrow on, if we do this, this is improvisation."

The decision to back Guaidó "was the right thing to do at the time," Breier said. "The mistakes may have been in the subsequent execution of everything that went around it." The PDVSA sanction, she said, was "the key error." From that point forward, you were following the Bolton-Mauricio philosophy of 'Let's hit him with everything we've got as quickly as we can.' And I would always go back and say, 'Great, you want to sanction military official *xyz*? What's the plan? Why would we sanction that official and not the other one? How does that fracture the military? How does that help us? What's the strategy?' And there was no answer. They had no answer."

Keith Mines described the Bolton approach as: "Just crash the economy and they'll somehow cry uncle." He called it "reverse rapture theology, where somehow you put pressure on the bad guys and they just leave and leave the good guys in charge. It was so much more complicated than that. It still is, and that was just never going to work."

Career State Department officials like Breier and Mines argued for thinking about sanctions within a broader context of diplomacy and negotiations. "I don't think anybody really caught that," Mines said. "I think that was just a little too sophisticated, if you will, for this administration. This is a blunt instrument kind of administration. So I think they just got very enamored, very caught up very early on the notion of sanctions, and that became really the one piece of the policy."

Less than a month after the oil sales ban, the White House announced sanctions against four Venezuelan governors.[7] Among them was Rafael Lacava, who had helped arrange the release of Joshua Holt less than a year earlier. "That was really spiteful," said Caleb McCarry, the Senate aide who negotiated the release. "My assumption was that the purpose of sanctioning Lacava was to send a signal: Don't think that you can get any kind of deal, even giving prisoners up, because we're coming for your head."

* * *

NINE DAYS AFTER Cúcuta, on March 4, Guaidó flew back to Caracas—defying Maduro to arrest him. It was a brave act. He walked off a plane, into the airport. The government did nothing and Guaidó was received by cheering supporters.

On March 7, the lights went out.

Guaidó denounced the years of government ineptitude that led up to the blackout. He tweeted that the end of the dictatorship would bring the light. But there wasn't much else that he could do. He was president in name only. He couldn't fire the head of Corpoelec or dispatch engineers to turn the power back on.

Instead, he tried to look presidential. He appointed ambassadors. He floated a plan to allow private investment in the oil sector. He tweeted. And he held rallies around the country. *Vamos bien! We're doing great!* News stories started to ask whether Guaidó was losing momentum, whether Maduro would simply outlast him. Guaidó declared that his movement was entering a new phase, then the final phase, then the definitive phase. The lights went out, came on, went out again. But Guaidó was on the sidelines, a president without a government.

* * *

ON APRIL 30 AT 5:46 A.M. Guaidó posted a video to Twitter. In the video he was standing outside, in the predawn darkness. He wore a dark suit, a white shirt, and no tie. Behind him was a group of uniformed soldiers armed with assault weapons. That was unusual enough, but what really grabbed your attention was that Leopoldo López was standing behind Guaidó. López had not been seen in public since he'd been sent to prison in 2014. Eventually he'd been moved to house arrest. But Leopoldo López at liberty in the streets of Caracas was news.

Once you got over the shock of seeing López out and about, you could listen to Guaidó's words. He seemed to be saying that the armed forces had turned on Maduro and that he'd taken control of a military air base at the center of Caracas called La Carlota. "Today as interim president of Venezuela, as the legitimate commander in chief of the armed forces, I call on all soldiers, all of the men and women, the military family, to join with us in this endeavor," Guaidó said in the video. "The definitive end of the usurpation starts today!"

That seemed momentous, but it was hard to follow the thread. This was often the case with Guaidó. He was an elliptical speaker, tripping over words and diving into tangents, and when he was done, you'd often scratch your head and wonder what he'd just said. "Be alert for the calls, for the call," Guaidó said in the video. "Already many soldiers have joined us. Our military family that has already taken the step. Everyone who is listening to us, everyone who will listen to us in the coming minutes: Now is the time. The time is now. The time not just to be calm and collected, at this time, courageous and collected, so that a calm comes to Venezuela. God bless you. We will keep moving forward to achieve freedom and democracy for Venezuela."

Word spread, and hundreds of excited Guaidó supporters started heading to the air base. But when they got there, they discovered that Guaidó hadn't taken over the air base at all. He hadn't even tried. Instead, he was *outside* the air base, on a highway overpass that overlooked the base. There was confused milling about as people congregated on the overpass, quickly outnumbering the small group of about forty soldiers with Guaidó. There was selfie-taking and posting to Twitter. The legislator Edgar Zambrano appeared wearing a gray suit with a canary tie. He enclosed López in a bear hug, then strode toward Guaidó, who theatrically clicked his heels in mock military pomp. They were boys playing at soldiers. The real soldiers, in green fatigues, were mostly very young.

They looked scared. Each one had a strip of blue cloth tied around his right arm, so that they could tell who was on their side. López and Guaidó wore them too. Like pinnies in a pickup soccer game.

And then there were the green bananas.

In one photo posted online, a heavy machine gun leaned unattended against the parapet-like wall of the overpass. Beside it were two plastic milk crates. One was overflowing with machine-gun belts, tossed in helter-skelter, like a suitcase packed in a hurry. The other was full of green bananas.

Whoever had planned whatever it was that was supposed to be happening that day hadn't thought far enough ahead to provide ripe bananas for the troops to eat while they defended the overpass from the enemy. Whatever their plan, like the bananas, they hadn't waited for it to ripen.

After a few hours in which they weren't attacked and no more troops showed up to join them, Guaidó and López simply drifted away. They walked to a nearby plaza, where Guaidó gave a short speech. Eventually Guaidó drove off in an SUV. López was given asylum in the home of the Spanish ambassador. The soldiers from the overpass took refuge in the Panamanian embassy.

It was Cúcuta all over again—no clear plan, stuck on a bridge, with no way forward.

Media reports called it a military uprising that failed or an attempted coup. But it was neither of those. No one rose up. The soldiers with Guaidó came from the small unit assigned to the National Assembly building. No brigades or divisions changed sides. No shots were fired.

Golpe is the word for coup in Spanish. This was a *nolpe*. Nothing.

* * *

IT WAS A rebellion on gossamer wings, built of wishes and moon dust.

Almost since Guaidó's swearing in, efforts had been under way, in Washington and Caracas, to entice top figures in the government to turn against Maduro. They soon got a response: Maikel Moreno, the chief justice of the Supreme Court, dispatched a representative to Bogotá, to make contact with Julio Borges, the exiled Venezuelan politician who served as one of Guaidó's chief diplomats. Borges and the man sent by Moreno, a lawyer, began discussing the text of a possible Supreme Court ruling that would back Guaidó and the National Assembly and pave the way for Maduro's exit. After a while, Moreno's representative said he wanted to talk to the Americans. A secret meeting was arranged with a U.S. official in Bogotá, on February 24, the day after the aid push at Cúcuta. Moreno's representative talked at length about the legal nuances of the proposed Supreme Court ruling. Finally he got to the point. If Moreno was going to flip, the man said, he needed something in return. Moreno wanted the United States to lift sanctions against him and other judges. And he insisted that the U.S. dismiss a money laundering indictment against Raúl Gorrín, the influential Venezuelan businessman who U.S. prosecutors claimed acted as a financial front man for Moreno and the first lady's three sons. The U.S. official replied that the sanctions could be lifted but not the indictment. (The U.S. sent a signal a few weeks later when it lifted sanctions against the wives of Gorrín and Gorrín's brother-in-law, who was also his business partner.)

On a separate track, López had made contact, through an intermediary, with Cristopher Figuera, the head of the Sebin, Maduro's intelligence police. Figuera visited López at his home, and according to López, they began hatching a plan to launch an uprising against Maduro. López told Figuera about the contacts with Moreno and urged him to reach out to the chief justice. At that point, the two threads of the conspiracy came together. Figuera met with Moreno and then the two of them spoke with the defense minister, Vladimir Padrino. Around the same time a pair of mid-level military officers reached out to López to express their unhappiness with the country's direction (these were the officers who would join López and Guaidó on the overpass).

It all amounted to a murky, half-formed conspiracy that never coalesced. Guaidó was to lead a large march in Caracas on May 1. López said that the plan called for Guaidó to appear with a contingent of soldiers and police who would declare their loyalty to the interim president. That would spark massive street demonstrations and the Supreme Court would then announce the ruling backing Guaidó. The defense minister would declare his support. Military units around the country would join in. And Maduro would be forced to go into exile.

But the bananas were green.

At the eleventh hour, at Figuera's insistence, the plot was moved up a day, to April 30. "At eleven o'clock at night on the twenty-ninth they call me and tell me the decision is that it's going to happen tomorrow," López told me (the call, he said, came from Figuera). López said that he didn't know why the plan had changed. "The decision was made by those who were in a position to lead the mobilization. I was a prisoner in my house." But when they pulled the trigger, nothing happened. Moreno and the defense minister denounced the putsch. Figuera fled to Colombia. Guaidó and López were left standing on the overpass.[8]

The episode was deeply embarrassing: a Keystone Kops koup.

And it didn't play well to the occupant of the White House.

Trump wanted fast results. He'd been told that Guaidó would sweep to power. But Maduro held on. In May, Trump spoke to Russian president Vladimir Putin by telephone, and Putin mocked Guaidó, saying that his claim to the Venezuelan presidency was no more legitimate than if Hillary Clinton had declared herself president of the United States after losing to Trump. It was a clever barb and Bolton believed that the phone call soured Trump on his Venezuelan adventure. But Trump had already complained to Bolton that Guaidó was weak and Maduro was strong.[9] In his comic-book fashion, Trump had made a more accurate assessment than the National Security Council or the State Department.

* * *

I sat down with Guaidó in July 2019. He had been loaned part of a floor in a Caracas office tower. He had a glassed-in office with a spotless white Formica desk and a Venezuelan flag. Guaidó was three days from his thirty-sixth birthday. Gray threads streaked his thick dark hair.

We talked about elevated expectations and the frustration of his followers.

"On January 4," he said, meaning the day before he became head of the National Assembly, "if we had talked, you probably would have told me that this was impossible, that it was David versus Goliath, but it was so effective that within days we had built up great expectations. That's not a bad thing. Now the important thing is to meet the challenge created by this hope." The opposition, he said, was in the majority. "When you're talking about who is the majority, who has the recognition, the dictatorship has been defeated," he said. This is what Venezuelans would call confusing magnesium with gymnasium. Yes, the majority of the population was against Maduro, but it hadn't been enough to push Maduro out of power. "We need to win," he said. "That's evident."

He said that Venezuela had gone backward a hundred years. "There are no antibiotics, you cook on a wood fire, there's no public transportation, you have to walk, there's no media or access to means of communication because there's no electricity."

Guaidó had started out the interview as a politician hitting his talking points, but as time went on, he relaxed. He talked about how he tried to find the time to spend with his daughter, Miranda; about how he questioned whether he was being a good father. He talked about the threats to his family: his brother had to flee the country; his mother went abroad for medical treatment. He said that out of his ten or so closest friends, only one remained in Venezuela.

Then he told me about a trip he'd made a few days earlier to a rural area near Caracas, where he met "the guy who fed the rabbits," a young man who raised rabbits to eat and sell. Everything was difficult for the guy who fed the rabbits: getting food for the rabbits, transporting the rabbits. He would be going somewhere to sell some rabbits and he'd be stopped at a checkpoint and the soldiers would steal the rabbits. He lived in a shack with a tin roof and a dirt floor. They cooked on a wood fire. He had a child and another on the way. His wife's sister had epilepsy and they couldn't afford to buy her medicine. Whenever they had two coins to rub together, they had to spend the money on some emergency. What impressed me was that for the few minutes that Guaidó had spent with the guy who fed the rabbits, he'd stopped being a politician long enough to listen to another person's story.

* * *

CÚCUTA AND APRIL 30 were the definitive tests for the notion of the *quiebre militar*, the break in the armed forces.

The problem was that it was never more than that—a notion. "On the analytical side of the U.S. government, there was no question in anyone's mind that the military was not going to respond to any of this stuff," Keith Mines told me. "That was part of where the hesitation about Guaidó came from. We knew he couldn't do it alone, and if the security forces didn't jump, it wasn't really going to work."

Chávez had turned the military into the Bolivarian Armed Forces, loyal to him and his party. He brought in Cubans to set up an intelligence operation within the military, efficient and brutal, to root out dissent. He promoted loyalists and built a system of political indoctrination. Maduro, who had no military background, was quick to send the message that any dissent would be answered with force. After Óscar Pérez, a former police officer, rebelled in 2017, firing shots and dropping hand grenades on government buildings in Caracas from a helicopter, he was hunted down and killed.[10] In 2019, a Navy captain, Rafael Acosta Arévalo, was arrested on suspicion of plotting against the government. He was tortured and beaten and rolled into court in a wheelchair so that the nation (and the officer corps) could see the consequences of rebellion. He died from his injuries the same day.[11]

Mines came to realize that the opposition had little real insight into the military world. "They would just admit, 'We are guessing. We do not know what their incentives are. We don't know how they're structured. We don't have personal contacts that might, you know, be bridge building.'"

When Mines told me that he and others in the government were aware that Guaidó's approach was based on a chimera, I asked him why the U.S. government had poured its resources into supporting him. "We just all got behind trying to find some way to make it work," Mines said. "None of us fell on our swords and said, 'Oh, this is just going to be a disaster.'" The way he described it, the administration's policy took on an institutional momentum. When it failed to produce results, there was always a fallback. "Whenever something was tried and failed, it was more sanctions," Mines said. "The answer was always more sanctions."

* * *

GUAIDÓ WAS A bubble that lasted less than four months, from January 23 to April 30. Suddenly Venezuela had hope. It had a young leader who promised that the time had come for change, who told people, *Vamos bien!* The American president talked about Venezuela. Any day the Marines would come and save them. Any day the avalanche of aid would arrive. Any day the military would turn on Maduro. After April 30, people disengaged. They came out to demonstrate less and less. The fever pitch of the first weeks had been too much to sustain. Life was hard enough. People were hungry. They had to stand in line for food or gasoline. Guaidó meant well, but he had promised quick results—instant gratification—and there was nothing to show for it.

26

Dead Houses

I flew to Caracas a few weeks after the non-uprising on the overpass. The country was seized with a kind of nervous exhaustion, whiplashed by the last several months: the flash ascent of Guaidó, the standoff at Cúcuta, the blackouts, the looting, the pantomime of April 30, the threats of invasion from Washington, the perpetual shouting from all sides, the dueling presidents, the social media frenzy. And all the time the economic free fall—no money no food no medicine no water. Always getting worse and never touching bottom.

On that trip and subsequent ones in 2019, I would often spend my days in Petare or another barrio where families were struggling to eat, even once a day, and then I'd return at night to my hotel or a friend's apartment in one of the wealthy parts of Caracas. There the restaurants were always full, the bars packed with stylish men and women, laughing, playing, flirting, doing business. Sometimes during the day, on my way to an appointment, I would pass a gym that had floor-to-ceiling windows. Inside you could see the fit people taking Spinning classes, sweating to keep the pounds off, even as a mile or two away, people were going hungry, agonizing over their malnourished children. It wasn't the fault of the people in the gym that they had enough to eat and wanted to stay in shape. Some people still had jobs, and you couldn't blame them for wanting to live in a country that was something like the country they used to live in. I came to see that there were many Venezuelas.

There was the Venezuela of shacks and one meal a day and there was the Venezuela of exercise classes and packed bars. There had always been that juxtaposition of money and poverty, but now the moneyed portion was shrinking—especially what had once been the comfortable middle class—and the group at the bottom was growing larger. Middle-class people were spending the savings they had in dollars and wondering what to do when they ran out. At the same time, a new kind of high-end store, called a bodegón, started to appear, selling imported goods with prices in dollars. They had fancy hams from Spain and extra big boxes of Frosted Flakes from Costco in Miami. Behind much of this traffic were mafias connected to the military and the top echelons of the government, which made it possible to fly in all these goods without paying import duties and allowed the stores to operate with no government interference. One bodegón I visited had boxes of Krispy Kreme donuts flown in the day before by private jet.

In Caracas there was electricity and gasoline. The government worked to maintain a degree of normalcy in the capital. The farther you went from Caracas, the worse things were. And the worst of all, everyone said, was Maracaibo. If in some parts of Caracas you could squint your eyes and pretend that the world was normal, in Maracaibo, you could open your eyes and imagine that you'd arrived in the zombie apocalypse.

* * *

WHEN MY PLANE landed in Maracaibo one morning in May 2019, ours was the only arrival all day in the second-largest city in the country, a city the size of Philadelphia. We filed off the plane into an empty airport. The lights were off. The air conditioning was off. The only sound was the chatter of suitcase wheels on linoleum. I looked out the windows in the arrival area at the empty tarmac. There were no other planes, only dormant, decrepit jetways extending out from the terminal like enormous blind caterpillars with open, regurgitant mouths. I followed the other passengers down the empty hall to the baggage area. We might have been the last passengers coming off the last flight from nowhere to nowhere. The baggage carousel lurched into motion; it sounded like a cement mixer loaded with marbles. A group of young

Mormon missionaries from other parts of Venezuela waited for their bags, overdressed for the heat in their dark suits and ties. One of them wore an argyle sweater vest. The restaurants and shops in the airport were closed. One shop window had a display of macrame bikinis and T-shirts with the image of the Virgin Mary.

As we drove in from the airport, the city felt depopulated. At least half the stores and businesses we passed were shuttered. There was no traffic, but there were long lines of cars at the gas stations. You had the sense that there were more cars waiting in line to buy gasoline than circulating on the streets. A line of people waited at a bank for their turn at the cash machine. The daily withdrawal limits hadn't kept up with inflation, so you could take out only enough money for a single bus fare. You had to come back the next day to withdraw the return fare. Parts of the city had no electricity because of the power rationing. If there happened to be other cars at an intersection where the traffic signals were out, you'd play chicken to see who would go first. Some drivers would cruise right through. Others would ease into the intersection, hesitating, foot on the brake.

* * *

DEAD HOUSES IS a novel by a Venezuelan writer named Miguel Otero Silva. It tells the story of a once-prosperous town that has been devastated by malaria—which was epidemic in Venezuela in the early twentieth century—and other diseases. By the time the action of the book starts, most of the town's residents have abandoned it, either for the graveyard or to start over again in another, healthier part of Venezuela. The main character is a young woman named Carmen Rosa, who ultimately heads across the country until she winds up in the newly discovered oil fields of eastern Venezuela. The book and a sequel about life in the oil fields tell the essential story of Venezuela. Poverty. Disease. Ruin. Refugees. Oil. Sudden riches. Repeat. The circular time of Venezuela mirrors the cyclical nature of oil. Prices go up, prices go down. And now we're back at the beginning. Otero Silva's book is called *Dead Houses* because the town of the story is full of them, fallen into ruin, left behind by the former occupants who had died or fled.

Everywhere I went in Maracaibo, people pointed to the empty, dead, and dying houses. A pollster named Efraín Rincón conducted a survey in late 2018 that attempted to measure the exodus from the city by asking people questions about family members who had left the country. He estimated that one-fifth of the city's population, more than 330,000 people, had emigrated. Maracaibo is close to the border with Colombia, and many people have family there. When life in Maracaibo became intolerable, it was natural for people to head across the border in search of something better. The proximity made it easier to leave. Rincón's survey probably underestimated the extent to which the city had emptied out, because it simply asked about people who had left the country. It didn't count the people who left Maracaibo for other parts of Venezuela where living conditions hadn't deteriorated as much. By the time I talked to Rincón, in mid-2019, his survey was also out-of-date. He'd conducted the survey more than six months before the devastating blackouts and the looting that affected Maracaibo more than any other city in Venezuela. Rincón told me that if you counted internal immigration and the likely surge of additional refugees in the months since the survey, it wouldn't be a stretch to think that a third of the city's population had left—more than half a million people in a city that had formerly had a population of 1.7 million. What the numbers covered over was the ripping apart of families. Some members would leave and others would stay. There were many times during my interviews when men—it was always older men—would start to weep as they told me of their children who had left the country or were preparing to leave.

Rincón told me about his own family. A typically large Maracaibo clan, they would gather each year, about ninety people, for the traditional Christmas Eve dinner. That was before the crisis. The previous December there had been only twelve people present. Nearly everyone else had left the country. There were more family members now in Florida than in Maracaibo. Rincón and I met over coffee in one of the two fancy hotels remaining in Maracaibo. It was like a hotel in a dream. The air conditioning was cranked to the max and food at the buffet was abundant. Near the end of our conversation, Rincón told me that he was leaving too. He'd taken a job in Mexico, and he and his wife were preparing to move. "It was a hard decision," he said. "You have no idea." Outside, the hotel swimming pool sparkled like a blue jewel in the sun.

* * *

OKAY: HERE'S HOW it works. You're driving down the street in Maracaibo and suddenly you see a giant hole in the ground, enormous, like the crater of a volcano, a wound in the earth. And you say, "Stop the car. What the hell is that?"

The answer, as though it was the most ordinary thing in the world to have a giant hole in the middle of your city, is "Oh, that's the Coquivacoa Hole."

In Maracaibo they have a hole so big that it has a name.

It's a monument to broken promises that go back long before Hugo Chávez.

When Carlos Andrés Pérez was president, during the 1970s oil boom, he conceived of a wondrous civic center for Maracaibo, a fitting emblem for the great city. Vast in scale, a marriage of culture and commerce, it would have office towers, a concert hall, a library, a stadium, and more.

It was to be called the Coquivacoa Civic Center, its name derived from an indigenous word for the area around Lake Maracaibo and the people who lived there. Plans were drawn up and a hole was dug, where foundations and subbasements and utilities and parking garages would go.

But dig the hole was all they ever did.

The project stalled.

Presidents and governors came and went.

The pit remained.

It's still there.

Stop the car.

I got out and approached on foot.

It had become a dump site. All along the lip of the crater, trash was piled up, spilling into the void. It was hard to say how far down the hole went, but it was an impressive distance. At the bottom, there was a jungle, with trees, deep green and shady, inviting, a respite from the beating sun. The trash along the rim was quotidian. An empty plastic bottle of a cleaning product called Full. Sardine tins. Tires. I peered into the depths. It felt prehistoric, outside time. A Lost World. From down be-low came the chirping and cawing of unseen birds and a rustling that might have been a large animal moving through the underbrush.

A movement drew my eye back to the crater's edge. A man walked toward me through rippling waves of heat. He was eating a banana and he dropped the peel on the ground. Why not? It was a garbage dump. He wore a purple polo shirt, neatly pressed blue jeans, and black es-padrilles with holes in the toes and on the sides. He bent over, stood up, bent over. He was collecting scraps of wooden lath from a pile of debris.

I said hello.

He told me that the wood was to cook with, since he'd had no gas at home for over a month. His name was Henry Real. He raised pigs, butchered them, and sold the meat. Like unbuilt civic centers and other broken promises, a shortage of cooking gas was nothing new. Gas shortages had been chronic for years, since before Chávez, but as was true with everything else, it was much worse now. Mostly these days, there was no gas to be had. Then, when the gas arrived, you had to wait in line for hours, perhaps all day, to buy a cylinder. That was at the government price. You could probably find a cylinder on the black market, but it would cost more than a month's wages.

I asked Henry about the pit.

His top front teeth were missing. He was tall and thin. He narrowed his eyes and looked without interest into the hole.

"The guys who were going to build here ate all the coppers," he said. *Coppers* is a Maracucho term for money. To say that they ate the cop-pers means that they stole the money. "We haven't had any water for two weeks," he said. He was talking about his house. "There's no law. No water. The country is destroyed." He spoke without anger, only resignation.

There was a lightness, an agility, in the way that Henry moved. I thought that he must be a good dancer. His pressed jeans spoke of a man who had not lost his self-respect. We walked back to the street. He had a graying Clark Gable mustache, and he wore his hair in a brush cut. His face was flushed and drops of sweat clung to his forehead, like water beading on the side of a glass.

At the curb there was a hand truck with a plastic milk crate. He bent down and loaded the wood into the milk crate. He also had a sack full of fruit and vegetable scraps. For the pigs. The sack buzzed with flies. A smaller plastic bag with bananas was knotted around the handle of the hand truck. The bananas were spotted with brown.

He looked down at his torn shoes and told me that he couldn't afford a new pair. "I'm forty-eight years old and I didn't think I'd ever see this," he said. He meant the city, the country, ruined like an old pair of canvas shoes, worn down to nothing. "But that's life. What are we going to do?" He said that he would sometimes see children scavenging for food in the trash along the edge of the pit. I could tell that it bothered him.

Off to one side of the pit was an army barracks. The barracks kitchen was where Henry collected the food scraps for his pigs. He pointed farther up the road. That way, he said, is the University Hospital. "But there's nothing there. No medicine. Nothing."

I asked him what was at the bottom of the pit. "Just trees and bushes and stuff." A flicker of interest crossed his face. "They've killed people down there." Who? "Homeless people."

A short stout woman in a black skirt and a black-patterned blouse walked toward us through the blast of sun. There was no one else around. Just Henry and me, standing still, and the woman, walking. She was walking in the street, beside the curb, looking down at her feet. When she reached us, she looked up.

"You haven't seen a large coin purse, have you?" She was on the verge of tears and she was breathing heavily.

Henry said no. I shook my head.

"*Ay dios!*" she said, and she left us, plodding along in the street. She walked stiffly on thick legs, as though she was afraid to keep going and not find what she was looking for and afraid to stop looking and give up hope.

We watched her go.

"I'd have given it to her if I'd found it," Henry said.

* * *

NIGHT. WE DRIVE along lightless streets. Families sit in front of their homes, on stoops, in chairs, at tables, talking, playing dominoes, passing the time. The white light from our headlights engulfs them for an instant, like a strobe, capturing scattered images—a hand raised to place a domino on the table, a mouth opened in laughter. The light washes over them and moves on, leaving them behind in darkness. This is life now, post-electricity, which is to say pre-electricity, rushing forward into the past.

We are lost, looking for a bar called Pa' que Luis. We climb a hill, turn a corner, and enter a sector with power. Electricity. *Luz*. Light. The city is an unfathomable jigsaw puzzle of circuits with invisible boundaries. On that side of the line, there is no light. On this side, there is. We keep going and cross into another dark sector. Is it power rationing or a localized blackout? Who knows?

All of a sudden the bar, Pa' que Luis, comes into view, straddling a corner, exploding like a bomb of light, illuminating everything around it. Spotlights are mounted high on the walls, pouring light onto the street. A softer, yellower light pours out the windows. When you've got it, flaunt it.

The eponymous Luis stands outside the door of his bar, a plastic cup of beer in hand. He is famous for the coldness of his beer and the warmth of his gaita.

Pa' que Luis is one of the centers of gaita, the music of this place, of Maracaibo. In better times, bands played here, musicians drank here. They wrote songs about this bar. There are photos on the walls of famous gaiteros.

The bar is brightly lit, too bright. But maybe that's what people want these days. Here is cold beer, conviviality, music, light.

It's Friday night, but few patrons have braved the darkness to wash up on this island of light. There are two couples at different tables. One of the couples seems happy—relieved to escape the hot, airless house, the darkened rooms, the mosquitoes, the waterless shower. The man sits on a stool and the woman stands facing him, squeezed between his knees. Two brown beer bottles, jeweled with sweat, are on the table. They drink beer, laugh, kiss. The other couple is distant. They sit on stools, half facing each other, distracted by the screens of their telephones: a different source of light.

I go to order beer. A powerful fan blasts air at my head. The barman asks how many beers I want. There are four of us, so I ask for four beers. He shakes his head. It takes me a while to understand: they've instituted a new system since the blackouts. What happened was that the lights would go out and people couldn't pay for the beer they'd drunk because the card readers had stopped working (cash had disappeared long ago). So now you tell the barman how many beers you expect to drink in the course of the evening and you pay ahead of time and he doles them out to you, round by round, marking your consumption down on a chit until you've reached your allotment.

A rare exercise in planning ahead.

Recorded gaita music plays loudly on enormous speakers. The man whose girlfriend is pressed between his legs sings along. Her face is turned up toward his. The bandstand is empty. Luis presides at the door. The distracted couple leaves and another one enters, deposits money, receives two beers as an advance on the night's drinking. They stand at the bar, under the fan. The man wears a pink polo shirt. She has tight-fitting bleached white jeans. He puts his arm around her waist. They are easy together. The bar is bright. The beer is cold. There is *luz*. A boot-black enters from the street and looks around. He has a tiny stool under his right arm and carries his kit in a wooden box. His hands are dark from polish. He walks the length of the room, like a person looking for someone he's expecting to meet in a crowded bar. Then he turns and walks back toward the door. "This place used to be full," the bootblack says aloud to the room, to the gaita, to the light. "I don't know what's happened here."

27

A Wooden Knife

In the early 1960s the leaders of Venezuela's fledgling democracy hired a group of urban planners from Harvard and MIT and asked them to design a new city that would rise out of the country's eastern wilderness. They called it Guayana City, and they placed it at the confluence of two great rivers: the Orinoco and the Caroní. They envisioned the city as a hub for industry and electrical power. They planned immense dams for the Caroní, with hydroelectric plants that would power the nation. They planned steel mills to take advantage of deposits of iron ore and aluminum mills to process locally mined bauxite. There was gold and diamonds in the hills.

The gringos came and drew long, wide straight avenues for their imagined city. Workers came from all over Venezuela, South America, and Europe. They built the dams and the power-generating plants and the mills and the streets and the houses. And people stayed and the city grew, and over time, the straight lines of the gringo planners were scribbled over with the crooked, wavy lines of the south.

You can look out on the city, on the straight lines and the crooked lines, from the apartment of María Nuria De Cesaris. She lives on a high floor of a building on the planned city's main avenue in its planned center. María Nuria is an urban planner, and she came to Guayana City in the 1970s to help coax a working city out of the straight and curvy lines. She worked for the Venezuelan Guayana Corporation, the giant government holding company that built the city and everything around it. She is an optimist by trade; she believes that plans are worth making and can be carried to fruition.

The city that grew up here was a special place. No other city in the country had so many college-educated professionals per capita— economists, engineers, architects, lawyers, doctors, administrators. It was a fast-growing city with plenty of problems. But what made it different, in María Nuria's eyes, was that a large number of its citizens had a pride of place and an awareness that the new city was unique. They were willing to discuss their problems, look straight at them, and make plans to deal with them.

When Chávez was elected, the city's strength became its weakness. Chávez didn't trust professionals. They weren't his people. They didn't owe him anything or want the old order turned upside down. They were bourgeois. That made him distrust the very idea of Guayana City. Chávez, María Nuria said, was determined to undo the good parts of the democratic governments that came before him. "If there is one unifying strand of the last twenty years of Chavismo, it's the conscious destruction of everything that was successful" before Chávez, she said. The educated, intentional, striving city stood as a kind of perpetual challenge. "It was too much in his face that you could build the country in a different way."

* * *

WHEN I FIRST went to Guayana City in 2013, its muscular vivacity was intact. The city of 2019 hardly seemed the same place. It was decayed, dirty, uncared for. The mills were stopped, robbing the city of its heartbeat. But it didn't have the desolation of Maracaibo. That was partly because gold was keeping it going. Guayana City was the jumping-off point for the enormous arc of licensed and illegal gold mines to the south. But the streets were mostly empty. The malls were deserted. Few restaurants were open. I went to an arepa shop that I'd been to six years before. It used to be known for its big selection of arepa fillings. This time they had almost nothing: an arepa with cheese, an arepa with shredded meat. The place was empty. The owner had been murdered a few years earlier and they were just hanging on.

The night I arrived, I took a drive around town. Long stretches of roadway were dark. Everything seemed covered in a layer of gray dust. Traffic signals were out. In a tiny triangle of land beside an intersection, someone had planted a patch of yuca. Anything to survive. In Guayana City I worked with a driver named Luis Rodríguez. He drove us across a causeway on the Caroní River that ran above the Macagua Dam, where giant turbines spun the nation's electricity. The streetlights were out on the road across the dam, which connected the two main sections of the city. "*En casa de herrero, cuchillo de palo*," Luis said. "In the blacksmith's house, a wooden knife."

Guayana City also had its holes in the ground, although none were as big as the Coquivacoa Hole in Maracaibo. A giant hole had been dug for a regional office of the Central Bank; it was to have had underground vaults to hold the gold from the Guayana mines. It was never built. I saw two giant holes excavated for shopping malls that were never constructed and one for a hotel. Some major projects had stalled after they began to rise from the ground. The most impressive was the cathedral. It sat on a prominent corner, along one of the city's main avenues. Pope John Paul II held a mass at the spot when he visited the city in 1985. A design for a cathedral was commissioned and construction began. And then work stopped. It sits there today, an enormous concrete base, with concrete columns two or three stories high on each side, hundreds of pieces of rebar rising from the top of each column, like the upraised arms of a congregation, reaching toward heaven.

Luis said, "Not even the works of God prosper here."

* * *

VENEZUELA WAS LIKE a clock that was winding down, losing time as the spring relaxed.

The first time I wandered into José Chacón's bookstore in Guayana City, he was talking with a couple of his regular customers—if you can use the word *customer* for people who never buy anything in a store that has nothing to sell. They were all men in their fifties or sixties, with time on their hands, and they were talking earnestly about matters of importance. The question was whether Chávez, in his wisdom, had wanted every state (there are twenty-three of them plus the capital district in Caracas) to have its own currency. Chacón said that Chávez had. One of the customers thought that Chávez had simply suggested it as a possibility. Another regular customer wondered if, whatever the comandante had said on the subject, allowing every state to issue its own currency might not cause certain problems. For instance, how to carry out transactions from state to state. That led to a conversation about the barter system. That was something else that Chávez had mused about: the end of money and the whole country's switching to a barter system.

Chacón was the manager of the Guayana City branch of a government-run bookstore chain called Librerías del Sur. Bookstores of the South. The chain sold inexpensive books from government publishing houses and lots of works by Venezuelan authors. When I lived in Caracas, there was a store in my neighborhood where I would often go to browse. Once, in a large, well-stocked branch near Plaza Bolívar in Caracas, I tried to buy a book by the Venezuelan novelist Renato Rodríguez. I took the book to the cash register. The woman at the register tapped some keys on her computer. "It says that the book is out of stock," she said.

We looked at each other. "What does that mean?"

"It's out of stock. I can't sell it to you."

"Okay. But it's right here."

"The computer says that it's out of stock."

"You're holding the book in your hand."

"I'm sorry. If it says it's out of stock, it's out of stock."

"There's several more on the shelf, where I got that one."

"It's impossible. We can't sell books that are out of stock. If you'd like to come back another day . . ."

The branch that Chacón managed was in the center of Guayana City, a block or two from some of the most powerful symbols of Venezuela's dashed dreams. There was the headquarters of the Venezuelan Guayana

Corporation, the state holding company that built the hydroelectric projects and the steel and aluminum mills (where the planner María Nuria De Cesaris had worked). There was the local headquarters of Corpoelec, the electrical utility. And there was the giant hole in the red earth that had been dug for the never-built branch of the Central Bank.

I happened to be walking past the big hole one day when I noticed the sign for the bookstore. It was located in a nearly empty shopping mall, next door to a shuttered vegetarian restaurant called Sprouts of Life. Elsewhere in the mall there was a closed beauty salon with zebra-striped furniture. A closed stationery store. A closed dental office with a name in English: White Smile. A motionless escalator with missing steps, like gapped teeth. Upstairs, there was office space that was used for services by an evangelical church called Luz de la Esperanza. Light of Hope.

It was dim inside Chacón's shop, not because the power was out but because the bulbs had burned out and not been replaced. The central air didn't work (Chacón told me that the condenser had been stolen from the roof of the mall). But it was the near absence of books that most drew your attention. I counted eight titles for sale. The books were set out on a table near the door, in piles of three or four copies each, fanned out to take up more space. Instead of books, the shelves held oversize models of insects made by a local craftsman. Each insect was about ten inches long, mounted in a diorama. There was a big grasshopper among leaves, a black ant crawling across grass. Some struck a whimsical note. An enormous mosquito played the maracas; a walkingstick played a snare drum. Each model had a label with the common and Latin name of the insect and details of its habitat and diet.

Chacón (his customers called him by his last name) had been trained as what he called an "activator." Part of his job was to "activate" culture in Guayana City. So, lemons into lemonade, the absence of books gave Chacón space for other things. Like giant insects. Another area of the store had an exhibit of pencil drawings by local art students: a still life of oranges; an Archangel Michael slaying a prostrate Satan. The doomed Satan had little wings shaped like the wings on the butterfly displayed among the insect dioramas. The Archangel Michael had wings that looked like large pieces of dry toast.

Chacón presided over all this from a high stool behind a counter in the middle of the store. Near the counter he kept an amateur portrait of Chávez in a simple black frame. Chávez stared out of the picture with a furious intensity. His eyes were asymmetrical—the left eye squinted, the right eyebrow was kinked like a checkmark. A vibrant scarlet beret rested over his furrowed brow like a thick dollop of raspberry sauce atop a sundae.

Chácon's face had a different sort of intensity, the illuminated face of the believer. He had jug ears that stuck out sideways, and the whites of his eyes went all the way around the brown irises.

In the Gospel according to Chacón, Chávez gave Venezuela the light of self-knowledge. "Before, we didn't know ourselves and the world didn't know us," Chacón told me one day. Chávez gave Venezuelans a constitution. Chávez cared about the poor, and he gave them a government that put them at its center. He told them that each person's opinion mattered and that the government belonged to them. "Chávez helped the people. I tell you sincerely, from my heart, because that's what Chávez did. He helped the people."

Chacón always voted for Chávez and then for Maduro. "He continued Chávez's legacy," Chacón told me. "He followed what was written. It's all been written down." Chacón was talking about Chávez's National Plans, his six-year blueprints for government. Chacón had studied them all. The first was in 2001. The next (also called the Simón Bolívar Project) was issued in 2007, and the next one was released by Chávez in 2012 when he was running for reelection. Maduro had one too, issued in 2019. They were full of wonderful promises for making Venezuela a great power, wiping out poverty, adding years to life expectancy, saving the planet.

Chacón was born in western Venezuela, and when he was a child, his family moved to Guayana City, drawn, like so many others, to the industrial metropolis springing up from the bare ground. Chacón still called it "the city of the future."

Chacón was a Citizen with a capital C, a man who believed in the idea of working to make the country a better place. He cared about humanity. (The fifth objective of Chávez's last National Plan was to "preserve life on the planet and save the human species.") He was a poll worker on election day. He organized his neighbors to keep their street clean. He taught classes as a volunteer in government programs that helped people who hadn't finished school earn high school diplomas or college degrees. He was currently teaching in a program for electrical engineering students. I was impressed: all this and electrical engineering too? It turned out that he was giving classes in political education. His students read and discussed the National Plans.

Chacón had always been a man of the left, believed that there was a better, fairer world that men could make for themselves. But until Chávez, he'd never seen anyone who could turn that promise into reality.

On Sundays Chacón used to watch *Aló Presidente*. "He had a giant brain," Chacón said. "He'd quote from some book of 500 pages or 1,500 pages. And the next day I'd come in here and I'd take a look at the book, to see if he got it right." Chacón made a fat space between his thumb and index finger to show the size of the books that Chávez read. "I'd write it down and I'd come in and take a look, and damn if he didn't have it right, such and such a thing, exactly as it was written. How about that?"

Here's what I struggled to understand about Chacón: how do you keep the faith when all around you there is misery and destruction? It was true, Chacón said, things hadn't worked out exactly as Chávez had planned it, but there was a reason for that: the hegemonic powers.

"Look around. They're destroying everything. They're like a hidden giant. They're like a spirit. They work behind the scenes. Sometimes you don't even know they're there. But how else can you explain why just about everything the government does is being destroyed? Let's be clear, this is a group of people that you're better off not even naming them because it can be dangerous." "They" controlled the dollar, the yen, the pound, the bolivar; "they" knew no borders, moving unseen from New York to London to Paris to Tokyo. Look at what the hegemonic powers had done to Libya. It was rich in oil and rich in farmland, just like Venezuela, and they'd fallen on it and devoured it. "They've got their tentacles everywhere. It's part of their chess game." Nothing was too large or too small. Who else could have been behind the looting of the air-conditioning systems from government offices all over Venezuela? "I know what I'm talking about," Chacón said. He gestured toward the dead air conditioner in his shop. "They stole this one too."

The ultimate goal was Venezuela's oil, the largest reserves in the world. How could you doubt it? Wasn't there a thing called the Monroe Doctrine? Operation Condor (the CIA-supported campaign of repression carried out by right-wing dictatorships in South America in the 1970s)?

That was the beauty of Chacón's paranoia, perhaps of all paranoias: on their own, each of the pieces was valid. Yes, there was an ultra-rich global elite that traveled easily from country to country. Yes, there was a Monroe Doctrine. Yes, his air conditioner didn't work. But it was the leap from each of those points to the chess game and the tentacles and the hegemonic powers that you were or weren't willing to make.

Chácon used to wear size 34 pants, but now he wore a 32. Chácon was a funny kind of optimist: he'd lost fifteen pounds, but he knew people who'd lost more.

It seemed contradictory: a paranoid optimist. But that was Chacón. On his side of the street, it was always sunny. The revolution could do no wrong. The other side was always out to spoil the good things the revolution did.

Chacón told me that he ate two meals a day. "It used to be, you ate mayonnaise, beef, all the tomatoes you wanted! You used to eat hamburgers, hot dogs, junk food like that, which is bad for you. Now we've learned how to eat better, how to eat healthy, about nutrition, how many calories you need, what you should be eating, that kind of thing. That's the sort of thing that the crisis has taught us. It's not that you get better nutrition. It's that we learned to eat healthier. We learned to give up lots of things that are bad for us. Especially sausages, which are so unhealthy. I still eat them, but not like before. It used to be, every day, that's all you'd eat. Now, at least, lentils are good for you. Before, nobody ate lentils. They were the cheapest thing there was. Legumes. They were practically free, and no one ate them. Nobody wanted lentils before this. Now everybody wants them because people learned that they're good for you. Squash too! People used to feed it to the animals. And it's really good for you! All this has really helped us learn a lot of stuff."

We talked about the boxes of food that the government distributed at low cost. "You get six kilos of rice, two of corn flour, four boxes of tea, three bags of powdered milk, a liter of oil, a kilo of sugar, pasta, three or four cans of tuna fish. That's worth more than a person makes in three months!" He had an inflated notion of the contents of the food boxes, judging from the stories that other people had told me. I asked if he remembered when he had received one last. It had been six weeks. Or maybe eight. But Chacón knew of people or had heard of people who were delivered a box every two to three weeks. Or maybe once a month. His optimism kept shining through. Like the cashier in the bookstore in Caracas, reality was no obstacle to his faith. The conversation turned to the great steel and aluminum mills that had once been the economic motor of Guayana City. Now they were all shut down. Chacón found the silver lining. If the mills weren't in operation, then they weren't polluting. "Maybe we'll all live longer." With the mills idle, he said, the workers could start farming garden plots in the land around the factories.

Chacón made "just a little bit" above the minimum wage. His wife also worked, and sometimes his oldest son brought in some money. Chacón owned two cars, but neither one was running because he couldn't afford the spare parts. Better to walk and eat than ride and go hungry. Chacón's oldest son was in college, studying industrial engineering. His son talked about finding a job where he could earn dollars. Chacón said he'd never touched a dollar—imperialist money—in his life. Well, maybe once. Chacón was a patriot. The bolivar was good enough for him. Now his son was talking about leaving the country. It broke Chacón's heart. Chacón got that look on his face that I'd seen so many times in the last few months in Venezuela—the look of the parent who couldn't bear the thought of being separated from his children. "I don't want him to go because—damn it, because I don't."

I think of Chacón as the Last Chavista. Not yet, not today, but someday. There he will be, all alone, everyone else having fled the country or gone off exhausted to collapse somewhere. There you'll see Chacón, sitting atop the great pile of rubble and ash, holding firm, chewing on the last lentil, and musing with undiluted delight about the time that the comandante went on television and remembered some phrase or fact that was printed on page 389 of some book, and when Chacón looked it up, sure enough, there it was, just like the comandante said.

On one of my visits to Chacón's shop I bought a book of poetry. A label on the back said: "Published during the time of economic war against Venezuela." The last time I saw Chacón he was alone in his store, with the insect models and the books fanned out on the table by the door, the portrait of Chávez, the broken air conditioner, and the burned-out lightbulbs, in the lonely shopping mall with the crippled escalator. Next door, Sprouts of Life. Upstairs, the Light of Hope.

Golden Hearts

In the Macro Centro, the young men stand around and sing: Oro. Oro. Oro. Oro. Oro. Gold. Gold. Gold. Gold. Gold. It sounds like this: *Oro-rororororororororororo*. The Macro Centro is a shopping mall in the center of Guayana City, and the young men are the barkers for the gold buyers who ply their trade inside a narrow souk in a corridor off to one side of the mall's entrance. There is a closed door guarded by a burly off-duty cop whose nickname is the Tiger. The buyers sit in tiny cells a bit larger than phone booths, each one with a scale, a drawer full of cash, and a money-counting machine. The barkers stand outside with their song of gold, drawing in the small-time miners fresh from the mines, who've come to sell. These are the gold panners, the guys who carry long steel bars up into the mountains to lever up boulders and look for gold nuggets underneath, grunts on a placer mine crew, men or women with a few grains of gold wrapped up in a scrap of paper. You can tell the miners by their rubber boots and their dirty clothes and the off-the-grid look in their eyes.

Ororororororororo. In New York City in the early 1990s the crack dealers on First Avenue would sing to you in the same way: *Smokedope-smokedopesmokedope*. My friend Paula said that the young men at the Macro Centro sounded like souls in torment.

The shops at Macro Centro are stripped to their minimum. Some stores sell only cell phone cases. Some sell only hats. The real business of the place is gold. At least a third of the stores are closed. I stop in a store that sells cheap Chinese hardware. I buy two small flashlights. The woman at the counter turns them on to show me that they work. A man puts a bunch of 500 bolivar notes into a counting machine. The bills are sepia, with Bolívar's face on them. The Bolívar on the bills is a placid, and self-satisfied Bolívar, with doe eyes and long sideburns. The machine whirs. Bolívar's face flicks by, like in a flip-book, except that his expression never changes. After the machine counts the bills, the man hands them to the woman who sold me the flashlights. She takes them and counts the same bills by hand. "You don't trust the machine?" I ask. Her hands move very fast. She finishes and says, "Money was made to be counted."

* * *

THE SPANISH CONQUISTADORS tromped all around this part of Venezuela looking for El Dorado and never found it, slaughtering and dying as they went. Today to get to El Dorado, you take Highway 10 south from Guayana City, toward the Brazilian border. The closer you drive to the town of El Dorado, the worse the road becomes. There are points where you must slow the car down to a crawl to navigate the potholes. The road into El Dorado is paved but it soon loses itself among the dirt streets, which are crowded with people and motorcycles and pickup trucks. As we come into town my friends tell me to stop taking video with my cell phone. The sindicato has eyes everywhere. The gold mines and the towns here are controlled by criminal gangs called sindicatos. The word *sindicato* means labor union, and the gangs started as corrupt construction unions that morphed into criminal enterprises. The boss of a sindicato is called a pran. The term comes from Venezuelan prisons, where a pran is an inmate who is the boss of the cellblock or, in many cases, the entire prison. The word may be an onomatopoeia, derived from the sound of a gun being fired: *pran pran pran*. The sindicatos and the prans took the code of violence from Venezuelan prisons and applied it to society at large. A pran named Fabio controlled El Dorado and the mines around it, up and down the Cuyuní River. Another pran controlled the highway and the mines south of El Dorado. The sindicatos were brutal, but they had established a kind of order in the interest of more efficiently carrying out the extraction and movement of gold.

The traffic leads to a boat launch on the Cuyuní River, where long, lanceolate aluminum boats crowd together. People embark here for the mines—miners, cooks, prostitutes, shopkeepers, itinerant peddlers, sindicato soldiers. There's a riverside market where you hear the wet *thwack* of fish being separated from their heads. River fish contaminated with mercury from the mines. The stores in El Dorado list their prices in grams of gold. Eight-tenths of a gram for five kilos of coffee, one and a half grams for ten kilos of powdered milk, everything in mining camp proportions.

* * *

I GOT ON a boat and headed upriver. The Cuyuní was a wide, flat ribbon of brown water with jungle pressing in on either side. The young man who sat in the rear by the outboard motor scarcely touched it, letting the boat run straight in the middle of the stream. We passed placer mines half hidden on the shore and rafts anchored mid-river, where shirtless men labored over clangorous pumps that suctioned up sediment from the bottom and vomited a brown sludge into sluice boxes. Small scarlet butterflies wafted past like burning snowflakes. At one point we passed a tiny canoe with an old indigenous man in it, fishing.

After a couple of hours, the boat dropped me at a clearing on the right bank and I hiked through the brush to the mining camp of a man named Donis Rodríguez.

Donis had one of the saddest faces I've ever seen. He had a bulbous nose, bloodshot eyes, elongated ears, brown, sunblasted skin, short hair, and a two-day scruff of beard. He wore an expression of the deepest forbearance. And yet he was friendly and open to strangers. He'd been repairing some equipment and there was a streak of grease on his right forearm. Donis operated a placer mine. He had a crew of seven men, plus a woman who cooked. He needed only six men to work the mine, but at any given moment at least one of the men was sick with malaria and couldn't work. They slept in hammocks slung side by side under tin-roofed ramadas and ate in an open-sided canteen. Donis's mine was a big crater in the jungle. The men used a pressurized hose to wash the sediment from the yellow sides of the crater. It collected in a pond and they pumped it up onto an enormous sluice, a couple of stories tall at the top. It was covered with green Astroturf. The sediment ran down the incline, and bits of gold were trapped in the fibers of the carpet. Once a month they washed the gold bits off the carpet and used mercury to separate the mineral from the soil and other impurities. The take for the previous month, Donis told me, was 400 grams of gold. This still wasn't pure gold, but it was the form of gold used locally as currency. At the time that I was there, 400 grams was worth about $12,000. Donis paid his crew (including the cook) 35 percent off the top, which worked out to $525 each. And he paid all the expenses of the operation, including food, fuel, and machinery.

On top of that, he paid 10 percent to the indigenous community whose land the mine was on and another large percentage to the sindicato. He paid bribes to the National Guard for every drum of fuel and more bribes for each piece of equipment that he brought upriver. It was like talking to a shopkeeper in New York City about all the taxes and fees he has to pay to stay in business. Except that the shopkeeper gains something in return—streets and schools and public transportation.

Recently Donis had a problem. He had bought a motor for one of the pumps he used in the mine, but when he brought it to his camp the motor didn't work. He went back to the man who'd sold him the motor, and the man refused to refund his money. After a while the dispute came to the attention of the sindicato. Donis and the man who sold him the motor were summoned to a meeting in El Dorado. A man from the sindicato acted as judge; he told each of them to argue their case. It was almost like going to court. The "judge" ruled that Donis should repair the motor and that the seller should pay the cost of the repair.

"The sindicato is really the government around here," Donis said. We stood beside the giant sluice box, where bits of gold were lodged among the plastic fibers. It was getting late; the sun had dropped out of sight behind the jungle. A cooling breeze blew downriver, and the sky seemed to soften as if it were a big blue cloud.

As I walked away from Donis's camp, I thought: the government is the mob and the mob is the government. Out here, the government's main function was to shake people down and extort money from them—such as in the bribes paid to the National Guard. The mob stepped in and, in its own brutal way, did some of the things that we expect a government to do—it collected taxes and enforced a kind of order. It was really a form of contracting out. The government found it more efficient to let the sindicatos keep order and keep the gold flowing than to go in and do the work itself. At the end of the day, the same people ended up lining their pockets.

For all the gold that moved through his hands, Donis said that there wasn't much left at the end of the month. "The big guys on top," he said, "step on the little guys underneath."

Everyone knew their place in the great flow of riches. The dirt-poor miners at the bottom, the sindicato tough guys, the privates and the officers in the National Guard, the prans, and far away, where they didn't have to get their boots dirty, the government officials who received their portion.

* * *

The last time that Néstor López had malaria, he hallucinated that he was running on the side of a mountain, through fields of flowers, until he saw his son, who took hold of him and led him home. His family told him later that he'd been raving about panning for gold; they bathed him with cool water to bring down the fever. Néstor estimates that he has come down with malaria more than forty times; and that last time was one of the worst.

Néstor lived in Tumeremo, a town north of El Dorado, and he'd done a bit of everything that had to do with mining for gold. He'd panned for gold, he'd worked in a placer mine, he'd been lieutenant to a pran in a sindicato, and he'd run cantinas and bordellos in mining towns. Néstor was small and wiry, with a gravelly voice. His nickname was Alto Pana, Best Friend. He knew everyone by name and was quick to lend a hand. Everyone in Néstor's family has had malaria many times. His youngest daughter, Aurora, who was five years old when I met her, had, by the family's count, come down with malaria seventeen times.

Malaria had once been eradicated in most areas of Venezuela, and the story of how it was done was a source of national pride. The disease had once been so chronic and widespread that it seemed like a permanent feature of the country, like oil. In the 1940s, the country developed an innovative public health program that involved the spraying of DDT and the deployment of rural health workers to distribute antimalarial medicine. It was so effective that it became a model for other countries to follow. Now malaria is epidemic again. In 2019, there were 400,000 cases reported in Venezuela, according to the Pan American Health Organization.[1] That was two and a half times more cases than in Brazil, which has almost eight times the population. The epicenter is in the gold mines, where mosquitoes breed in the jungle. There are still some government workers who provide antimalarial pills, but they often sell them to supplement their salaries. The miners, to save money, will take just enough pills for their symptoms to go away and then face a relapse later on.

* * *

IN THE TOWN of Las Claritas, south of El Dorado, a woman came down from the mines and arrived at a house where several friends had gathered. The woman was distraught. She told her friends a story whose beginning they already knew. One day, a nephew of the local pran became infected with HIV. The pran ordered his men to find the woman who had infected his nephew. The nephew, it appeared, had slept with one of the women who sold coffee in the streets of Las Claritas. These coffee women are a common sight all over Venezuela. They carry chrome thermoses and stacks of tiny plastic cups, and they sell sweet, weak hot coffee for a few bolívars. In any town, of almost any size, you can see the coffee women. They sit on plastic stools on street corners or in the plaza or they stand on the center line of the highway at the entrance to town, selling coffee to drivers who slow down at the checkpoints. Now the men from the sindicato rounded up all the coffee women in Las Claritas. They gave them a beating and put most of them on a bus out of town. That was the part of the story that everyone knew. You couldn't hide it—one day the coffee women were there and the next day they were gone.

But now the woman who had come down from the mine told her friends the part of the story they didn't know. She told them what happened next. One of the coffee women was HIV positive. She and three other women were taken to a mining town called El Portón. The residents of El Portón, the miners and cooks and shopkeepers and bar owners—were called out to the main street. The four women were brought out and the men from the sindicato beat the women with bats or clubs. Then they took chainsaws and cut them to pieces. The woman who came down from the mine had seen this happen. As she told the story, her whole body shook. She couldn't stop crying. What she had witnessed is called *escarmiento*, which means punishment, and, in particular, a punishment that is meant to teach a lesson. The dictionary of the Royal Spanish Academy offers this definition: "To learn from one's own or another's experience in order to avoid making the same mistakes." Don't do as this woman did or you will pay the same price. Why four women? Why not just the one? To increase the horror. In the mines, when a person falls afoul of the sindicato, they say that the person ran a red light. As though it was a minor infraction whose penalty turns out to be death. I was told this by a person who was there when the woman came down from the mine and told her story. Her body shook and she couldn't stop crying. I asked the person who told me to repeat the details to make sure that I'd understood. I didn't want to believe the story. The person grew impatient with my questions. "This happens all the time there," the person said. "There" was in the mines.

* * *

A YOUNG MAN wanted to leave the sindicato. He told his boss, who told the pran. He wanted to go home. But the rule of the sindicato is that no one leaves the sindicato. The young man was beaten. Another young man was summoned. The second young man was a backhoe operator at a mine controlled by the sindicato. He was told to climb into his machine and dig a hole. Then the first young man, the one who wanted to go home, was led to the hole and pushed in. He was in bad shape, but he was conscious. The men from the sindicato ordered the backhoe operator to fill the hole. He did what he was told. He later said to the person who told me this story: "I did something that I didn't want to do."[2]

* * *

THE PEOPLE WHO told me these stories—and I heard many others—asked me not to print their names because they were afraid. Fear is the main product of the mines, much more than gold. Most people come out of the mines about as broke as they went in. But they all come out more afraid. There is no data on the number of people who have gone to the mines and never come back. Periodically there are massacres when two armed groups—sindicatos or the Colombian guerrilla groups that have established themselves in the mining area—fight over territory. These massacres make headlines, with photographs of piles of bodies. Nothing much happens and they are forgotten by everyone except the relatives of the dead men and women. Until the next massacre. But the people who die in escarmientos or the casual and constant violence that visits itself on the mines—they leave no record.

Néstor López lived for a time in a mining settlement called La Franela, far up the Cuyuní River. One day Néstor went to see the local pran about some business. Some members of the sindicato arrived, leading a boy, about sixteen years old. They took the boy inside to where the pran was waiting. Néstor heard three shots. *Bam bam bam.* It was an execution.

Some time later Néstor heard about a man who was looking for his son, who had disappeared. The description matched the boy that Néstor saw. I asked Néstor if he'd said anything.

"What could I say?" Néstor replied. "He feels pain for his son. If I say something, he's going to make an accusation, and then they'll kill me and there'll be a hole in the ground for me too."

As the country's economic situation grew worse and oil production went into free fall, the government became desperate for a new commodity that it could sell for the hard currency it needed to sustain a minimum level of imports and the flow of graft that bought the loyalty of groups within Chavismo. That's when it turned its attention to the gold mines. It took steps to capture more of the gold produced by smaller artisanal mines, and it established mills to process the rock and sediment taken from larger mines. In theory, all the gold produced, just like oil, belonged to the government. But in practice, a portion went to the government, a portion went as kickbacks to government and military officials, and a portion stayed with the sindicatos or the Colombian guerrilla groups.

What mattered to the government was that the gold kept flowing. The sindicatos and guerrillas were like contractors, whose job was to ensure a relatively efficient and constant production of gold. Violence was just another industrial by-product, like the mercury in the rivers, that had to be tolerated.

Through negligence, corruption, and mismanagement, the Maduro government presided over the destruction of the oil industry. The Trump administration's sanctions were the coup de grace. PDVSA had a specialized workforce, unions, labor safeguards, and environmental regulations. By turning to gold mining as a substitute, Maduro replaced a modern, highly technical industry with a lawless, unregulated enterprise where workers had no rights, no regular salary; where they were beaten or raped or killed; where they were exposed to an epidemic of malaria; where environmental devastation was the norm, with jungles stripped and rivers poisoned with mercury; where indigenous rights were violated.

Maduro, the worker president, had created a perfect workers' hell.

Gold mining, as it was practiced in southeastern Venezuela, was the country's economic model taken to its most extreme expression—extracting a raw material from the ground at any cost.

The day that I took the boat up the Cuyuní River from El Dorado, a small jet left Caracas and flew to an airport in Fort Lauderdale, Florida. Customs agents there found 230 pounds of gold, worth $5 million, hidden in the nose section of the plane. The pilot and a passenger were arrested. A few weeks earlier, a similar amount of Venezuelan gold was taken from a plane that landed at Heathrow Airport in London. The gold was molded into ingots. Six of them were fashioned in the shape of hearts.[3]

29

Newsprint

There was a bus graveyard in Guayana City, next to a public transit termi-nal. The dead buses—I counted fifty-eight—were parked in rows. Some had been in accidents: a shattered windshield, a crumpled grill. Most of them seemed to have simply broken down. They were being cannibalized for parts. They were all red, made by a company called Yutong and bought from China. Under Chávez, China loaned billions of dollars to Venezuela; Venezuela in turn took the money and bought Chinese buses and washing machines and satellites. It was a great deal for Chi-nese manufacturers. Not so good for Venezuelans, including those who wanted to ride buses. All over the country you would run across grave-yards like this one, full of red Yutong buses. I don't know if the buses were lemons or if they weren't maintained. Either way, they didn't last long. Next to the bus graveyard was a bus depot surrounded by a high wall. Inside I could see more damaged buses. Painted on the sides of some of them, in big white letters, were the words *Don't touch*.

There was also an ambulance graveyard in Guayana City. I counted thirty-nine dead ambulances parked outside the city's emergency dis-patch center. You couldn't tell what was wrong with them, but you could see that they hadn't moved for a long time. Weeds grew up around them. Some had flat tires and some had the tires removed. They had slogans on them, from the days when they were driving around responding to emergencies. "Fake calls destroy lives." "Free 24 hours." I saw only one ambulance that looked like it was still functioning. It was parked in a different area, as if to isolate it from the broken-down ambulances. The tires were smooth as a Spaldeen—no tread at all.

* * *

MY FRIEND CLAVEL tells this story:

One night she woke up and saw that a house on her street was on fire. The Guayana City Fire Department has only one working fire truck (in a city with a population greater than 700,000), although there is also a crew of firefighters based at the Sidor steel mill. Clavel started calling around and finally someone gave her a number that she could call for a fire truck. Eventually a fire truck came. She thinks it came from the steel mill. Another neighbor made some calls and was able to summon an ambulance. A woman and her adult son lived in the house that caught fire. By the time the firefighters found them and brought them out, they were unconscious. They put them in the ambulance, but the ambulance had no oxygen. The ambulance took the woman and her son to a hospital. But the hospital turned them away—it didn't have the supplies or the equipment to treat them. The ambulance drove to another hospital, farther away. By the time the ambulance arrived, the woman and her son were dead.

The cause of death that was given was smoke inhalation.

* * *

DRIVING ONE DAY in Guayana City we passed a pickup truck that had caught fire. It was parked on the side of the road. The body of the vehicle was charred, and flames were shooting up from the engine block. Some people stood around watching it. We kept going. Half a mile farther on we came upon a fire station and I asked Luis, who was driving, to pull into the driveway. I figured I'd be a good citizen and report the fire. It was a big fire station. Luis told me that it had once been used as a school for firefighters. The wide, open-fronted garage had three stalls, which would be where the fire trucks were kept. It was empty. A phrase was painted in red block letters on the back wall:

Cuando el clarín de la patria llama hasta el llanto de la madre calla.
When the clarion of country calls, even a mother's tears are silenced.

The concrete floor of the garage was swept clean.

I started up a paved walk to the building. On the pavement at my feet there was a scuffed, half-erased emblem. It showed two firefighters attacking a flame that looked like a man-size artichoke. Above the flame was a round symbol containing a ladder and a fire helmet. The words surrounding it read *Guayana City Fire Department*, and below that was a slogan: *Discipline and Abnegation*. I continued up the walk, pushed the glass door open, and entered the building. A firefighter in a blue uniform sat at a desk to the right of the door.

I told him about the pickup truck on fire. I pointed down the road and said that it was less than five minutes away. The firefighter turned on a radio and spoke into it. He named the street and asked if anyone had received a report of a vehicle on fire. A staticky voice responded in the negative. He turned off the radio. His uniform was very clean. It was a little faded, maybe from being washed repeatedly. You could tell that he was a neat person, that he had discipline. I wondered if he was the one who had swept out the garage. He was fair-skinned, and his hair was cut short. I looked around the entryway to the firehouse. It was clean and quiet and peaceful. Amber light from the low sun slanted through the glass door and the window by his desk.

He said that he and a colleague were the only ones on duty at that firehouse. In any case, they had no vehicle to use to respond to emergencies. Not even a car. I asked how long he'd been a firefighter. He said ten years. When he started, they had six ambulances and several fire trucks. Now they had no ambulances at all and there was just one fire truck for the entire city. It was kept at a different firehouse. If there was a big fire, the firefighting unit from the steel mill would be called. I felt sorry for him. A firefighter without a fire truck. That was abnegation. He was pleasant to talk to. He projected a sense of calm.

He thanked me for coming in.

* * *

As I TRAVELED around Venezuela in 2019, it dawned on me that the country had become the Republican dream fulfilled. Some people called Venezuela a failed state. Others called it a mafia state, taken over by a criminal gang that was interested only in maximizing profits from drug trafficking, money laundering, and other illicit pursuits. But it was neither of those things. It was a state reduced to the absolute minimum. Maduro had started the process, and the Trump White House had helped him carry it toward completion. Or perfection. In the United States the Republican dream was to starve the beast, to cut government financing so deeply that most of the things that we expect a government to do become impossible. Then theoretically society and private initiative can flourish, unencumbered. This was Venezuela. There were almost no services, no fire trucks, no ambulances. Public hospitals and clinics barely functioned. Poor people still received some benefit payments and pensions, but they were worth so little that they could hardly be called support. People were on their own, left to fend for themselves, free to exercise personal responsibility. Residents filled the potholes on their streets, carted off their own garbage, hired private security guards to protect their neighborhoods. Government-run factories, farms, and stores were shut down. Desperate to promote some kind of economic activity, and despite its socialist rhetoric, the government had quietly been increasing the ways the private sector could participate in the oil industry and other areas that were previously reserved for the state. In the gold mines, the government had outsourced most state functions to the sindicatos. The irony was that Republicans in the United States considered Maduro their enemy. They should have been applauding him. He was a fellow traveler.

* * *

DAVID NATERA IS a stubborn man. He is tall and narrow-shouldered and loose-jointed in an Ichabod Crane sort of way. He's stiff-necked and irascible. He didn't get to be seventy-eight years old by bending in the wind. "I'm one of the ones that isn't going anywhere!" he told me. He was emphatic. "We have roots here." Natera was comparing himself to other Venezuelans of his class and station who had moved to Miami or Madrid or Bogotá. He wasn't about to leave and give the government the satisfaction of being rid of him. Of shaking the pebble from its shoe.

Natera, was a lawyer like all the men in his family, but in 1977 he came to Guayana City and started his own newspaper. He called it *El Correo del Caroní, The Caroní Post*—after the newspaper founded by Bolívar, *The Orinoco Post*. Back in the 1970s the city was growing so fast (or not fast enough) that there was a housing shortage. For the first two years, Natera slept in his office.

Natera blames his fellow patricians in Caracas for Chávez's rise. He is still bitter that they backed Chávez in 1998, loaning him their private jets and giving him airtime on their television stations, thinking that if he was elected they could control him. "Chávez won in the Caracas Country Club! The elite put Chávez there!" But Chávez slipped out of their control. "The Venezuelan people are very good and generous and trusting," he said. "They weren't prepared for anything as perverse as this."

We were sitting in his office. He was behind a desk covered with books and knickknacks and stacks of old copies of *El Correo del Caroní*. Natera was dressed in a loose-fitting white linen shirt and white slacks, with white socks, a black leather belt, and loafers. His head was bald on top, with patches of white hair on the sides. He had a narrow face, long earlobes, and watery brown eyes behind rectangular rimless glasses. The backs of his hands were foxed like an old newspaper forgotten in a drawer.

For forty-two years, Natera had written every editorial the paper ran. He also owned a television station and a radio station. But he had no income because he couldn't sell any ads. No one would buy them—they were afraid of angering the government. Natera kept his threadbare media empire alive out of stubbornness, principle, and pride. "With my own savings!" He was wealthy once and maybe still was. But he drove an old beat-up white Dodge Grand Caravan and he'd sold some real estate to keep things going. "No one can understand why during all these years, everything that I ever had, everything that I earned *in my life*, everything that I had here or that I saved in dollars, I spent to keep all this going." He pounded the desktop with the flat of his hand.

In the middle of the Orinoco River, in front of Bolívar City, the state capital, where Natera was born, there is a stone outcropping that rises from the water. It's called the Rock in the Middle. Natera is like that rock. "The corrupt person, the thief, wants everyone else to be like him, he wants to get you on the same level that he's on," Natera said. "In the world of the corrupt man, the best thing is for everyone to be corrupt. If there's one person who says no, then, damn it, they've got to kill him."

There is no paper mill in Venezuela that produces newsprint. If you want to print a newspaper, you must import paper. For years, under Chávez, the government used currency controls to make it harder for unfriendly newspapers to get the dollars they needed to buy and import newsprint. Then in 2014, Maduro created a government-run company to be the sole importer and distributor of newsprint. Natera, on principle, refused to buy from the government monopoly. He saw what was coming. He knew that if they sold it to you today, they could hold it back tomorrow. To stretch his reserves of newsprint, he cut back on the number of pages in the paper and then went from printing daily to once a week. In 2017, he stopped printing altogether. (Other newspapers were slowly strangled by the government's newsprint monopoly, and most have now shut down their print editions.)

Natera maintained a skeleton staff, and *El Correo del Caroní* lived a precarious existence online. He had two part-time reporters and a part-time editor.[1] Despite immense obstacles, they managed to produce some of the best news coverage in the country. They'd done exposés on the environmental impact of gold mining, on violence and disappearances in the mines, on the murder of Pemón Indians by the army, on the decline of the steel and aluminum mills. For all of his grumpiness, Natera was revered by the people who worked for him. He'd stood by them, paid their salaries, given young reporters a place to learn and experienced reporters a place to keep publishing, even as the media landscape in the country dwindled to almost zero.

El Correo del Caroní was an old-fashioned operation: newsroom in front, press in back. The door to the press bay squeaked, but that was the only thing here that needed oiling. Natera kept two men on the payroll to maintain the press, even though it hadn't run in almost two years. "It's perfectly oiled so that it's ready when it's time to turn it on again," Natera said. There were two rolls of paper mounted on the press ("Ready to go!" he said in English) and five more on the spotless concrete floor next to the machine. These five rolls were still wrapped in brown paper, with the mark of the Crofton paper mill of British Columbia inked on the side. When he stopped printing in 2017, Natera held these rolls in reserve so that when the government falls, he can be on the street the next day with a special edition. Natera is a stubborn man. I asked him when he expected to print again. "When the country demands it!"

Every day Natera comes to the newsroom and passes through the squeaky door into the press bay. He stands on a low metal step at the base of the machine, puts both hands on the press, palms downward, bows his head, and says a prayer to the Holy Trinity. "Watch over us," he says, "protect us and keep us safe from all danger."

30

The Screw-up at Macuto

Juan Guaidó had run out of steam. The people hadn't risen up to drive out Maduro. The military hadn't jumped to the opposition. The United States hadn't invaded.

Guaidó and Leopoldo López (now living in the Spanish ambassador's house) were keenly aware that they were losing momentum.

They needed to find another way. In June they reached out to J. J. Rendón, a Venezuelan political consultant living in Miami, who had a reputation as a master of the political dark arts. Rendón had helped elect Juan Manuel Santos president in Colombia and Enrique Peña Nieto in Mexico. But he'd also run into controversy. In 2014, Rendón resigned from Santos's reelection campaign following news reports that he'd received millions of dollars from drug traffickers seeking a conduit to the government (Rendón denied the accusations).[1]

Now they instructed Rendón to try to find another way out of Venezuela's impasse.

By August or September Rendón had made contact with Jordan Goudreau, a Canadian-born U.S. Army veteran who had served for fifteen years as a Green Beret, with tours in Afghanistan and Iraq. Goudreau had left the military in 2016 and eventually moved to Florida, where he formed a security company called Silvercorp USA. The company didn't seem to have much business, but Goudreau posted photographs online that showed him performing security at a rally attended by President

Trump. He was also a security contractor at the fundraising concert in Cúcuta, the night before Guaidó's attempt to carry aid across the border. "Controlling chaos on the Venezuela border," Goudreau wrote on Instagram, with a photo that showed him at the concert.

Rendón began talking to Goudreau about organizing a mercenary force to invade Venezuela and, in Rendón's words, "extract" Maduro. Rendón told me later that he'd done a thorough vetting of Goudreau. But Goudreau had no track record to suggest that he was capable of organizing a major international operation. "He looked clean," Rendón told me.

They spent several weeks hammering out the details, and on October 16, 2019, they signed a highly unusual document: a contract to invade Venezuela.

According to the contract, Silvercorp, Goudreau's company, would be paid $213 million "to capture/detain/remove Nicolas Maduro" and, in his place, "install the recognized Venezuelan President Juan Guaidó."

Stop a moment and think about that word: *install*.

Five months after the debacle of April 30, when a poorly thought out and clumsily executed effort to provoke a military uprising ended in embarrassing failure, Guaidó had given up on pushing out Maduro on his own and had hired a foreigner to "install" him in the presidential palace.

The contract—which was kept secret at the time—spelled out rules of engagement and identified targets (Maduro and others) that could be "neutralized." It required foreign fighters to wear Venezuelan uniforms and cover their faces "to protect the face of the project as Venezuelan only."

The contract was signed by Goudreau, Rendón, who was identified as the High Presidential Commissioner for General Strategy and Crisis Management, and a Venezuelan legislator close to Guaidó named Sergio Vergara,[2] who had been working with Rendón.

It was also signed by Guaidó.

Goudreau made an audio recording of a video conference he had with Guaidó, in which they discussed signing the contract. In the recording, Goudreau asked Guaidó if he had any concerns. Guaidó gave a nervous laugh and responded, in English: "A lot of concerns, but we're doing the right thing for our country." There was discussion of the need to sign two copies of the document, in its English and Spanish versions, and to scan and send the signed contracts. At the end of the recording, Guaidó said, "Let's go to work!"

Guaidó has denied signing the contract. But it was negotiated and signed by his representatives and it would have had no validity without his signature—he is the only person named in the document as a party to the contract (his name appears twice).

But shortly after it was signed, the deal fell apart.

The contract required the Guaidó government to pay Silvercorp a $1.5 million retainer within five days of signing. They never paid it.

Goudreau insisted on being paid. Rendón said that he gave Goudreau $50,000 to string him along. Finally in early November there was a blowup. Rendón said that he met with Goudreau and presented him with a letter canceling the agreement. (It's worth asking why the contract needed to be canceled if Guaidó had never signed it.) He said that Goudreau refused to sign the letter and stormed out.

Rendón said that he didn't hear from Goudreau again for several months.

* * *

But Goudreau was busy. Before negotiating the contract with Guaidó and Rendón, he had joined forces with Clíver Alcalá, a former Venezuelan army general. Alcalá had been close to Chávez, but he broke with Maduro and went to Colombia, where he started to gather together deserters from the Venezuelan military. According to reporting by Joshua Goodman of the Associated Press, Goudreau and Alcalá met in Bogotá in mid-2019 and began to make plans for an invasion of Venezuela to overthrow Maduro.[3] Goudreau recruited a pair of Green Beret friends, Luke Denman and Airan Berry, to help train the Venezuelan recruits at camps in Colombia.

By early 2020, however, the conspiracy began to unravel.

On March 24, the Colombian police seized a vehicle full of weapons on the Caribbean coast. The cache included assault rifles, laser sights, night-vision goggles, silencers, body armor, and helmets.

Two days later, the U.S. attorney general, William Barr, announced that the Justice Department had indicted Maduro and several others in what it called a "narco-terrorism conspiracy." One of the people indicted was Goudreau's partner, Clíver Alcalá. The indictment accused Maduro and the others of shipping large amounts of drugs to the United States as part of a plot that "prioritized using cocaine as a weapon against America." The State Department put a $15 million bounty on Maduro's head and offered rewards of $10 million for Alcalá and two others named in the indictment.

The day that the indictment was announced, Alcalá posted a video on Twitter, saying that he was in Colombia and that he intended to surrender to U.S. authorities. And then he dropped a bombshell. He said that Guaidó and Rendón had signed a contract with American military advisors to liberate Venezuela and that the weapons seized by Colombian police had been intended for that purpose. "We had everything ready," Alcalá said.

Two days after that, Diosdado Cabello, the powerful Chavista politician, went on television in Venezuela and gave a detailed account of Alcalá's planned invasion.[4] He named Goudreau and the two American trainers. He showed images from Goudreau's social media feeds. He said that the operation had been infiltrated and he played a video of a soldier from one of the training camps who had been captured when he sneaked back across the border into Venezuela.

On May 1, the Associated Press published its article exposing the connection between Alcalá and Goudreau.

After all that—the seized weapons, the indictment and surrender of Alcalá, the television appearance by Cabello giving details of the conspiracy, and the AP article—you might have thought that would have been the end of the story.

Incredibly, it was not.

On the night of May 3, Venezuelan security forces announced that they had confronted a boatload of armed invaders at the coastal town of Macuto, near Caracas. Officials said that they had killed eight combatants and captured two.

At about the same time, a video was posted to Twitter, declaring the start of an invasion to liberate Venezuela. It starred Jordan Goudreau.

"At 1700 hours a daring amphibious raid was launched from the border of Colombia deep into the heart of Caracas," Goudreau said in the video. He wore a gray polo shirt and trousers and a gray New York Yankees cap. He was with a former Venezuelan military officer named Javier Nieto, who said that the invasion was code-named Operation Gideon.

Goudreau and Nieto, however, were not participating in the raid. The video, with trees or bushes in the background, appeared to be made somewhere in Florida, perhaps a park or a backyard.

The next day the Maduro government announced an even more startling development. It said that it had captured a second boatload of invaders, at an idyllic Caribbean beach town called Chuao. This time there were no casualties. Officials showed photographs of the captured men lying facedown on the ground. Among the invaders were the two American trainers recruited by Goudreau, Luke Denman and Airan Berry.

* * *

THE MADURO GOVERNMENT crowed. Its wildest conspiracy tales had been proved true. For years it had talked of shadowy conspiracies hatched by gringo imperialists and right-wing Colombians in cahoots with the Venezuelan opposition—and here it was, amazingly, all wrapped up with a bow. The government painted the botched operation as a second Bay of Pigs, the ill-fated 1961 invasion of Cuba backed by the U.S. government. But this was, at most, a Bay of Piglets, a ripple on the tide.

Venezuelans started calling it, after the spot where the first boat was intercepted, *la chapuza de Macuto*—the Macuto Screw-up.

Goudreau accused Guaidó and Rendón of backing out of their deal and he went public, providing images of the contract, with Guaidó's signature, to a Miami-based Venezuelan journalist named Patricia Poleo, who posted them online.

Guaidó claimed that the bungled invasion was a hoax perpetrated by the Maduro government. Rendón went on television, falling on his sword, trying to shield Guaidó.

But there were too many questions without answers. Who signs a contract to invade their country? Who leaves that kind of paper trail?

Or was the point to create a paper trail? Did someone want something to hold over Guaidó's head? Or was someone looking to undermine Guaidó and make him look foolish and reckless?

Or was it simply what it appeared to be—an incredibly naive and badly executed effort to hire a mercenary force to solve the problem that the opposition hadn't been able to solve on its own?

At a news conference in Caracas, Maduro showed a video of a propaganda-style interrogation of Luke Denman, one of the captured Americans. Denman said that his objective on arriving in Venezuela was to take control of an airport so that Maduro, once captured, could be flown to the United States. The interrogator spoke choppy English. He asked Denman, referring to Goudreau: "Who commands Jordan?" With an exaggerated roll of the eyes that seemed intended to contradict his words, Denman replied, "President Donald Trump."

Maduro accused Trump of giving the direct order for the invasion. U.S. officials have repeatedly denied knowledge of Goudreau's activities and evidence that the United States was involved in mounting the operation remains sketchy. Five months after the botched invasion, in October, Goudreau filed a lawsuit in Florida state court in Miami, seeking to force Rendón to pay him the remainder of the $1.5 million retainer. In the lawsuit, Goudreau said that he met three times with an obscure Trump administration official to discuss obtaining a license to export weapons for the invasion. According to the lawsuit, Goudreau believed that the plan had U.S. government approval. And it said that no one associated with Guaidó had told him to stand down.

Denman and Berry were sentenced in Venezuela to twenty years in prison.

Jordan Goudreau dropped out of sight.

I was talking to a Venezuelan friend living in New York about Guaidó and the strange contract that led to the fumbled invasion. She expressed what many Venezuelans were thinking: "These guys aren't willing to go the distance," she said. "They want to outsource everything."

* * *

IN THE DISNEY cartoon "The Sorcerer's Apprentice," Mickey Mouse is a drudge, hauling water in the sorcerer's workshop. When his boss takes off for the night, Mickey puts on the sorcerer's pointed blue cap, brings a broom to life, and orders it to carry water in his place. Mickey sits in the wizard's big chair and falls asleep while the broom keeps going, hauling bucket after bucket of water, until the workshop floods. Guaidó was Mickey Mouse in a blue cap with moons and stars, dreaming of sitting in the presidential chair and waking up to find himself underwater. Goudreau was the broom: once he was brought to life and ordered to do Guaidó's work of removing Maduro, he wouldn't stop.

* * *

"THERE'S A BIT of Ahmed Chalabi among these guys," Keith Mines, the former State Department official, told me. He was comparing the hardline elements of the Venezuelan opposition to the Iraqi politician who claimed that Saddam Hussein had weapons of mass destruction in order to provoke a U.S. invasion. "Their idea was, we are going to go through the motions of all this stuff, play it straight, but just so you know, it's probably not going to work, and at the end of the day, you're going to need to invade. That was clearly where their hearts were." Mines meant that all of the opposition's initiatives in 2019—Guaidó's swearing in, the Cúcuta aid push, the non-uprising on the overpass—were simply meant as placeholders until Trump pulled the trigger on military action. In meetings with U.S. officials, opposition leaders would point to the Maduro government's ties with Iran and the presence (in reality, minimal) of Hezbollah in the region, and they would stress Venezuela's role as a transshipment point for drugs. "They were always trying to go that direction of 'There's a threat to the United States that you need to deal with.'"

But there was never any serious consideration of military action by the administration. Jim Mattis, who was defense secretary for Trump's first two years in office, refused to dedicate any resources to planning military action in Venezuela, arguing that it was a distraction from real threats elsewhere. After Mattis was gone, defense officials continued to take the same line.[5]

Nonetheless, it was astonishing to hear Mines evoke Chalabi, whom he'd known when he was posted to Iraq in 2003. Chalabi's lies and the willingness of U.S. officials to be duped by them, or to go along with them, helped trigger decades of war that led to the death of more than 4,400 U.S. soldiers and hundreds of thousands of Iraqis.[6]

"We gave them just enough encouragement," Mines said of the Venezuelan opposition. "I don't think we ever disabused them of that. And again, I think their assumption was always, 'We will go through the motions, you know, maybe we get lucky.' But they didn't really think they would. And then at the end of the day, when nothing works, the United States will finally just say, 'The heck with this, we have to invade.'"

We were back to the eternal show of Venezuela, back to Chávez's breaking ground for a hospital that would never be built. The point was not to bring the humanitarian aid across the bridge at Cúcuta, it was to make a show of trying. The goal was not to stage a military uprising on April 30. It was to create the appearance of an uprising.

The point wasn't to be president, it was to appear to be president.

* * *

GUAIDÓ AND HIS wife, Fabiana, named their daughter Miranda, after the founding father who was betrayed by Bolívar's act of treachery. The curse that Francisco de Miranda pronounced on Bolívar at the start of the Venezuelan independence struggle still echoes down the centuries: *bochinche, bochinche. Nothing but noise and chaos.*

In the years before the war of independence, the island of Trinidad, which was under British control, had been a safe haven for colonial Venezuelans conspiring against the Spanish crown. Miranda was living in London then, and he employed an agent in Port of Spain, named Pedro Josef Caro, who sent him reports as one conspiracy after another fermented and fizzled. One of these dispatches was dated April 29, 1799, but it could have been written yesterday. "The pity of it is that our countrymen have no agreed-upon plan, nor do they act with aforethought," Caro wrote. "And they are more inclined to change their Master than to be free: that is my judgement. They believe that it is the same to shout 'Independence! Independence!' as to be independent, and that they will become so simply by emerging from the Spanish yoke, even as they submit to another for protection."[7]

Blackout

After the nationwide blackouts in March, the four Corpoelec exiles who returned to help bring the electrical system back to life—Juan Carlos, Antonio, Luis, and Francois—stayed on at the utility as advisors.

Pretty soon they discovered that no one wanted to hear their advice.

"I'm very disappointed," Juan Carlos told me in October. "When someone hires you as an advisor, they don't have to do what you say, but you expect them to at least listen to you." Juan Carlos has a facade of extreme calm. On this occasion there was anger behind it, simmering up from a deep frustration. "You called me to help, but you won't let me help. I'm not going to play the fool."

One of the first pieces of advice that the four of them had offered was that the company urgently needed to improve employee morale. That included meaningful raises to stop the loss of experienced workers. They took their proposal to Delcy Rodríguez, the vice president who had been put in charge of the recovery operation. They never heard back.

Juan Carlos ticked off some of the problems that remained unaddressed. "You go to the offices of Corpoelec and 25 percent of the people are at work and they leave at two o'clock to make some money on the side. The same thing is happening in the power plants." He said that in Guayana City there were only two workers assigned to do maintenance on close to twenty electrical substations. There was one old pickup truck available for them to use, and when it broke down, the workers paid for the repairs on their own. I asked how they could afford to do that on a Corpoelec salary. He said that the workers used the vehicle to do odd jobs on the side to make extra money—so it was in their interest to keep the truck operating. To do their job properly, these workers needed a vehicle with a bucket lift. The bucket trucks had all broken down and never been fixed. Throughout the company, routine maintenance schedules had been allowed to lapse. It was urgent that they be reinstated. "There is still no maintenance plan," Juan Carlos told me more than six months after the blackout. "You're just putting out fires."

* * *

FRANCOIS MORILLO HAD been eager to dig in after being away from the utility for a few years—he was certain that he could find plenty of ways to make the company more efficient. "They said, 'Okay, but you can't look at *xyz*, because those managers are untouchable,'" Francois told me. He walked away. The inertia that existed before the blackouts had taken over again. It was the same short-termism—while the necessary minimum of electricity continued to flow, there was no willingness to do any more. Just enough was good enough. "Everything we did was to get back to March 6," Francois said, referring to the day before the first blackout. "And on March 6 the electrical system was already in crisis."

Francois had been a leftist all his life. Like his workmates he believed that Chávez had set the country on the right path—the path to socialism. Francois told me that the utilities that preceded the formation of Corpoelec had a kind of internal caste system. If you belonged to the right social group or the political party that was in power at the moment, your path to advancement was clear. Francois wasn't part of that clique, so he felt held back. Under Chávez, things changed. Francois became the head of operations at the Guri hydroelectric plant and then manager of the Bolívar region, where all the large generating plants were located. It seemed to me that what he was describing at the utility was what had happened all over the country—one elite stepped in to take the place of another. Party membership was a ticket to advancement. At the same time, Francois wasn't a yes-man. He had an independent streak and wasn't about to accept everything that occurred in the name of Chávez's revolution. At its peak, he told me, Corpoelec had about 50,000 employees, but it really needed only half that many.[1] He had no patience for the profligate patronage and corruption and incompetence. "Sometimes people confuse socialism with the idea that you have to accept everything," Francois said. "That's not socialism. You have to have standards."

After the blackouts, once Francois saw that there was no hope of getting anything constructive done at Corpoelec, he returned to the job that he'd taken after he'd been driven out of the company the first time.

Francois worked as the director of planning at a government-run vocational school known as INCES. The school had branches all over the country. Created long before Chávez, it used to be called just INCE— National Institute of Training and Education. Chávez added an *S* for *socialist*: National Institute of Socialist Training and Education. There is an old joke that says that capitalism is the exploitation of man by man and socialism is exactly the opposite. I don't know if Francois was familiar with it, but his description of the difference between INCE and INCES made the joke obsolete.

"The INCE prepared people to be slaves, mere workers, without freedom," Francois told me. "It was so you could go to work for a big company and the company could get rich off of your labor." We met in a spare office at the institute's Guayana City headquarters. He wore a white buttoned shirt and an Apple Watch, and his manner had something of both an engineer's precision and a teacher's empathy. He said that under Chávez, with the transformation to INCES, there was a change in orientation. "Now when we train people, the goal is that they can become their own bosses so that they can say, 'I have the training and I can get together with four other workers and we can start our own company.' Or they can go out and teach their trade directly to the people." Francois chopped at the desk with big hands as he spoke. "But in practice, it's the same as before. They go to work for a company and the company screws them over."

* * *

THE FIRST TIME that I'd spoken with Antonio Martini, he told me: "If Venezuela falls in this struggle of transformation, then all of Latin America falls with her. A lot of countries and a lot of social movements look to Venezuela as an example: *If Venezuela can do it, then we can too.* If Venezuela falls, then there's no more model to follow."

I dropped in a few times to see Antonio at the office that he and his wife, Mercedes, had rented in a shopping mall. They were struggling to find a way to make a living. They'd started a business doing career and life coaching; Mercedes did some graphic design; and they'd created an online travel agency. You had to admire their initiative. No one was traveling. The businesses that might have needed graphic design services were closing. And the prospects for coaching clients couldn't have been too rosy. On one of my visits, we discussed the terrible shape the country was in—out-of-control corruption, the tanking economy, the mess that the government had made of Corpoelec. We talked about the way that Antonio and his friends had tried to make a contribution and then had been ignored in favor of politics as usual. I asked Antonio how he would vote if there were a presidential election today. Without hesitation, he said that he would vote for Maduro. Mercedes said that she would do the same. I was stunned. How could that be, after everything that we'd been talking about?

"We believe that socialism is the only path to build the America that we want," Antonio said, meaning America in the hemispheric sense. "A united America, an America where respect and solidarity are the norm. So we would be going against our convictions if we voted for the opposition."

We'd also talked about how calling yourself a socialist or wearing a red T-shirt didn't make you a socialist and about how so many of those who filled the ranks of the United Socialist Party of Venezuela—Luis Motta Domínguez, the former energy minister, for example—were no more socialist than Donald Trump was. "The phrase 'to each according to his needs, from each according to his abilities' still resonates for me," Antonio said. "That's the place that we want to get to, but the course that we're traveling—let's just say that our ship is being blown from side to side by strong winds that have taken it a little off course, but the ship is still moving, it's still advancing."

Here was a guy who'd been unfairly fired from the job he loved by a corrupt and incompetent bully who had been appointed because the president thought it was more important to play politics and placate the factions within his party than to guarantee reliable electrical power for the citizens of the country. Here was a guy who'd seen the electrical grid that he'd worked for decades to build and sustain be ruined by bad management and corruption—with great suffering for ordinary people as the result. And yet he said that he'd still vote for the people who had done all that.

"I don't think that the problem is the socialist system," Mercedes said. "We're human beings. People become sick with power, they become sick with greed, and that distorts everything." I pointed out that this had been going on for almost twenty years. "It makes you sad to see how the system that we believed in has become so perverted, the results being what you see today," Mercedes said. "It makes you sad because this isn't the socialism that we dreamed about."

I asked if this conversation could be quoted in the book I was writing.

There were things, Antonio said, that were best discussed among a small group of friends. There was the risk that someone would conclude that you had crossed the line between being critical and being counter-revolutionary. Mercedes said that it made her afraid. I asked again if they were comfortable with the conversation appearing in the book. There was some nervous laughter.

"Then it will be part of written history," Antonio said.

* * *

A FEW DAYS after my conversation with Antonio and Mercedes, I was back in Caracas and I had breakfast with Enrique Márquez, an opposition politician from Zulia state. Márquez had a reputation for being open-minded and not orthodox. He had opposed the decision to boycott the May 2018 presidential election and he'd supported Henri Falcón, the opposition candidate who ran in defiance of the boycott. He also maintained contact with people in the Maduro government, believing that the country would advance only through communication and dialogue. These positions did not make him popular among some of his fellow oppositionists. It was Márquez who had left the stage after Guaidó's swearing in, concerned by the way it had been concealed from the rest of the opposition. We sat on a terrace at a restaurant called Rey David. We ordered the criollo breakfast, and it was enough food for an entire day: arepas and butter and shredded beef and eggs and sweet plantains. Life in Venezuela was full of invisible lines. There were the lines in Maracaibo during the power rationing, separating parts of the city that had electricity from those that did not. There were the lines between gang territories in Petare where you could be killed if you stepped on the wrong side. And there were the lines between places that didn't have food and those that had more food than you could eat.

The Chavista leadership, Márquez told me, had no scruples: they were capable of doing virtually anything in order to survive, to stay in power. He wanted me to understand that this lack of scruples wasn't the product or the symptom of some kind of criminality—it wasn't the unscrupulousness of a drug trafficker or someone who paid a bribe to win a government contract. The Chavista leaders saw themselves as actors in a great drama of good versus evil, David versus Goliath. And this epic contest justified any form of action in the name of staving off defeat and preserving the chance to one day prevail absolutely. Márquez told me about a recent conversation that he'd had with Héctor Rodríguez, a young Chavista governor. Rodríguez was considered to be one of the more ambitious and promising of a new generation of Chavista leaders. He was also perceived to be a potential moderate, someone who could perhaps build a bridge between Chavismo and the opposition. Márquez said that Rodríguez had told him: "We have a geopolitical role. If we lose Venezuela, then we lose Cuba, then we lose Nicaragua, and then we lose all of Latin America for the revolution. Therefore, we cannot lose Venezuela. We are determined to stay in power."

This was the corollary of the idea that animated policy makers in Washington—Venezuela could be the domino that made all the leftist governments in the hemisphere fall over.

Márquez disagreed with the notion, prevalent among many of his co-oppositionists, that the Maduro government was first and foremost a conglomeration of criminals whose main objective was to continue profiting from various forms of corruption and illegal activities, like drug trafficking. "These are people who are very dogmatic," Márquez said. "They have a gigantic dogma in their heads. It justifies all of their actions, in their minds. If I have to kill, I will do it, simply because it's part of my fight against imperialism. If I have to destroy Venezuela, it doesn't matter. Venezuela will be reborn later in the fight against imperialism. It doesn't matter what happens."

They were true believers.

I admit that I feel a kind of envy of Antonio and Mercedes and the others—Juan Carlos, Francois, and Luis. After my first conversation with Antonio, I wrote in my notebook: "I wish I could believe in something like socialism or god." I envy the simplicity of belief. Of an ordered world that obeys rules, whether of a god or socialism or some other ism. But I have a newspaper reporter's occupational handicap: I believe only in the truth. The truth of a journalist is not simple. It requires digging and talking to lots of people who say conflicting things. The world is a complex place, and the job of the journalist—as well as the job of the citizen—is to try very hard to understand the world as it is. More than three decades ago, in Mexico City, I had a long conversation with the Cuban author and film director Jesús Díaz. Jesús said to me: "We have to see the world as it is, not the world as we want it to be." This struggle had become the center of Jesús's life. About a year after we talked, Jesús would break with the Castro government and go into exile in Spain. More recently, the historian Timothy Snyder wrote that history is complex and difficult, while fables—those that nations or ideologies tell about themselves—are appealing and easy to live with. "Authoritarianism begins," Snyder wrote, "when we can no longer tell the difference between the true and the appealing."[2]

You could say that Antonio is naive or that his faith is a blind one. But he is also a person of good faith. He believes in making an effort to make the world a better place. Antonio—drummed out of Corpoelec and still believing. Mercedes, watching the destruction of the country and being afraid that if she spoke up something bad would happen to her—and still believing. Lentil-eating Chacón, cinching his belt and teaching about the National Plans that have never come close to being fulfilled—and still believing.

I don't feel that same envy for the Delcy Rodríguezes or the Héctor

Rodríguezes of this world. Their Manichean fantasy is different in its consequences. Andrés Izarra, the former cabinet minister, told me that in 2013, on the night of the presidential election to replace Chávez, the early returns showed Maduro behind. Izarra said that he listened to Delcy and Diosdado Cabello talk about what to do if Maduro lost: No matter what the outcome, they said, the government would not surrender power to the opposition.

Maduro had inherited from Chávez a government stripped of checks and balances, without a separation of powers. Chávez had filled the Supreme Court with loyalists, and they reliably ruled in favor of the government. Judges at other levels were kept in line. For years, the legislature was a rubber stamp with a tame Chavista majority. The Chavistas also controlled the electoral council, allowing them to set rules and conditions that suited them. Chávez and Maduro after him liked to boast about how many elections they'd won and how they'd created a democracy that put people first. But after so many years in power, they could conceive of only one sort of democracy—one that had them always as the winners.

* * *

AFTER JUAN CARLOS retired from Corpoelec, following his run-in with Motta Domínguez and the bogus allegation of sabotage, he and his wife started a business, making and selling cleaning products. They made liquid soap and laundry detergent and dish soap and floor cleaner and disinfectant. They mixed the products in their garage and poured them into plastic bottles for sale. People liked the products, and they did well. But they needed salespeople. Antonio and Mercedes signed up. They had their life coaching and graphic design businesses and their online travel agency. But that wasn't enough. So now they added cleaning product sales to their résumés. Francois signed up too; he needed something to supplement his salary at INCES and his Corpoelec pension. When Luis Dimas was kicked out of Corpoelec, he'd started selling chicken parts. He bought whole chickens and cut them up and wrapped the parts in plastic and delivered them to people's homes. It was a custom business—you could pick what you wanted, thighs, breasts, or a mix.

As the economy grew worse, however, Luis couldn't survive on chicken parts alone. He too joined Juan Carlos's sales team.

Juan Carlos had spent decades operating enormous hydroelectric plants, with their dams and reservoirs and turbines, connected to hundreds of miles of high-tension lines marching across the landscape. Now he made cleaning products. It was quite a change, but there was something about it that suited him. It fit his engineer's temperament. And no politics and no bosses were involved. And he could do it all in his garage. Juan Carlos told me: "That's how Henry Ford got started."[3]

Venezuela Agonistes

By the start of 2020, Venezuela's healthcare system was barely functioning. Close to half of the country's doctors, some 30,000 of them, had emigrated.[1] Medicines were unavailable or in short supply. Hospitals frequently had no electricity or running water. Equipment was out-of-date or broken. When the Covid-19 pandemic hit, it was clear that Venezuela would have to take strong measures or face disaster.

On February 27, Maduro announced that he had created a commission to lead the country's coronavirus response, to be led by Vice President Delcy Rodríguez. (This was a day after Trump, in Washington, announced that Vice President Pence would lead the U.S. virus task force.) Two weeks later, on March 13, officials said they had detected the first two cases of Covid-19 in the country. Three days after that, Maduro announced a nationwide stay-at-home order—the first in Latin America. Maduro shut the airports. He used his close relations with China to arrange for the donation of half a million antibody tests, while other countries in the region were struggling to buy tests on the open market. Cuba provided advice and sent doctors.

In one sense, Venezuela was lucky. The country was already isolated. There were hardly any international flights. People were leaving Venezuela, not going there. At first it seemed that there were few cases of Covid-19. But it was only a matter of time. People who live day to day and have no food at home can't stay inside for weeks or months waiting for the pandemic to subside. They have to go out and make a few bolivars to buy food. And people who have no running water and no soap can't wash their hands. So while Covid was slow to take off in Venezuela, its spread inevitably accelerated.

By December 2020, Venezuela said it had a total of about 105,000 cases and 900 deaths. But there was good reason to be skeptical of the official data. Colombia, with about double the population, was reporting 1.4 million cases and 38,000 deaths. The antibody tests the government used as its principal detection method were not designed to give an accurate picture of the infection rate. For that, the government needed diagnostic tests, but it administered those in much smaller numbers.[2]

By now authoritarianism had become a vocation and the government criminalized infection. Venezuelan refugees returning from other parts of Latin America were labeled as bioterrorists, intentionally bringing infection back to the country.[3] The government strictly controlled the number of returning refugees allowed to reenter the country, forcing hundreds to wait at the border on the Colombian side. Returnees were placed in quarantine facilities, in crowded conditions, without basic hygiene or adequate food or attention.

Throughout the country, people who had Covid symptoms or tested positive were often forced into similar quarantine facilities. Many people opted instead to conceal their condition and stay at home, to recover or die there.

The government acted aggressively to control information as well. It began arresting reporters and medical personnel who posted information on social media that questioned or contradicted the official data. Early on, a young community journalist named Darvinson Rojas posted a few tweets suggesting that a small number of locally reported cases had been left out of the official government count. The FAES, Maduro's feared special forces police, showed up at Rojas's house at night, claiming that they'd received a report of a person with Covid at his address. They took him away and detained him for twelve days.[4]

Doctors and nurses who questioned the readiness of the healthcare system or the government's low case counts were intimidated and harassed. Information was a powerful tool. If the government controlled the information, it could control the narrative—how many cases, how many deaths, who to credit and who to blame.

You could question the effectiveness and appropriateness of the government's measures, but it was clear that Maduro was governing. He ordered a quarantine and took steps to enforce it. He used his relations with other countries to secure aid. Government officials gave daily briefings and Maduro went on television regularly to discuss the virus and the measures the country was taking. Governments throughout the world were struggling to develop an effective response to the virus. Maduro's government had been quicker to act and more aggressive than many others. It was hard to square this with the persistent characterization of Venezuela as a failed state or a state captured by organized crime. Maduro's failures were of a different nature than those of the United States or neighboring Brazil, where Trump and the Brazilian president, Jair Bolsonaro, denied the seriousness of the pandemic and undermined efforts to combat it. Maduro governed as an authoritarian, criminalizing the disease, jailing journalists and doctors, and increasing the repression against his political opponents.

When the Covid-19 pandemic reached Venezuela, I was in contact via WhatsApp messages with Hilda Solórzano, the woman in the Petare slum who lived in a tiny shack with her husband and seven children. Her life had been difficult before. Now everything was worse.

"Things are crazy here," Hilda wrote one afternoon. "No work. No food. I don't know what I'm going to do. At least we ate something yesterday in the afternoon. Today we haven't eaten anything." I asked what they'd eaten the day before. "Lentils." And the day before that? "Rice." Hilda's kids used to receive daily meals at school. But that stopped when the government shut down the schools because of the virus. That night I wrote to Hilda again, to ask if they'd had anything to eat. She replied: "Yes. I got some rice and I gave it to the kids so that they wouldn't go to bed on an empty stomach."

There were rumors of people in the neighborhood coming down with Covid, and it was hard to tell what was true. Hilda was worried about her children. "I'm afraid because three of the children have asthma and another three are underweight, so they don't have the defenses they should. But I trust in God that everything will come out okay." She had so many children it seemed that one or more of them were always sick. At one point Gregorio, her youngest, the boy whose teeth had turned black and fallen out, came down with a fever that wouldn't subside and had to spend the night in a hospital. Hilda had no medicine to give her children, not even acetaminophen.

She told me that they hadn't had cooking gas for more than a week. She'd been cooking on a wood fire, on the ground. They would collect scraps of wood in the street or farther up on the hill where there were trees and underbrush.

While all this was going on, the price of oil crashed when Saudi Arabia and Russia started a price war. Venezuela's already low oil revenues fell even further. The cost of pumping oil in Venezuela was higher than the price on the world market. Storage tanks filled up and analysts predicted that Venezuela would have to stop pumping oil altogether because it had nowhere to put it and nowhere to sell it. At the same time, the country's decrepit refineries stopped producing gasoline. Maduro arranged to buy several tankers of gasoline from Iran. But that was only a stopgap. The United States sought to block Iran from sending further shipments, and in much of the country it became nearly impossible to buy gasoline. Maduro allowed some service stations to sell gasoline at international prices, in dollars. The Venezuelan birthright of cheap gasoline—the citizen's most direct connection to the liquid oil in the ground—had ended. At the same time, the bolivar kept plunging and the dollar, the yanqui greenback, was increasingly used as the country's everyday currency. At one point, the minimum wage, in bolivars, equaled less than a dollar a month.[5]

All the while the United States kept turning the screws, targeting sanctions at Russian and Iranian efforts to help Maduro sell oil. There were a few lonely voices calling for an easing of sanctions during the pandemic—but they were ignored.

While all this was going on, Guaidó was reduced to watching from the sidelines. There was little that he could do. He was a fictional president running a fictional government. He promised to distribute a few thousand face masks and surgical gloves to medical workers. He taped a short speech that was posted on the internet, where he said, "Venezuela is in our hands," and then added, "You can count on me." But that made the difficult truth even more evident. Venezuela was *not* in his hands, and there was virtually nothing that he could be counted on to do. He was as powerless as almost everyone else in the country.

And then came Jordan Goudreau's invasion and the revelations about the contract with Guaidó. I noticed that some pro-opposition online media outlets stopped referring to Guaidó as the country's interim president. They went back to calling him the leader of the National Assembly. He'd been demoted.

The responsibility for the disaster in Venezuela lies with Maduro, and Chávez before him. Chavismo has been in power for more than two decades. They own the wreck of Venezuela. It is of their making. Maduro built a government that is brutal, cruel, and destructive. But the opposition has made many errors along the way. For much of 2019 and 2020, opposition supporters responded sharply to any criticism of Guaidó, characterizing it as aiding the enemy. But what Guaidó needed most was criticism. He needed to hear from people outside the limited circle that was guiding him. Silencing criticism was another lesson that the opposition learned from the Chavistas.

"We can't keep playing at being a government on the internet," said Henrique Capriles, the opposition politician who had run for president against Chávez in 2012 and Maduro in 2013. He had remained mostly quiet during Guaidó's turn in the spotlight, but toward the end of 2020 he spoke out. "Either you're the government or you're the opposition. You can't be both."[6]

In any case, the term in office of Guaidó and the legislators who served with him was coming to an end. The country was due to hold National Assembly elections in December 2020. Maduro used the pandemic as cover to step up repression. The Supreme Court seized control of several opposition parties, removed their leaders, and installed new ones amenable to the government. Maduro was creating a bespoke opposition that could run candidates in the election and create the appearance of a contested vote. But this time Maduro cracked down on the left as well. The courts took over several leftist parties that had begun to voice criticism of the government, and leftist leaders were thrown in jail. I wondered if Maduro was creating an opportunity for his critics.

Chavismo lived off the deep divisions that it had mined in Venezuelan society. In prison would the two sides find common ground?

Guaidó and most other opposition leaders again called for an election boycott, as they had during the presidential election in 2018. Less than a third of voters cast ballots in the December election. The Chavistas won 90 percent of the seats. "Nothing is going to happen if you call on people to do nothing," Capriles had said in criticizing the boycott. But in the face of nothing, it wasn't clear what the alternative was for Venezuelans desperate to have something.

* * *

AND THE AMERICANS? It was like watching the Venezuelanization of U.S. policy making. So much was improvised, done without thinking things through, without preparation, ignoring the facts, hoping that it would all work when your own experts said that there was little chance of success.

"Everybody's revisiting whether this whole thing was a good idea or not," said Keith Mines, the former State Department official. "There was always an argument for there just not being a way to work this thing of a parallel government. I mean, it had never been done before. And I think now we kind of understand why. Because it just doesn't—it doesn't work."

It was the old gringo trait of being sure that you knew what was right and what another country needed and how to fix what was wrong. Or of thinking that you could exploit another country for your own ends. Venezuela had become a second Cuba, a cat's-paw that could be used to swing an election in Florida. For more than fifty years the embargo against Cuba hadn't changed things for the better on the island—but how many votes had you gotten in that time? And if the oil embargo on Venezuela had to last fifty years—why not?

Uncle Sam had a long history in Latin America, playing at empire, playing at dominoes. For the United States too, the past and the present could merge.

Still, Trump's Venezuela strategy paid off again in Florida. He won the state in 2020, helped by a large-scale misinformation campaign targeting Hispanic voters with the message that the Democrats were socialists and that Joe Biden, Trump's opponent, was a pawn of Maduro.[7] Three weeks before election day, Trump had tweeted: "Our country cannot survive as a Socialist Nation, and that's what the Democrats want it to be. The USA will never become a large scale version of Venezuela."

But Florida turned out not to be the decisive state, and in the aftermath of the election, there was a startling juxtaposition for those who wanted to see it. Venezuela held its National Assembly election one month after the presidential election in the United States. While Trump and his Republican allies tried to overturn the U.S. result, Maduro again fulfilled a Republican ideal, holding an election in which only one side was allowed to win.

Guaidó also did Trump one better. Having boycotted the December election, Guaidó declared the vote invalid. The assembly then passed a resolution extending, for at least a year, the terms in office of the legislators, including Guaidó—who could then maintain his claim to be the country's interim president. Under the constitution, those terms expired on January 5, 2021, and on that day, in Caracas, the new crop of mostly Chavista legislators, brushing aside Guaidós's maneuver, was sworn in. The next day, January 6, in Washington, a pro-Trump mob attacked Congress, trying to stop the certification of Biden's presidential victory— a last spasm in Trump's efforts to extend his own time in office. Trump eventually left the White House, still claiming to have won the election, while Guaidó continued to exercise his ephemeral presidency. In the midst of it all, Trump allies like the lawyer Sidney Powell had been peddling a conspiracy theory that software created for Hugo Chávez had been used in U.S. voting machines to steal the presidential election.[8] A meme circulated: Trump had warned that if Biden won the election, the United States would become like Venezuela—and with the Capitol riot, he was proved right.

* * *

ONCE IN OFFICE, Biden quickly made good on a campaign promise: his administration ruled that as many as 320,000 Venezuelans living in the United States would be eligible to stay without risk of deportation for at least eighteen months.[9] The designation, known as temporary protected status, was likely to be extended for a longer period, as had been done with immigrants from other countries who in the past were granted a similar protection due to ongoing conflict or natural disaster.

The immigration protection had long been sought by Venezuela advocates, but Trump—despite his aggressive stance toward Maduro—did not approve it. Instead, his administration moved to strip the protection from immigrants that had benefited from the designation, including those from El Salvador and Haiti, as part of his broader attack on immigration.

Meanwhile, with Biden in the White House, Maduro began sending signals. In April 2021, his government transferred six former executives of Citgo, the U.S.-based and Venezuela-owned refining company, from prison to house arrest. The men, known as the Citgo 6, had been jailed on corruption charges and included five naturalized U.S. citizens and a Venezuelan who had been a U.S. resident.[10] The U.S. had long expressed concern over the treatment of the men. A few days later, the Chavista-controlled National Assembly appointed a new electoral council, including two opposition-aligned figures on the five-person panel. Previously the opposition held only one seat on the council.[11]

At the same time, the opposition was becoming more fluid. Capriles and Stalin González (the former second vice president of the assembly—he had refused to go along when the legislature moved to extend the terms of its members) emerged as leaders of a more pragmatic wing of the opposition. Rather than insisting on the immediate exit of Maduro, they took a more gradual approach, prioritizing negotiations and talking to the government about creating conditions for fair elections, including international observers. Both Chavismo and the opposition, González told me, would have to move toward the center to find common ground.

But there was little indication early on that Biden was considering a significant change in direction. Antony Blinken, Biden's secretary of state, said in his Senate confirmation hearing that the United States would continue to recognize Guaidó as Venezuela's legitimate president and he supported the use of sanctions. "Maybe we need to look at how we more effectively target the sanctions that we have so that regime enablers really feel the pain of those sanctions," Blinken said.[12] On Cuba policy too, Biden showed no interest in using political capital to revisit Obama's opening, which Trump had turned back.

Democrats were stunned by their shellacking in Florida. Besides losing the presidential vote in the state, two incumbent (and moderate) Democratic congresswomen lost their seats in majority Hispanic Miami-Dade County, where Republicans had aggressively pressed their "all Democrats are socialists" campaign (there were other factors, as well, including a better Republican get-out-the-vote effort). This meant any administration move toward Venezuela that could be portrayed as an overture toward Maduro or a softening of support for Guaidó could cost the Democrats votes in the midterm election and beyond.

"They see it as a third rail," said a person who discussed Venezuela policy with an administration official. "They know nothing good is going to come of this."

But Donna Shalala, one of the two House members who lost in Miami-Dade County, told me that Biden needed to show real progress against Maduro in Venezuela in order to shield Democratic candidates against red-baiting and persuade more Hispanic voters. "The only way to do that is to demonstrate in at least one socialist country that we're prepared to get something done," Shalala said. "Unless they want to write off Florida . . . But I just don't think they're going to do that."

* * *

"IT PAINS ME to say that Venezuela is just a piece of land with a group of people living on it who haven't been able to build a nation and create a national spirit, with the principles and values and the culture of a nation and a national identity," José Vicente Haro, the human rights lawyer who had been kidnapped and tortured, told me. Venezuela falls always into the same trap, opting for the strongman, the caudillo, a savior on a white horse. "In Venezuela," José Vicente said, "there are many people and very few citizens."

His words took me back to a conversation I'd had almost seven years earlier, on election day in October 2012, when Chávez ran for the last time. I was at a polling station in a Caracas barrio called Catia. I spoke to a woman named Esther Silva. She had purple ink on her right pinkie, to show that she had voted. Turnout was very high. Esther was seventy-one years old and she'd been able to use a special line for senior citizens. Even so, it took her an hour to enter and vote.

Esther had never voted for Chávez. He had some good ideas, she said, but the underlings he assigned to carry them out made a hash of everything (this happened to be a criticism that many Chavistas voiced as well—the comandante was never to blame). On this day Esther had voted for Capriles. She had hopes that the country was poised for a change. She turned out to be wrong, but her words have stayed with me. "I want to be a citizen," Esther said. "I'm tired of being 'the people.'"

* * *

CYCLES. THE BOOM and bust of oil. The circular time of Chavismo, with its revolutionary fantasy and its gaze fixed in the past, the golden age of Bolívar, the glorious failure of Chávez's coup. The bicycle of corruption, keeping the wheels turning, one crooked deal financing the next. Poverty has its cycle too. Poverty grabs on to you and won't let you go.

It seemed like every time Hilda started to get a little bit ahead, poverty grabbed her and dragged her back.

After I met Hilda, she started her baking business again, the one she'd had before her daughter Yara was killed. She made rolls and pastries in her tiny shack and sold them in the neighborhood. She made birthday cakes with fancy decorations. A relative of her husband helped out, selling the rolls Hilda made. She was doing well and the family was eating better. Hilda was full of energy, upbeat. Then the relative ran off with the money from two weeks of sales. Without the money, she couldn't buy ingredients. A man in the neighborhood was going to lend her money to buy equipment, but he was killed in a shooting. Eventually Hilda had to give it up anyway—the cost of ingredients had gone so high that people couldn't afford to buy what she made.

She took a sewing course offered by the government. She bought a sewing machine and started making clothes. She made clothes for her family and then to sell. She was like a one-woman factory, busy all the time. With the money she made, she went to buy fabric. As she left the store she was held up. The muggers took the fabric, the rest of her money, and her cell phone.

Venezuela too kept getting pulled back. Each boom led to a bust that left the country worse off than it was before. Oil was a curse. Venezuelans seemed to know only one way. They weren't citizens so much as clients. The government existed to dole out the dwindling oil money. For all that it wanted to pretend that it was something new, Chavismo was more of what came before. And now the opposition had learned the lessons of Chavismo all too well.

One day in 2019, I was talking with Hilda's eighteen-year-old daughter Hilmaris. She was tall and looked like her mother, with long black hair and shy, probing eyes. I asked Hilmaris what the future looked like to her.

"The way things are, it's very hard to say, 'Tomorrow something is going to happen and Venezuela is going to change,'" Hilmaris said. "You have to go on, little by little, creating an ideology or a consciousness that something's going to happen, that we can move forward, that we can be more humble and more kind, as Venezuelans. We have to change our way of thinking, because maybe Maduro will stay on as president and Venezuela will stay the same—or maybe they'll overthrow Maduro and Guaidó will take his place, but Venezuela could still stay the same."

She said that Venezuelans were too conformist. It was a word that I heard many times as I traveled around the country. I asked what she meant. She said that Venezuelans were too willing to go along with things as they were, accepting whatever they were given without insisting on something better. That was one of the perplexing things about the petrostate. Venezuelans expected their government to spread around the oil money, but they were often willing to accept a meager portion—a box of food that didn't come when it was supposed to, a pension that bought a few eggs.

Hilmaris said, "As Venezuelans, we have to change in order to change Venezuela."

* * *

VENEZUELA'S GREATEST MODERN painter was Armando Reverón. He lived on the beach near Caracas and painted a world drenched in the savage white light of the Caribbean, a light that seemed to chase away all color from the landscape. Reverón went mad and lived a happy, odd, marginal existence, painting and creating. "Painting is truth," Reverón said once. "But light blinds you, it drives you crazy, it torments you, because you cannot see light."[13] I think that what Reverón meant was that truth was elusive because you could approach it only through something that you could not see. Reveron's greatest paintings are almost pure light—sketchy figures and palm trees stripped of color, washed clean, lost in the glare.

I said at the outset that I thought of Venezuela as the shouting country. I have another way of seeing it. I think of Venezuela as a country of light—Reverón's blinding, revealing, concealing light on the littoral, the golden light of Caracas evenings filtered through the dark green leaves of mango trees, the diffuse light of the immense savannah. I noticed, as the crisis worsened, that some news photographers seemed to be having a hard time portraying life in Venezuela, so they fell back on a visual trick. They began to use filters to make their subjects darker and shadowy. I think that they felt that the brightly lighted country in front of their lenses didn't comport with the misery that they encountered as journalists. As I traveled around Venezuela while the country collapsed, I had the opposite concern. I feared that the stories that I was collecting were too dark, too violent, unrelentingly without hope, and I struggled to square them with the light-filled, raucous, noisy country that I'd lived in a few years before. I encountered a country of darkness, of blackouts, a country that seemed to be running away from the light.

Back in 2012, I took a reporting trip to the plains in the southwestern state of Apure. It was the rainy season, and the plains were experiencing their annual flood. The waters rose and covered the land. What had been earth was now water. The flood filled the tall grass plain and the grasses changed from land plants to water plants, waving in the current just as they used to wave in the wind. We passed through a rough settlement, a few houses lost in the plain. I went down with the children from the settlement to a low place and we jumped into the water, swimming above what was dry land a few days before. The children laughed, their round, innocent faces held above the smooth water. Above us the dome of blue sky, some wisps of cloud. I'd gone there to write a story about drug traffickers and hidden airstrips. This part of the country had been taken over by outsiders with guns, and the people who lived there had no choice but to go along. There was fear all around, like I would later find in the gold mines. And yet, there was the laughter of the children and also the perseverance and bravery of people who had been there before and would be there after. That was a dark story too. And all those days that we spent on the plains, we were surrounded by a kind of liquid light, brilliant, limpid, clear as the water. It was possible there, on the flooded plain, to feel like a witness to the first days of creation, when the world hadn't decided yet if it was going to be land or water, so it was both at once.

ACKNOWLEDGMENTS

With the deepest gratitude, I acknowledge all those in Venezuela who, over many years, shared their stories with me—for their infinite generosity, their openness, their courage, their trust, and their hope for better times.

I thank my close collaborator and friend Patricia Torres for her patience, her hard work, for countless conversations and many miles traveled together—and for her faith in me and this book. María Iguarán provided timely help with reporting, research, and transcriptions. Trish Hall gave me invaluable advice and encouragement. Paula Ramón helped me get through the hard parts. Julio Bianchi taught me how to make arepas.

I especially thank the journalists and drivers who worked with me in Venezuela in 2019 and 2020. In Caracas: Carlos Peña, Jacobo Nasra, Omar Mora, Luis Atencio, and Francisco del Avila. In Maracaibo: Nataly Angulo, Sheyla Urdaneta, and Henry Matos. In Guayana City: Clavel Rangel, María de los Ángeles Ramírez, Luis Rodríguez, and Andrés Jesús Rodríguez. In Cumaná: Nayrobis Rodríguez.

A profound thank you to George Witte, my editor at St. Martin's Press, and to David Vigliano, my agent.

Thanks to everyone on the foreign desk at *The New York Times*, in particular my editors, Greg Winter and Marc Lacey; and to Joe Kahn for sending me to Venezuela.

Thanks for help with research to Sam Goldsmith, Hilda Peña, Gaspar Le Dem, and Tracy Connor; for fact-checking to Ghada Scruggs; for fixing in Maracaibo to Alejandro Calmen; for reading and commenting on the text to José Luis Paniagua; and for comments on individual chapters to Brian Ellsworth, David Goodman, Francisco Monaldi, and Michael Penfold.

Thanks to Romy Neuman for math and fact-checking help; to Emma Neuman for her interest and encouragement; and to Max Neuman for his organizing skills and many conversations that helped sharpen my thoughts and words.

Over coffee one morning in Café Arábica in Caracas, Luis García Mora asked what my book was about. I told him, and he said: "Ah, I see. You're going to write from the heart." I hope that I have fulfilled his expectation.

NOTES

PROLOGUE: MENE GRANDE

1. There were other wells drilled before Zumaque 1, but it is considered the first commercially successful well. The image of a pumpjack's motion as diastole and systole was used by Ross Macdonald in *The Moving Target*.

CHAPTER 3: BLACKOUT

1. Venezuela is known for its beauty pageants and international beauty queens, and before the crisis, there was a thriving beauty industry that promoted superficial enhancements, including plastic surgery.
2. Darlene Rivas, *Missionary Capitalist: Nelson Rockefeller in Venezuela* (University of North Carolina Press, 2002), 120.

CHAPTER 4: TO BE BOLÍVAR

1. Columbus's arrival off South America and his association of it with the Terrestrial Paradise are discussed in: Bartolomé de Las Casas, *Historia de las Indias* (Project Gutenberg). Margarita Zamora, *Reading Columbus* (University of California Press, 1993), 141–51. Samuel Eliot Morison, *Admiral of the Ocean Sea* (Little, Brown, 1942), 532–58.
2. Martín Fernández de Enciso, *Suma de geografía*.
3. Elías Pino Iturrieta, ed., *Historia mínima de Venezuela* (Colegio de México, 2018), 22.
4. Pino Iturrieta, *Historia mínima*, 25. Aldemaro Romero Jr., Susanna Chilbert, and M. G. Eisenhart, "Cubagua's Pearl-Oyster Beds: The First Depletion of a Natural Resource Caused by Europeans in the American Continent," *Journal of Political Ecology* 6, no. 1 (1999): 57–78. Aldemaro Romero, "Death and Taxes: The Case of

the Depletion of Pearl Oyster Beds in Sixteenth-Century Venezuela," *Conservation Biology* 17, no. 4 (2003): 1013–23.

5. I have relied on numerous texts on the lives of Miranda and Bolívar and the war of independence, including: John Lynch, *Simón Bolívar: A Life* (Yale University Press, 2006). Marie Arana, *Bolívar: American Liberator* (Simon & Schuster Paperbacks, 2013). William Spence Robertson, *The Life of Miranda*, vols. I and II (Cooper Square Publishers, 1969; originally published in 1929). Juan Uslar Pietri, *Historia de la rebelión popular de 1814* (Monte Ávila Editores Latinoamericana, 2007; originally published in 1962). John V. Lombardi, *The Decline and Abolition of Negro Slavery in Venezuela 1820–1854* (Greenwood Publishing Corp., 1971).

6. Pino Iturrieta, *Historia mínima*, 101.

7. Pino Iturrieta, *Historia mínima*, 120.

8. The classic text on Bolívar worship is Germán Carrera Damas, *El culto a Bolívar* (Grijalbo, 1989).

9. Eduardo Blanco, *Venezuela heroica, tomo primero* (Ediciones del Nuevo Mundo, 1979), 85–86.

10. Tomás Straka, *La épica del desencanto: Bolivarianismo, historiografía y política en Venezuela* (Editorial Alfa, 2017), 109–111.

CHAPTER 5: BLACKOUT

1. A Chavista legislator named Luis Tascón uploaded the names of the petition signers to a website, which government officials used to identify and purge workers they considered disloyal. It became known as La Lista Tascón, Tascón's List.

CHAPTER 6: CRUDE

1. Rómulo Betancourt, *Venezuela, política y petróleo* (Academia de Ciencias Políticas y Sociales, 2007), 60. On March 18, 1923, three months after the gusher at Cabimas, a story appeared in *The New York Times* under the headline "Biggest Oil Well Yet." It said the well was "conceded to be the most productive in the world." That may not have been quite accurate, but it was a lot of oil and a sign of more to come.

2. Terry Lynn Karl, *The Paradox of Plenty: Oil Booms and Petro-States* (University of California Press, 1997), 80.

3. Franklin Tugwell, *The Politics of Oil in Venezuela* (Stanford University Press, 1975), 182.

4. Karl, *Paradox*, 81.

5. Thomas Rourke, *Gómez: Tyrant of the Andes* (Halcyon House, 1936), 187–88.

6. Betancourt, *Venezuela*, 38–40.

7. Mariano Picón Salas, "La aventura venezolana," *Suma de Venezuela* (Monte Ávila Editores, 1988).

8. For immigration policy that favored white Europeans, see John V. Lombardi,

Venezuela: The Search for Order, the Dream of Progress (Oxford University Press, 1982), 50–51. Pérez Jiménez alluded to this policy in an interview in 1998 with the television journalist Óscar Yanes; he said that the large number of international beauty queens from Venezuela was the direct, although unintended, result of European immigration, which was encouraged "to improve the ethnic component" of the country. The United States rewarded Pérez Jiménez's anticommunism and favorable treatment of the oil companies by awarding him the Legion of Merit in 1954. Larry Rohter, "Marcos Pérez Jiménez, 87, Venezuela Ruler," *New York Times*, September 22, 2001.

9. Ruth de Krivoy, *Collapse: The Venezuelan Banking Crisis of 1994* (Group of Thirty, 2000), 259.

10. Karl, *Paradox*, 71 and 112.

11. Teodoro Petkoff, "Esto le sacó la piedra," *Tal Cual*, September 20, 2004.

12. Karl, *Paradox*, 116–17.

13. Oil production had been falling since the early 1970s—first as foreign oil companies slashed investment in anticipation of the industry's eventual nationalization and later in response to OPEC production cuts—a factor that made the economy's eventual downturn more severe. The production drop in the 1970s and 1980s was paralleled decades later by a decrease in production during the Chávez years, another period of record high prices. In both instances, the nation tried to plug the gap by borrowing money (Francisco Monaldi, interview).

14. Karl, *Paradox*, 146–48.

15. Krivoy, *Collapse*, 261.

16. Karl, *Paradox*, 156–57.

17. Krivoy, *Collapse*, 260.

18. Karl, *Paradox*, 164.

19. Janet Kelly and Pedro A. Palma, "The Syndrome of Economic Decline and the Quest for Change," *The Unraveling of Representative Democracy in Venezuela*, ed. Jennifer L. McCoy and David J. Myers (Johns Hopkins University Press, 2004), 207–208.

20. "What Dutch Disease Is, and Why It's Bad," *The Economist*, November 5, 2014. Jeffrey D. Sachs and Andrew M. Warner, "Natural Resource Abundance and Economic Growth," Working Paper 5398, National Bureau of Economic Research, December 1995.

21. Karl, *Paradox*, 91.

22. Karl, *Paradox*, 91.

CHAPTER 7: THE MAN UNDER THE PALM TREE

1. Another friend of mine tells a joke that is almost identical to D.'s story. In the joke, an economist encounters a fisherman on the beach. They have a conversation similar to the one that D.'s father had with the man beneath the palm tree. The joke is an evergreen. D. says that his story is true—the man and the coconut tree and

the camping trip were all real. In both cases, joke and family lore are rooted in something essential in the way Venezuelans perceive their reality.

CHAPTER 8: FIRST, I WANT TO SAY GOOD MORNING

1. "The most striking aspect of the 1961 Constitution was its reaffirmation of state intervention and extreme presidentialism." Terry Lynn Karl, *The Paradox of Plenty: Oil Booms and Petro-States* (University of California Press, 1997), 105. "The 1999 constitution maintained and even deepened centralized, presidential control over the country, along with a statist approach to economic affairs." Jennifer L. McCoy, "From Representative to Participatory Democracy? Regime Transformation in Venezuela," *The Unraveling of Representative Democracy in Venezuela*, ed. Jennifer L. McCoy and David J. Meyers (Johns Hopkins University Press, 2004), 279. For an alternate view, that "the 1961 constitution was aimed at limiting presidential powers," and "the 1999 constitution increased the presidential powers dramatically," see Francisco Monaldi and Michael Penfold, "Institutional Collapse: The Rise and Decline of Democratic Governance in Venezuela," *Venezuela Before Chávez: Anatomy of an Economic Collapse*, ed. Ricardo Haussmann and Francisco Rodríguez (Pennsylvania State University Press, 2018).
2. Alianza Regional por la Libre Expresión e Información, "Herramientas del estado para el control de la información: Cadenas nacionales," 62–68.
3. Rhonny Zamora was interviewed by Patricia Torres.

CHAPTER 9: IRREVOCABLE, ABSOLUTE, TOTAL

1. A second, never built phase of the Bolivarian Cable Train would have included two additional stations and an additional two-thirds of a mile of track.
2. The account of the Bolivarian Cable Train's jerry-rigged operation during a Chávez campaign event is based on public documents, news accounts and videos, as well as interviews with people who worked on the cable train project, including Jorge González, the Doppelmayr engineer, and three others who spoke on condition of anonymity because they feared reprisals or because they were not authorized to discuss the project. Haiman El Troudi, the former transportation minister, did not respond to emails. Presented with a detailed summary of the events, representatives of Doppelmayr in Austria refused requests to discuss the company's involvement in preparing and executing the simulacrum. "Doppelmayr does not comment on local politics," Thomas Kurz, a Doppelmayr manager on the project, said in an email. Julia Schwärzler, a Doppelmayr spokeswoman, refused to comment or make company personnel available for interviews. In the video of the Channel 8 broadcast of the cable train event it

is easy to see that there is no thick hauling rope pulling the train. If you look closely, it is possible to see the thin cable that was used in its place.

3. "Odebrecht and Braskem Plead Guilty," Department of Justice Office of Public Affairs press release, December 21, 2016.

4. Nicholas Casey, "Maduro Becomes Latest Leader Accused in Huge Bribery Scheme," *New York Times*, October 12, 2017. Euzenando Prazeres de Azevedo also said that Odebrecht had made secret donations to the campaign of opposition presidential candidate Henrique Capriles, a charge that Capriles denied. Joseph Poliszuk, "Las confesiones de Odebrecht," Armando.info, June 3, 2018.

5. Diego Oré, "Stalled Brazilian Odebrecht Projects Decay in Venezuela," Reuters, May 31, 2017.

6. Jan-Werner Müller, *What Is Populism?* (University of Pennsylvania Press, 2016), 21.

7. Terry Lynn Karl, *The Paradox of Plenty: Oil Booms and Petro-States* (University of California Press, 1997), 90.

8. After Chávez's final campaign rally, he was scheduled to visit several locations where his supporters were gathered around the center of Caracas. Temir Porras and Rafael Ramírez told me that Chávez was so exhausted and so close to collapse after the rally that the rest of his schedule was canceled. The dark jacket that Chávez wore on the stage belonged to Ramírez, who'd given it to Chávez to wear to protect him from a downpour during a rally a few days earlier.

CHAPTER 10: THE BARRIO

1. Most forms of birth control have a documented failure rate, including tubal ligations, which are most likely to fail among younger women. Centers for Disease Control and Prevention, webpage on contraception. Shilpa Vishwas Date, Jyoti Rokade, Vidya Mule, and Shreedher Dandapannavar, "Female Sterilization Failure: Review over a Decade and Its Clinicopathological Correlation," *International Journal of Applied and Basic Medical Research* 4, no. 2 (2014): 84–85.

CHAPTER 11: LITTLE BIRD

1. "Betancourt Term Begins in Caracas," *New York Times*, February 14, 1959.

2. "Castro Takes Oath as Premier of Cuba," *New York Times*, February 17, 1959.

3. On Maduro's rise within Chavismo: Rory Carroll, *Comandante: Hugo Chávez's Venezuela* (Penguin Books, 2013), 120–21.

4. There were other reasons for Chávez not to choose Diosdado Cabello. Cabello was widely perceived as corrupt; and he had previously lost a gubernatorial election to Henrique Capriles, the opposition politician who had run a strong campaign for president against Chávez earlier in 2012 and who was likely to be the opposition candidate if a new presidential election was necessary.

CHAPTER 12: BLACKOUT

1. The time stamp on Rubio's tweet was 5:18 P.M. EST, which, on that date, was 6:18 P.M. in Venezuela, or about an hour and 28 minutes after the lights went out.
2. "CHAMP—Lights Out," Boeing news release, October 22, 2012.
3. "Strategic Primer: Electromagnetic Threats," American Foreign Policy Council, 2018.
4. "Coordinating National Resilience to Electromagnetic Pulses," Executive Order 13865, March 26, 2019.
5. Rebecca Smith, "Assault on California Power Station Raises Alarm on Potential for Terrorism," *Wall Street Journal*, February 5, 2014.

CHAPTER 13: THINGS ARE NEVER SO BAD

1. Alejandro Werner, "Outlook for Latin America and the Caribbean: New Challenges to Growth," IMFBlog, January 29, 2020. Total economic contraction through 2020, which includes the impact of the Covid-19 pandemic, was estimated to be 75 percent (personal communication with IMF officials).
2. These illustrations are painted broadly and the reality is much more complex. In employment, millions of people work in what is known as the informal economy—as street vendors, for example. Many people lost full-time jobs at corporations or businesses that pay taxes and are government-regulated, and fell into the informal economy. In commerce, many stores shut down and others stayed open and saw their sales shrink.
3. "Venezuela Food Security Assessment," World Food Program, February 23, 2020.
4. N. Gregory Mankiw, *Principles of Economics*, 2nd ed. (Harcourt College Publishers, 2001), 723.
5. The contraction was 35 percent. Claes Brundenius, "Whither the Cuban Economy After Recovery? The Reform Process, Upgrading Strategies and the Question of Transition," *Journal of Latin American Studies* 34, no. 2 (May 2002): 365–95.
6. The Central Bank of Venezuela reported that inflation was 130,060 percent in 2018 and 9,586 percent in 2019. In contrast, the April 2021 World Economic Outlook published by the International Monetary Fund estimated that inflation was 65,374 percent in 2018 and 19,906 percent in 2019. "Venezuela's Inflation Tumbles to 9,586% in 2019: Central Bank," Reuters, February 4, 2020. "World Economic Outlook: Managing Divergent Recoveries," International Monetary Fund, April 2021.
7. Inflation in Colombia was 3.2 percent in 2018 and 3.5 percent in 2019. "World Economic Outlook: Managing Divergent Recoveries," International Monetary Fund, April 2021.
8. On the day I made this calculation, in August 2021, the exchange rate was about 4,000,000 bolivars to the dollar. But getting a true sense of the devaluation is com-

plicated by the fact that Maduro knocked off five zeros from the bolivar in 2018. If we add the zeros back on, the equivalent exchange rate in 2012 bolivars would be Bs 400,000,000,000 to the dollar. That is the rate that I used to show the depreciation between 2012 and 2021. It is worth noting here that Chávez had previously (in 2008) removed three zeros from the currency. As a result, it would take 100 million of the August 2021 bolivars to equal one bolivar on the day that Chávez took office in 1999. Removing zeros was, in part, an attempt to pretend away the effects of inflation and depreciation. To imagine what it would be like if the dollar had lost value in a similar way, consider that in 1999 the cost of a dozen eggs in the United States was roughly $1. If the dollar had undergone a similar loss of buying power to that of the bolivar, that same dozen eggs would have cost $100 million in 2021.

9. "Refugee and Migrant Response Plan 2020 for Refugees and Migrants from Venezuela," UNHCR-IOM Office of the Joint Special Representative for Venezuelan Refugees and Migrants, May 2020.

10. OPEC, Annual Statistical Bulletin, 2005, 2008, 2010, 2014, 2018.

11. The price was $7.76 a barrel in mid-February 1999, the month that Chávez was first sworn in. Historical price data was compiled by the Baker Institute for Public Policy at Rice University, Center for Energy Studies, based on information from the Venezuelan Ministry of Energy and Petroleum. Prices are for the Venezuelan crude oil basket, which differs from international benchmark prices.

12. OPEC, Annual Statistical Bulletin, 2020.

13. Francisco Monaldi, Igor Hernández, and José La Rosa Reyes, "The Collapse of the Venezuelan Oil Industry: The Role of Above-Ground Risks Limiting FDI," Baker Institute for Public Policy, Rice University, February 2020. OPEC, Annual Statistical Bulletin, 2017, 2019, 2020. Francisco Rodríguez, "Crude Realities: Understanding Venezuela's Economic Collapse," venezuelablog.org, September 20, 2018.

14. OPEC, Annual Statistical Bulletin, 2020.

15. Víctor Álvarez, interview, 2015.

16. Bolivarian Republic of Venezuela, 2016 Annual Report, Form 18-K, Exhibit D, Securities and Exchange Commission, December 21, 2017. The rainy day account was known as the macroeconomic stabilization fund.

17. William Neuman and Patricia Torres, "Venezuela's Economy Suffers as Import Schemes Siphon Billions," New York Times, May 5, 2015.

18. Baker Institute data.

19. The great New York Yankees catcher, Yogi Berra, is said to have described a popular restaurant this way: "Nobody goes there anymore; it's too crowded." Bruce Weber, "Yogi Berra, Yankee Who Built His Stardom 90 Percent on Skill and Half on Wit, Dies at 90," New York Times, September 23, 2015.

20. It was easy to determine how many international flights there were in a day: you could count them on the arrivals board in the airport.

21. Ruth de Krivoy wrote a fascinating postmortem on the banking collapse. Ruth de Krivoy, Collapse: The Venezuelan Banking Crisis of 1994 (Group of Thirty, 2000).

CHAPTER 15: KIDNAPPED

1. Angus Berwick and Sarah Kinosian, "Special Report: Elite Police Force Spreads Terror in the Barrios of Venezuela," Reuters, November 14, 2019.
2. "Human Rights in the Bolivarian Republic of Venezuela," Office of the United Nations High Commissioner for Human Rights, July 5, 2019.
3. "Resolucíon 28/15, Medida cautelar No. 127-15, Asunto José Vicente Haro y Pierina Camposeo respecto de Venezuela," Comisión interamericana de derechos humanos, August 28, 2015.
4. "Report of the Independent International Fact-Finding Mission on the Bolivarian Republic of Venezuela," Office of the United Nations High Commissioner for Human Rights, September 15, 2020.
5. José Vicente Haro and his lawyer, Francisco José Banchs Sierraalta, submitted an account of Haro's kidnapping by the FAES in a letter dated October 8, 2018, to the Inter-American Commission on Human Rights. The letter was provided by Haro.

CHAPTER 17: MEANS WITHOUT PRODUCTION

1. Baker Institute data.
2. Calculated in 2013 dollars, Venezuela's oil revenues during the Chávez-era boom, from 2000 to 2013, totaled $832 billion; inflation-adjusted revenues (in 2013 dollars) during the earlier boom, from 1974 to 1985, totaled $461 billion. While some analysts point to a later start for the 2000s oil price boom, the windfall for the Chávez government started immediately. When Chávez took office in February 1999, the price of Venezuelan crude was $8 a barrel; a year later, it was $26.
3. Banco Central de Venezuela.
4. "Inaugurado el tramo Caracas-Cúa del Sistema ferroviario central 'Ezequiel Zamora,'" news release, PDVSA, October 15, 2006. "Plan Socialista Nacional de Desarrollo Ferroviario," Instituto de Ferrocarriles del Estado, PowerPoint presentation, June 2013. Víctor Amaya, "Un elefante blanco al borde de la autopista," *Tal Cual*, February 10, 2016. "Plan ferroviario nacional: El tren como eje de desarrollo," Prensa Bolivariana, September 13, 2012.
5. *Aló Presidente* No. 296, September 30, 2007, todochavez.gob.ve.
6. Luigino Bracci, "Seis nuevos hospitales especializados comienza a construir el Gobierno Bolivariano," Agencia Bolivariana de Noticias, September 30, 2007.
7. Patricia Marcano, "Barrio Adentro IV: Seis hospitales prometidos y olvidados," larazon.net, March 2016. "Exministra de salud imputada por supuestas irregularidades," EFE, June 19, 2014.
8. The saga of the paper mill, Pulpaca, and the aluminum rolling mill, Serlaca, are described in Brian Ellsworth and Eyanir Chinea, "Special Report: Chávez's Oil-Fed Fund Obscures Venezuela Money Trail," Reuters, September 26, 2012. Maduro announced the appointment of the new manager, with the admonition "Cúmplase, avance," during a television appearance on November 29, 2019. On April 18, 2020,

a Twitter account, @Alcasa_CVG, belonging to the government aluminum company Alcasa, showed photographs of trucks removing machinery from the Serlaca plant site. The government said that the rolling mill would be installed in a different location, but the effect was that after many years and hundreds of millions of dollars, the plant site was being abandoned.

9. "Tercer puente sobre el Orinoco es 20 veces más caro que el más alto del mundo," *El Estímulo*, January 1, 2017. "Avanza construcción del tercer puente sobre el Río Orinoco," Transportation Ministry news release, October 27, 2013. *Aló Presidente* No. 316, August 3, 2008, todochavez.gob.ve.

10. In a speech in Porto Alegre, Brazil, on January 30, 2005, Chávez rejected capitalism and said that socialism was the path forward. The first reference that I have found to the phrase *twenty-first-century socialism* was in a speech in Caracas on February 25, 2005, when Chávez said: "What is socialism? Which of so many types of socialism? . . . We must invent a twenty-first-century socialism, we must invent it."

11. "Fact Box: Venezuela's Nationalizations under Chávez," Reuters, October 7, 2012. "AES Is to Sell Utility Stake to Venezuela," *Wall Street Journal*, February 9, 2007. "Venezuela Buys Majority of Seneca," UPI, February 13, 2007. Larry B. Pascal, "Developments in the Venezuelan Hydrocarbon Sector," *Law and Business Review of the Americas* 15, no. 3 (2009): 531–73.

12. Tom Hals, "Venezuela Settles $1.2 Billion Creditor Claim to Protect Citgo," Reuters, November 25, 2018. Jim Finkle, "Rusoro Says Awarded $1.2 Billion over Venezuelan Seizure of Gold Assets," Reuters, August 23, 2016. Marianna Parraga, "PDVSA Ordered to Pay Conoco $2 Billion After Venezuela Oil Nationalization: Arbitration," Reuters, April 25, 2018. Marianna Parraga, "Venezuela Must Pay Conoco over $8 Billion: World Bank," Reuters, March 8, 2019.

13. Ellsworth and Chinea, "Special Report: Chávez's Oil-Fed Fund Obscures Venezuela Money Trail." "El rol del Fonden en la corrupción venezolana," Transparencia Venezuela, October 2020.

14. Francisco Rodríguez, "Ecuador and Venezuela This Week," Torino Economics newsletter, September 24, 2018.

15. "Mensaje a la Nación del Comandante Presidente Hugo Chávez desde la República de Cuba," March 4, 2012, todochavez.gov.ve.

16. "Acto con motive del Día Internacional del Trabajador," April 30, 2008, todochavez. gob.ve.

17. María Ramírez Cabello, "Producción de Sidor cayó a cero en 2019 bajo control de Maduro," *Correo del Caroní*, January 20, 2020. We know about Sidor's decline because of the diligent and courageous reporting of María Ramírez and other journalists of the *Correo del Caroní* in Guayana City, who have spent years covering the region's state-owned heavy industries.

18. For Sidor's workforce at the time of the nationalizations, "Factobox: Steelmaker Ternium Sidor in Venezuelan Takeover," Reuters, April 9, 2008. For the steelmaker's post-takeover workforce, William Neuman, "Rival Factions in Strike Underscore the Fissures in Post-Chávez Venezuela," *New York Times*, October 6, 2013.

19. One of the most notorious cases of a labor leader who was jailed and harassed is that of Rubén González, who worked at the government-run iron ore mining company Ferrominera. In 2018, González was arrested for leading a protest over deteriorating conditions in the steel industry; he was tried in a military court and sentenced to almost six years in prison. González was freed in late 2020 when Maduro released dozens of people considered to be political prisoners. Angus Berwick and María Ramírez, "'My Life's Work': Venezuelan Union Leader Vows to Defend Workers After Pardon," Reuters, September 3, 2020.
20. Neuman, "Rival Factions."

CHAPTER 18: PIÑATA

1. This chapter is based on hundreds of pages of court documents relating to multiple cases, including indictments, criminal complaints, affidavits, plea agreements, hearing transcripts, and forfeiture agreements, as well as documents of the Treasury Department's Office of Foreign Assets Control.
2. Shiera's guilty plea was announced first. "Miami Businessman Pleads Guilty to Foreign Bribery and Fraud Charges in Connection with Venezuela Bribery Scheme," Department of Justice Office of Public Affairs press release, March 23, 2016. "Businessman Pleads Guilty to Foreign Bribery and Tax Charges in Connection with Venezuela Bribery Scheme," Department of Justice Office of Public Affairs press release, June 16, 2016.
3. Besides the convictions of Rincón and Shiera, federal prosecutors have won at least fourteen additional guilty pleas in cases deriving from the investigation of the two businessmen, including other contractors who paid bribes and employees at PDVSA or its procurement subsidiary who received them. Some indicted individuals have not appeared in U.S. court and have been charged or are under investigation in Spain in unrelated corruption inquiries there, including Nervis Villalobos, a former vice minister of energy in Venezuela, and Rafael Reiter, a former PDVSA head of security.
4. News outlets in Venezuela reported that Santilli was shot and killed in September 2020 while sitting in an SUV in a drugstore parking lot; an assailant on a motorcycle approached and opened fire, the reports said. In February 2021, U.S. prosecutors moved successfully to have the case against Santilli dismissed "in light of the defendant's death."
5. U.S. Energy Information Administration and OPEC Monthly Oil Market Reports.
6. "Former Venezuelan National Treasurer Sentenced to 10 Years in Prison for Money Laundering Conspiracy Involving Over $1 Billion in Bribes," Department of Justice Office of Public Affairs press release, November 27, 2018.
7. The deal was structured as a loan, but it was really just a currency transaction. Gorrín's partners acted as the lenders and PDVSA acted as the borrower. In this case the "lenders" acquired 7.2 billion bolivars, from Venezuelan companies

or individuals that needed dollars. The "lenders" then gave those bolivars to PDVSA, which exercised an option to repay the "loan" in dollars at one of the official exchange rates in effect at the time. PDVSA, as "borrower," gave the "lenders" $600 million as payment for the "loan." The "lenders" then paid off the companies or individuals who had given them the bolivars. The value of those bolivars at the black-market rate was just $43 million. The deal involved a group of upper-class Venezuelans who have come to be known as bolichicos, for their ties to the Chavista government. They include Francisco Convit, the grandson of one of Venezuela's most famous scientists; Convit was indicted but remains at large. Another bolichico who took part in the deal was Alejandro Betancourt, who in 2019 hired Trump's personal lawyer, Rudy Giuliani, to meet with Justice Department officials and seek to persuade them not to indict him (Betancourt has not been charged). Kenneth P. Vogel and Ben Protess, "Giuliani Represented Venezuelan Investor in Discussion with Justice Dept.," *New York Times*, November 26, 2019.

8. Gorrín was also identified as "Conspirator 7" in U.S. media accounts. Jay Weaver and Antonio Maria Delgado, "Media Mogul with Miami Mansion Emerges as Key Suspect in Venezuela Corruption Case," *Miami Herald*, August 25, 2018.

9. The three sons of the Venezuelan first lady Cilia Flores are Walter, Yosser, and Yoswal Gavidia Flores. A factual proffer in a federal money laundering case against a Swiss banker named Matthias Krull describes a meeting at Gorrín's Caracas office in which Gorrín allegedly introduced Krull to the brothers, who ranged in age at the time from their mid-twenties to their mid-thirties. They wore backward baseball caps and conspicuous gold chains. The brothers are skydiving enthusiasts. They move in a world of money, power, and leisure. You can get a glimpse of Los Chamos sometimes on their friends' social media accounts, tanned and bearded and fit, at the beach, at a remote nature park, on a skydiving trip. Their mother had been a follower of Chávez since the beginning. Children of Revolution, children of privilege, they seem to live a never-ending adolescence, gliding through a permanent summer.

10. To keep his Treasury business going, Gorrín had continued to pay tens of millions of dollars in bribes to one of Andrade's successors as national treasurer, Claudia Patricia Díaz Guillén, according to prosecutors. In 2020 a superseding indictment was filed charging Gorrín, Díaz Guillén, and her husband, Adrian José Velásquez Figueroa, with corruption and money laundering.

CHAPTER 20: NOT ANYMORE

1. Patricia Zengerle, "Kerry Meets Venezuela's Maduro amid Vote Tensions," Reuters, September 26, 2016.

2. Lesley Wroughton, "U.S. Names Special Envoy to Colombian Peace Process," Reuters, February 20, 2015.

3. Rory Carroll, *Comandante: Hugo Chávez's Venezuela* (Penguin Books, 2013), 43–44.

4. Shannon said that he had not heard a recording or seen a transcript of the call between Fidel Castro and Chávez, but that he was told about it at the time. A second person with knowledge of the call confirmed that it had occurred.

5. Juan Forero, "Documents Show C.I.A. Knew of a Coup Plot in Venezuela," *New York Times*, December 3, 2004.

CHAPTER 21: MAXIMUM PRESSURE

1. Jane Mayer, "The Danger of President Pence," *The New Yorker*, October 16, 2017.

2. Marc Caputo, "Trump Packs Foreign Policy Team with Cuba Hardliners from Florida," *Politico*, August 31, 2018.

3. Jenna Johnson and John Wagner, "Trump Won't Rule Out a Military Option in Venezuela," *Washington Post*, August 11, 2017.

4. By late 2018, none of the senior U.S. officials in Washington with direct responsibility for Venezuela policy, at the National Security Council and the State Department, had so much as set foot in the country, and that lack of experience would continue through the end of the Trump administration.

CHAPTER 22: EXODUS

1. The coalition was often identified by its Spanish acronym, MUD, for Mesa de la Unidad Democrática.

2. Capriles, whose maternal grandparents were Jewish refugees from Europe, also is reportedly descended from a half brother of Bolívar.

3. The border closing followed an old playbook: blame immigrants and provoke a fight with your neighbor to distract from problems at home. Maduro started out by deporting hundreds of Colombian residents from Venezuela. Even though the border was officially closed, Colombian immigration data continues to show large numbers of people crossing at border posts, and many more entered illegally. William Neuman, "Colombians Flee Venezuela's Crackdown on Immigrants," *New York Times*, August 27, 2015.

4. There are various sources for data on Venezuelan immigration and refugees in Colombia. The data given here is from a Migración Colombia report titled "Distribución de Venezolanos en Colombia 2020." The numbers from 2014 and 2015 may be undercounts, but the trend they establish is clear. Another data set is contained in the Gran Encuesta Integrada de Hogares (GEIH) produced by Colombia's Departamento Administrativo Nacional de Estadística (DANE). Estimates of Venezuelan immigrants taken from the GEIH data tend to be larger than the official immigration figures, in part because they may include Colombian citizens who resided previously in Venezuela. Either way the trend is similar. The GEIH data, sorted for people who reported being born in Venezuela and who lived in Venezuela five years prior to the survey date, shows that the number of such people in Colombia increased from 290,000 in 2017 to 890,000 in 2018 and 1.6 million in

2019. This analysis of the GEIH data is contained in Dany Bahar, Meagan Dooley, and Andrew Selee, "Venezuelan Migration, Crime, and Misperceptions: A Review of Data from Colombia, Peru, and Chile," Washington, D.C., Migration Policy Institute and Brookings Institution, September 2020.

5. Following the battle of Bomboná, in Colombia, on April 7, 1822, Bolívar and his army continued toward Quito. He was in Tulcán, Ecuador, near the site of the present-day Rumichaca Bridge, on June 12, according to a set of orders penned by his secretary. "Documento 6770, Oficio de José Gabriel Pérez para el general Antonio Obando, fechado en Tulcán el 12 de junio de 1822," archivodellibertador.gob.ve.

6. "Nacionalidad y puerto mes a mes para página web del MDI 2010–2020," Ministerio de Gobierno, Ecuador.

7. In 2021, the UN High Commissioner for Refugees estimated that there were 420,000 Venezuelan refugees in Ecuador; barely a decade earlier, the 2010 Ecuadorian census had found less than 5,000 Venezuelans living in the country. Giaconda Herrera and Gabriela Cabezas Gálvez, "Ecuador: de la recepción a la disuasión. Políticas frente a la población venezolana y experiencia migratoria 2015–2018," in Luciana Gandini, Fernando Lozano Ascencio, and Victoria Prieto Rosas, eds., *Crisis y migración de población venezolana. Entre la desprotección y la seguridad jurídica en Latinoamérica* (Universidad Nacional Autónoma de México, 2019), 128.

8. Average monthly Venezuelan entries into Colombia in the first half of 2017 equaled 44,000 and increased to an average of 88,000 a month in the second half of the year, according to data from Migración Colombia. At Rumichaca, 12,714 Venezuelans crossed into Ecuador in June 2017 and 25,565 entered in July, 15 times as many as in July the previous year.

9. According to the World Bank, Venezuela's population was 29.3 million in 2012 and it peaked at slightly more than 30 million in 2015.

CHAPTER 23: SWEARING IN

1. The account in this and subsequent chapters of the events that led up to and followed the swearing in as interim president of Juan Guaidó is based on interviews with dozens of people, including Elliott Abrams, Diego Arria, Kimberly Breier, Pedro Mario Burelli, Juan Cruz, Fernando Cutz, Stalin González, Juan Guaidó, Tomás Guanipa, José Vicente Haro, Leopoldo López, Enrique Márquez, Keith Mines, Miguel Pizarro, J. J. Rendón, Edward Rodríguez, David Smolansky, James Story, and Chúo Torrealba; as well as current and former White House and State Department officials, a Latin American diplomat, and others in Venezuela and Washington who spoke on condition of anonymity. It is also based on contemporary news reports, social media, U.S. government documents, and the memoir of John Bolton, *The Room Where It Happened*. Not everyone who spoke to me will recognize their version of events in the account related here. In some cases, versions conflicted and I weighed the evidence and tried to build an accurate composite from many inputs.

2. López was arrested in 2014 and charged with inciting violence at a protest. Although he had called on demonstrators to be peaceful, the government said that he used subliminal messages to urge his followers to violent acts. He was convicted and sentenced to more than thirteen years in jail. One of the prosecutors on the case later fled the country and said that the trial was a farce and that evidence was faked; former national prosecutor Luisa Ortega has also said that López was wrongfully accused and convicted. López was moved at various times between prison and house arrest.

3. A series of strategy sessions was held in late 2018 in the Caracas residence of the Chilean ambassador, where the López lieutenant Freddy Guevara was living as an asylum seeker. The meetings included other Popular Will leaders and occasionally representatives of other opposition parties; López often participated through a video call.

4. "Secretary Pompeo's Call with Venezuelan National Assembly President Juan Guaidó," State Department, Office of the Spokesperson, readout, January 10, 2019.

5. "Acuerdo sobre la declaratoria de usurpación de la presidencia de la república por parte de Nicolás Maduro Moros y el restablecimiento de la vigencia de la constitución," Asamblea Nacional, January 15, 2019.

6. John Bolton, *The Room Where It Happened* (Simon & Schuster, 2020), 253–56.

7. It was once fashionable among leftist parents in Latin America to name their children after Soviet leaders.

8. In the power-sharing agreement in the National Assembly, the body's top leadership posts were distributed among different parties. At this time the top three positions were assembly president Juan Guaidó of Popular Will; the first vice president, Edgar Zambrano, of Democratic Action; and the second vice president Stalin González, of A New Era. The comparable posts in the U.S. House of Representatives would be the speaker, the majority leader, and the majority whip.

9. The day after the United States recognized Guaidó as president of Venezuela, a story ran in *The New York Times* with the headline "After Tarnished Election, Opposition Figure Becomes Congo's President." It said that the U.S. had welcomed the swearing in of Félix Tshisekedi as president of the Democratic Republic of Congo, although his election victory was "widely considered to be illegitimate." A different candidate, Martin Fayulu, was considered by observers to have been the winner. Tshisekedi had the backing of the outgoing president, Joseph Kabila, and his victory was certified by the constitutional court, which refused Fayulu's request for a recount. The day of the court decision (which was also the day of Guaidó's swearing in), the state department issued a statement saying that the U.S. was "committed to working with the new DRC government." The *Times* reported that the residents of two cities where Fayulu had strong support were barred from voting. It also reported that Fayulu was endorsed by two other opposition leaders who had been banned by the government from running because of their popularity. It didn't sound very different from Maduro's victory in Venezuela, after banning other candidates and skewing the rules so far in his favor that the op-

position called a boycott. The *Times* story said that the United States and some African countries had decided to accept Tshisekedi's victory "to promote stability over potential chaos." Two months later, Tshisekedi was in Washington, where he met with Pompeo and discussed "promoting stability and security and attracting American investment in the DRC," according to the State Department. So why did the U.S. reject the outcome of one bogus election while it embraced the winner of another? It appeared that the U.S. was primarily interested in maintaining the cooperation of the Democratic Republic of Congo in the fight against the Islamic State. The U.S. didn't seem to care very much who occupied the presidential palace as long as they didn't get in the way of that cooperation. It's also worth noting that there is no large voting bloc of Congolese Americans in Florida or any other swing state.

10. Juan Guaidó, "Juan Guaidó: Venezuelans, Strength Is in Unity," *New York Times*, January 30, 2019.

CHAPTER 24: AVALANCHE

1. A 2021 report by the Office of the Inspector General of the U.S. Agency for International Development determined that the use of military aircraft to transport aid to Cúcuta "was not justified by operational needs as commercial transportation was available and less expensive." The report also determined that some aspects of the agency's Venezuela aid efforts were "not driven by technical expertise or fully aligned with the humanitarian principles of neutrality, independence and being based on needs assessments." "Enhanced Processes and Implementer Requirements Are Needed to Address Challenges and Fraud Risks in USAID's Venezuela Response," Office of Inspector General, U.S. Agency for International Development, Audit Report 9-000-21-005-P, April 16, 2021.

2. "Comunicado sobre los recientes acontecimientos en torno a los esfuerzos por ingresar ayuda humanitaria a Venezuela," news release of the Colombian president's office, February 23, 2019.

3. Interview with a U.S. official.

4. More than a thousand miles from Cúcuta, there was another standoff at a much smaller border crossing between Venezuela and Brazil. Two pickup trucks with boxes of food drove a few feet into Venezuelan territory and then retreated back into Brazil without unloading. Nonetheless Guaidó declared on Twitter that the aid had gotten through. "Attention, Venezuela!" Guaidó tweeted. "We officially announce that the first shipment of humanitarian aid has NOW ENTERED at the border with Brazil. This is a great achievement." But it wasn't true.

5. Michelle Carbert, "Canada, Lima Group Allies Reassert Opposition to the Use of Force in Venezuela amid Threats of U.S. Military Intervention," *The Globe and Mail*, February 25, 2019.

6. Luis Andrés Henao, "Venezuela's Maduro to Throw Concert Rivaling Richard Branson," Associated Press, February 18, 2019. Aid Live Foundation 2019 Annual Report.

CHAPTER 25: BUBBLE

1. Francisco Rodríguez, "Crude Realities: Understanding Venezuela's Economic Collapse," venezuelablog.org, September 20, 2018. Francisco Monaldi also noted the effects of these early sanctions on PDVSA: Francisco Monaldi, "The Death Spiral of Venezuela's Oil Sector and What Can Be Done About It," *Forbes*, January 24, 2018.

2. Francisco Monaldi, "The Collapse of the Venezuelan Oil Industry and Its Global Consequences," Atlantic Council, March 9, 2018.

3. John Bolton, *The Room Where It Happened* (Simon & Schuster, 2020), 251.

4. "Perverse policies and extreme mismanagement explain the bulk of Venezuela's collapse," said an article coauthored by Ricardo Haussmann, a Venezuelan economist at Harvard who was an advisor to Guaidó. Sanctions, it said, "are a means to put pressure on the regime to negotiate the return to democracy and constitutional rule. Oil sanctions are designed to restrict their access to the resources with which to continue its oppression." Ricardo Hausmann and Frank Muci, "Don't Blame Washington for Venezuela's Oil Woes: A Rebuttal," *Americas Quarterly*, May 1, 2019.

5. Edward Wong and Nicholas Casey, "U.S. Targets Venezuela with Tough Oil Sanctions During Crisis of Power," *New York Times*, January 28, 2019.

6. Paul Ronzheimer and Giorgos Moutafis, "Bild-interview mit Venezuela-Hoffnungsträger Juan Guaidó," *Bild*, February 1, 2019.

7. "Treasury Sanctions Governors of Venezuelan States Aligned with Maduro," Treasury Department news release, February 25, 2019.

8. Much ink was spilled over what turned out to be a nonevent. It's likely that the plot, such as it was, was compromised. Elliott Abrams, the State Department's special representative for Venezuela, told me that U.S. officials had heard from so many people about the nascent conspiracy that they wondered whether Maduro hadn't heard of it as well. Moreno told a confidant that he had alerted the head of military intelligence about the plot. Moreno also told the confidant that Figuera had exposed himself by going to Maduro and urging him to hold new elections. The account in this chapter of the April 30 plot is based on interviews with López, a person who spoke with Moreno shortly after the events, other sources in Venezuela and U.S. government officials. It also relies on news reports, including: Anthony Faiola, "Inside the Secret Plot to Turn Senior Venezuelan Officials Against Maduro," *Washington Post*, May 13, 2019. Anthony Faiola, "Maduro's Ex-Spy Chief Lands in U.S. Armed with Allegations Against Venezuelan Government," *Washington Post*, June 24, 2019. Kejal Vyas, Juan Forero, and José de Córdoba, "Venezuelan Businessman Joined Plot to Oust Maduro—and Escape Sanctions," *Wall Street Journal*, May 27, 2019. Nicholas Confessore, Anatoly Kurmanaev, and Kenneth P. Vogel, "Trump, Venezuela and the Tug-of-War Over a Strongman," *New York Times*, November 1, 2020. "La conjura de los testaferros," Armando.info, May 7, 2019.

9. Bolton, *Room*, 276 and 283.

10. Brian Ellsworth and Eyanir Chinea, "Rogue Ex-policeman, Six Others Die in Venezuela Forces Raid," Reuters, January 16, 2018.

11. "Detailed Findings of the Independent International Fact-Finding Mission on the Bolivarian Republic of Venezuela," United Nations Human Rights Council, September 15, 2020 (A/HRC/45/CRP.11), 183–87.

CHAPTER 28: GOLDEN HEARTS

1. Sean M. Griffing, Leopoldo Villegas, and Venkatachalam Udhayakumar, "Malaria Control and Elimination, Venezuela, 1800s–1970s," *Emerging Infectious Diseases* 20, no. 10 (2014). Pan American Health Organization / World Health Organization, "Epidemiological Update: Malaria in the Americas in the Context of COVID-19 Pandemic," June 10, 2020, Washington, D.C.: PAHO/WHO.

2. Stories of atrocities in the mining area are difficult, by nature, to confirm. In some cases I was able to find multiple witnesses to some of the accounts that I collected. In the case of the two accounts presented here, the people who told me what happened had spoken previously to others, and I was able to confirm that the details of their stories had remained consistent. They had not altered from one telling to the next. The person who told me of the death of the four women in El Portón did not want me to speak to the woman who gave her account of the escarmiento, for fear that the woman might tell the sindicato who my source had been.

3. Federal court papers, Southern District of Florida. Lucia Binding, "104 Kg of Gold 'Linked to Drugs Cartel' Seized at Heathrow Airport," *Sky News*, July 21, 2019.

CHAPTER 29: NEWSPRINT

1. In 2020 *El Correo del Caroní* increased its staff to include five reporters.

CHAPTER 30: THE SCREW-UP AT MACUTO

1. The news stories reported on testimony by a leader of the Rastrojos drug trafficking gang to U.S. investigators that he paid Rendón $12 million to intercede with government officials on behalf of several traffickers. Rendón denied taking the money. Julia Symmes Cobb, "Colombia President's Election Strategist Quits over Bribe Claim," Reuters, May 5, 2014.

2. Guaidó announced the appointment of Rendón and Vergara as "special presidential commissioners" at a news conference in Caracas in August 2019. Rendón's portfolio was commissioner of strategy. They were part of what amounted to a presidential cabinet, which Guaidó called his "centro de gobierno," and which he said would be under the direction of Leopoldo López. "Guaidó anuncia la creación de un 'centro de gobierno,' con Leopoldo López a cargo," EFE, August 28, 2019.

3. Joshua Goodman, "Ex-Green Beret Led Failed Attempt to Oust Venezuela's Maduro," Associated Press, May 1, 2020.

4. Cabello was also charged in the Maduro indictment, and there was a $10 million reward for his capture.

5. Juan Cruz, the former NSC official, and former State Department officials told me that Mattis refused to plan for military action against Venezuela. John Bolton, in his memoir, describes a similar reluctance at the Defense Department during his tenure.

6. For U.S. casualties: U.S. Department of Defense Casualty Status Report. For Iraqi casualties: Sabrina Tavernise and Donald G. McNeil Jr., "Iraqi Dead May Total 600,000, Study Says," *New York Times*, October 11, 2006. Salman Rawaf, "The 2003 Iraq War and Avoidable Death Toll," *PLoS Medicine* 10, no. 10 (October 15, 2013), e1001532.

7. *Archivo del General Miranda, Negociaciones, 1770–1810, Tomo XV* (Tipografía Americana, 1938), 426.

CHAPTER 31: BLACKOUT

1. A Corpoelec news release in 2013 cited a workforce of 50,000 employees: "El Ministro Jesse Chacón invitó a la fuerza laboral del SEN a ser protagonistas del plan 100 días," Corpoelec news release, April 30, 2013.

2. Timothy Snyder, *The Road to Unfreedom* (Tim Duggan Books, 2018), 278. For his discussion of national fables, see pages 76–78.

3. Juan Carlos went on to take a job, in 2020, as a vice president with the Venezuela Guayana Corporation, working to revive the heavy industries, such as the steel and aluminum mills, based in Guayana City. That gave him less time to spend on the cleaning supply business.

CHAPTER 32: VENEZUELA AGONISTES

1. "FMV asegura que alrededor de 30.000 médicos se han ido del país," *Tal Cual*, September 13, 2019. In 2014 there were approximately 66,000 doctors in the country: "PAHO's Response to Maintaining an Effective Technical Cooperation Agenda in Venezuela and Neighboring Member States," 70th session of the regional committee of WHO for the Americas, CD56/INF/12, September 5, 2018.

2. Christine Armario, Scott Smith, and Fabiola Sánchez, "Venezuela's Go-To Test for Fighting Virus Raises Questions," Associated Press, April 17, 2020. Angus Berwick and Vivian Sequera, "In Run-Down Caracas Institute, Venezuela's Coronavirus Testing Falters," Reuters, April 17, 2020.

3. A Twitter account of the Strategic Command of the Venezuelan Armed Forces, @ceofanb, in a tweet on July 12, 2020, called returning migrants who weren't observing quarantine bioterrorists and urged Venezuelans to turn them in. The

website of Diosdado Cabello's television program, *Con el Mazo Dando*, published an article highlighting the campaign to report returnees.

4. Angus Berwick and Sarah Kinosian, "Venezuela Wields a Powerful 'Hate' Law to Silence Maduro's Remaining Foes," Reuters, December 14, 2020.

5. "Venezuela Raises Minimum Wage in Fourth Year of Hyperinflation," Reuters, May 3, 2021.

6. Henrique Capriles Facebook livestream "Mensaje a los venezolanos," September 2020.

7. Ben Jacobs, "Why 'Socialism' Killed Democrats in Florida," *New York*, November 17, 2020.

8. Aaron C. Davis, Josh Dawsey, Emma Brown, and Jon Swaine, "For Trump Advocate Sidney Powell, a Playbook Steeped in Conspiracy Theories," *Washington Post*, November 28, 2020.

9. Lara Jakes and Anatoly Kurmanaev, "Biden Grants Protections for Venezuelans to Remain in U.S.," *New York Times*, March 8, 2021.

10. Luc Cohen, "Venezuela Releases Former Citgo Executives to House Arrest," Reuters, April 30, 2021.

11. Regina García Cano, Jorge Rueda, and Joshua Goodman, "Venezuelan Lawmakers OK Opposition Members to Election Board," Associated Press, May 4, 2021.

12. Hearing transcript, Senate Committee on Foreign Relations, January 19, 2021.

13. "La pintura es la verdad; pero la luz ciega, enloquece, atormenta, porque uno no puede ver la luz." Eugenio Montejo, "La luz de *Los espacios cálidos*," *El taller blanco y otros ensayos* (Sibilina, 2012), 106.

INDEX